Photo by: Chelsie Hutto

Tribute to Paula Ramsey
"Mom"

Paula Ramsey, founder & owner of "A Lady's Day Out" has gone to be with her sweet savior. On August 22, 2000 she lost her battle with cancer. Mom's life was an example for many. We can all be assured her rewards were great and that the Father welcomed her home with open arms and a big "Thank you" for a life spent glorifying Him and bringing many into the Kingdom.

"A Lady's Day Out" was Mom's vision. As with most things in her life, she was willing to share this with me. We traveled from one exciting town to the next—finding treasures and experiencing so much together for more than 10 years. I was blessed to have shared these times with my mom and hold them dear in the quiet places of my heart.

The loss of my best friend, business partner and mother is great, and the pain is deep. Our family has lost our "rock," but our faith in the Lord is strong, and we take comfort in knowing we will someday join her again in heaven.

I will miss our adventures together, but I am thankful for the times we shared, and I feel blessed to have had a mom that others could only dream of. I have always been and will continue to be proud of my mother for her love of the Lord, her right choices, her ability to lead by example and the contributions she made here on earth. Mom had an unconditional love for all of her children, and as her daughter, I will miss that attribute the most.

We will continue to publish "A Lady's Day Out" books and see her vision through. A percentage of all book sales will go to charity in Mom's memory. Thank you for celebrating her memory with us. Each time you pick up this book or any of our others, we hope you think of Mom and her inspiration—Jesus Christ.

Jennifer "Jenni" Ramsey

Beverly Bremer Silver Shop
(See related story page 43.)

Michael Gibson Antiques & Design, Inc.

(See related story page 19.)

V

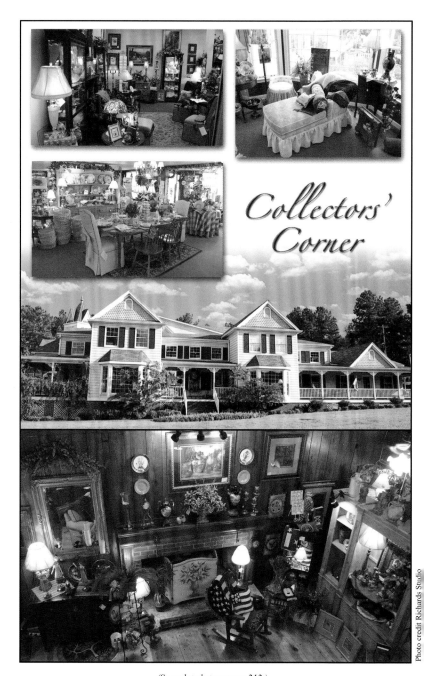

Collectors' Corner

Photo credit Richards Studio

(See related story page 212.)

VI

The Avenue®
(See related story page 189.)

VII

Jane J. Marsden
Antiques & Interiors

(See related story page 20.)

Impressions
A BRIDAL SALON

(See related story page 25.)

Susan Lee
(See related story page 26.)

The Plantation Shop
(See related story page 21.)

Old Town Antiques & Gifts
(See related story page 211.)

Crowne Plaza Hotels & Resorts – Macon
(See related story page 64.)

Pura Vida USA
(See related story page 128.)

Chef Audrey
(See related story page 307.)

The Old Governor's Mansion
(See related story page 202.)

City of Smyrna
(See related story page 253.)

The Shoppes of Plum Tree Village
(See related story page 252.)

Celebrity On Paces
(See related story page 27.)

Jolie Home
(See related story page 146.)

The Gardens at Great Oaks
(See related story page 249.)

★ **Atlanta Metro** (including Buckhead,
  Sandy Springs, Chamblee, Vinings)

2. Athens/Watkinsville
3. Blue Ridge
4. Bolingbroke/Juliette
5. Covington
6. Dahlonega
7. Dawsonville
8. Decatur
9. Helen/Cleveland/Sautee-Nacoochee
★ Macon
11. Madison
12. Marietta/Woodstock /Canton

13. Milledgeville
14. Newnan/Old Town Sharpsburg
15. Perry
16. Rome/Cave Spring
17. Roswell
18. Smyrna
19. Social Circle
20. Stone Mountain
21. Warm Springs/Pine Mountain
22. Warner Robins

Available Titles

After enjoying this book, we are sure you will also love our other books:

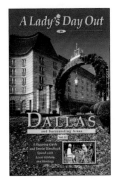

"A LADY'S DAY OUT IN DALLAS AND SURROUNDING AREAS"

From the glitz and glamour of Dallas to the Historic Square of Gainesville, we found the most delightful shopping, scrumptious dinning, luxurious bed & breakfasts and inns and so much more! Let us guide you through the Big "D" and 20 charming surrounding towns and cities. This book is a must for visitors and "Dallas Natives" alike. Featuring Dallas and the enchanting towns of Allen, Carrollton, Cedar Hill, Coppell, DeSoto, Duncanville, Flower Mound, Forney, Frisco, Gainesville, Garland, Irving, Lancaster, Lewisville, McKinney, Plano, Richardson, Rockwall, Sherman & Waxahachie. Hard Cover — *270 pages - $19.95*

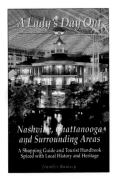

"A LADY'S DAY OUT IN NASHVILLE, CHATTANOOGA AND SURROUNDING AREAS"

From the rolling hills and mountains to Music City USA or the world's largest freshwater aquarium, Tennessee has got it going on! Discover Tennessee like you've never experienced it, with the help of our 19th book. "A Lady's Day Out in Nashville, Chattanooga and Surrounding Areas." You'll find the best shopping, lodging, eating and pampering services that each town has to offer, while learning the area's history, its special attractions, its extraordinary people and its calendar of events. This book is a must-have for those planning a getaway to: Nashville, Chattanooga, Bell Buckle, Brentwood, Clarksville, Clifton, Cookeville, Crossville, Dickson, Fayetteville, Franklin, Gallatin, Goodlettsville, Hendersonville, Lawrenceburg, Lebanon, Leipers Fork, Lynchburg, Murfreesboro, Pickwick, Savannah, Shelbyville, Signal Mountain and Waynesboro. Hard Cover — *280 pages - $19.95*

"A LADY'S DAY OUT ON NORTHWEST FLORIDA'S EMERALD COAST"

Sparkling, emerald green waters along miles of pristine sugar white sand beaches make the Emerald Coast breathtaking! You'll find beachside restaurants, shopping treasures, relaxing accommodations and sun-kissed attractions among the unhurried world along the Gulf. This book is the perfect companion guide to adventurers exploring the warmth and hospitality of Apalachicola, Carillon Beach, Destin, Fort Walton Beach, Grayton Beach, Gulf Breeze, Mexico Beach, Navarre Beach, Niceville, Pace, Panama City Beach, Pensacola, Pensacola Beach, Port St. Joe, Rosemary Beach, Sandestin, Santa Rosa Beach, Seagrove Beach, Seaside, Shalimar and Valparaiso. — *237 Pages - $19.95*

"A LADY'S DAY OUT IN THE RIO GRAND VALLEY AND SOUTH PADRE ISLAND"

Discover why the Rio Grand Valley and South Padre Island are the perfect places for a "two-nation vacation"! With one set of roots planted deeply in Mexico, and the other firmly in Texas, this book is loaded with magnetic "Beinvenidos" appeal. Tourists from the Northern United States flood to the Valley during the winter months to enjoy the warmer temperatures and delightful lifestyle. Vibrant shopping, casual eateries, charming attractions and wonderful accommodations makes this book a must have when planning an afternoon, weekend or week long getaway in Alamo City, Brownsville, Edinburg, Harlingen, Hidalgo, La Feria, Los Fresnos, McAllen, Mission, Pharr, Port Isabel, Port Mansfield, Raymondville, Reynosa, Rio Grande City, Roma, South Padre Island and Weslaco. — *176 Pages - $19.95*

"A LADY'S DAY OUT IN THE TEXAS HILL COUNTRY, VOLUME II"

Spiced with local history and heritage; this book is our latest edition for the Texas Hill Country. Featuring the best bed & breakfasts, inns, cottages, art galleries, antiques, tearooms, restaurants, unique boutiques, specialty shops, attractions and entertainment the Hill Country has to offer. Find out why the Texas Hill Country is a favorite destination for all. Plan your trip by using this book and you'll be sure to guide yourself to the best and most unique towns and shops the Hill Country has to offer. Featuring the wonderful towns of Bandera, Boerne, Medina, Vanderpool, Blanco, Brady, Brownwood, Early, Burnet, Buchanan Dam, Comfort, Fredericksburg, Goldwaite, Hamilton, Johnson City, Stonewall, Junction, Kerrville, Ingram, Lampasas, Llano, Marble Falls, Kingsland, Mason and Wimberley. — *250 Pages - $18.95*

"A LADY'S DAY OUT IN MISSISSIPPI"

Southern charm and uniqueness drip from the pages of this Shopping Guide and Tourist Handbook. We have found true Mississippi treasures! As always great shopping, dining and lodging fill the pages of this book in this fascinating state. Bay St. Louis, Biloxi, Canton, Cleveland, Columbus, Jackson, Natchez, Ocean Springs, Oxford, Pass Christian, Picayune, Vicksburg and Waveland are all covered. — *212 Pages - $17.95*

"A LADY'S DAY OUT IN TEXAS, VOL. III"

Features 37 new "GET-A-WAY" Texas towns—most are new and not covered in Texas, Vol. II—brimming with fascinating history and delightful, unique shopping. Inside you'll find all the details about romantic bed & breakfasts and inns, fabulous antique shops, lovely art galleries, home décor, gift shops and exciting entertainment, tearooms, soda fountains and much more. — *276 Pages - $18.95*

— BOOKS SOON TO BE AVAILABLE —
"A Lady's Day Out in Northern New Mexico"

Book Order Form

A Lady's Day Out, Inc.
8563 Boat Club Road • Fort Worth, Tx 76179
Toll Free: 1-888-860-ALDO (2536)

Please send _____ copies of **"A LADY'S DAY OUT IN ATLANTA, MACON & SURROUNDING AREAS"** at $19.95 per copy, plus $2.00 postage for each book ordered. (Tax included.)

Please send _____ copies of **"A LADY'S DAY OUT IN DALLAS & SURROUNDING AREAS, VOL. II"** at $19.95 per copy, plus $2.00 postage for each book ordered. (Tax included.)

Please send _____ copies of **"A LADY'S DAY OUT IN NASHVILLE, CHATTANOOGA & SURROUNDING AREAS"** at $19.95 per copy, plus $2.00 postage for each book ordered. (Tax included.)

Please send _____ copies of **"A LADY'S DAY OUT ON NORTHWEST FLORIDA'S EMERALD COAST"** at $19.95 per copy, plus $2.00 postage for each book ordered. (Tax included.)

Please send _____ copies of **"A LADY'S DAY OUT IN THE RIO GRANDE VALLEY & SOUTH PADRE ISLAND"** at $17.95 per copy, plus $2.00 postage for each book ordered. (Tax included.)

Please send _____ copies of **"A LADY'S DAY OUT IN THE TEXAS HILL COUNTRY, VOL. II"** at $18.95 per copy, plus $2.00 postage for each book ordered. (Tax included.)

Please send _____ copies of **"A LADY'S DAY OUT IN MISSISSIPPI"** at $17.95 per copy, plus $2.00 postage for each book ordered. (Tax included.)

Please send _____ copies of **"A LADY'S DAY OUT IN TEXAS VOL. III"** at $18.95 per copy, plus $2.00 postage for each book ordered. (Tax included.)

Please send _____ copies of **"A LADY'S DAY OUT IN TEXAS VOL. II"** at $17.95 per copy, plus $2.00 postage for each book ordered. (Tax included.)

MAIL BOOKS TO:

NAME: _____

ADDRESS: _____

CITY_____ STATE_____ ZIP_____

AMOUNT ENCLOSED: _____
CREDIT CARD ORDERS CALL: 1-888-860-ALDO (2536)
www.aladysdayout.com

A Lady's Day Out

IN

Atlanta, Macon & Surrounding Areas

A Shopping Guide & Tourist Handbook

— featuring —

*Atlanta • Athens • Blue Ridge • Bolingbroke • Canton
Cave Spring • Cleveland • Covington • Dahlonega
Dawsonville • Decatur • Helen • Juliette • Macon
Madison • Marietta • Milledgeville • Newnan
Old Town Sharpsburg • Perry • Pine Mountain
Rome • Roswell • Sautee Nacoochee • Smyrna
Social Circle • Stone Mountain • Warm Springs
Warner Robins • Watkinsville • Woodstock*

by Jennifer Ramsey

*Cover features Swan House at Atlanta History Center
(See related story on page 39.)*

CREDITS

Editor/Author
Jennifer Ramsey

Director of Research & Sales
Jennifer Ramsey

Editors & Writers
Michelle Medlock Adams
Gena Maselli
Jenny Harper Nahoum
Barbie Jenkins
Todd Winkler

Administrative & Production
Kay Payne
Mary Manzano
Laura Pender

Research & Sales
Nena Prejean
Tere Carter
Susan Calico
Kim Jacobs
Gayle Norris
Linda Williams

Paid advertising by invitation only.

Produced by
A Lady's Day Out, Inc.

Printed in the United States of America
By Armstrong Printing Company, Austin, Texas

Table of Contents

Note from the Author .... *v*

True Southern Soul, Shopping & Fun *1*

Georgia's Peaches—Its People *5*

Discover Atlanta *14*

Discover Macon *44*

Discover Athens/Watkinsville *74*

Discover Blue Ridge *91*

Discover Bolingbroke/Juliette *104*

Discover Covington *109*

Discover Dahlonega *121*

Discover Dawsonville *133*

Discover Decatur *142*

Discover Helen/Cleveland/Sautee Nacoochee *152*

Discover Madison *166*

Discover Marietta/Woodstock/Canton *180*

Discover Milledgeville *190*

Discover Newnan/Old Town Sharpsburg *208*

Discover Perry *215*

Discover Rome/Cave Spring *226*

Discover Roswell *243*

Discover Smyrna *253*

Discover Social Circle *263*

Discover Stone Mountain *271*

Discover Warm Springs/Pine Mountain *278*

Discover Warner Robins *301*

Index *311*

Cross Reference *314*

Note from the Author

What a blessing it has been for A Lady's Day Out to venture into another new state. Georgia is a sweet state, and I quickly came to adore it. The breathtaking beauty of the North Georgia Mountains, the sophistication of Atlanta, and the rich history of the Historic Heartland region are each unique and mesmerizing in their own right, but collectively, they are irresistible and what I have come to know as "Georgia."

After spending more than a year compiling this book, I would not dare claim to be as knowledgeable as a native, but I am no longer just a "visitor" either. My designation would fall somewhere in between. With that said, let me share with you some insight of what I've learned in my travels.

Atlanta is a wonderful, diverse, "BIG" city with all the perks we have come to expect. Yet, it also has a rich history that has been embraced and showcased well. Spending time in Atlanta is a must, but having a game plan is the only way to go. With so much to see and do in this wonderful city, plan your time and trip wisely using "A Lady's Day Out in Atlanta, Macon and Surrounding Areas" as your guide. Because of its size and traffic, you will have a much more enjoyable visit when you do.

When you venture beyond the city of Atlanta in any direction, you'll find true Southern hospitality permeates every nook and cranny. From the engaging people to the historical buildings and everything in between, we found the real South in all its glory! The towns featured in this book overflow with rich history, delightful shopping, delectable dining, and the Southern charm we all crave. A day in any one of these towns will only leave you wanting more, so plan to spend a few days in each, giving yourself time to embrace and appreciate all its splendor. Whether it is strolling through the downtowns and shopping in quaint boutiques and art galleries or relaxing in a bed and breakfast or a mountain cabin, we found something for everyone to enjoy. In the towns just north of the city, the beautiful Blue Ridge Mountains add another ingredient to our enchanting Southern mix. The mountain lakes and streams are great entertainment for those who enjoy fishing or river rafting, but are also very soothing to the soul for those looking for a quiet retreat. They possess a peaceful beauty I found very comforting.

I loved it all, and I know you will too. Have a great time and I will anxiously await the reports of your adventures. E-mail us at aladysdayout@aol.com.

Jennifer "Jenni" Ramsey

True Southern Soul, Shopping & Fun

Welcome to Atlanta and her gorgeous surrounding neighbors. Even the city's name seems to roll off the tongue with a slow Southern drawl. This Peach State capital and its surrounding towns are an amazing mixture of cobblestoned historic sites and upscale shopping; music legends and charming folklore; spirited celebrations and yummy peach pies! When Ray Charles sang "Georgia On My Mind," he coined a perfect phrase for the charm and magnetism of this beautiful place that is oh so hard to forget. In visiting Atlanta metro and all of her sophisticated communities, we found treasures in every corner of the city, from exclusive couture and artistic masterpieces to stenciled furniture and hand-thrown pottery. We lunched at adorable tearooms and dined in top-rated restaurants we know you will love. We rummaged in quaint antique shops and sashayed through Buckhead's chic boutiques. Every day was as much fun as the last!

Atlanta is an international business center, one of the world's top decorative markets, a trendsetting fashion mecca, and home to the "world's busiest airport." But it is also a gentle city that successfully blends its forward thinking ideas with its "Old South" traditions. The echoes of war are remembered throughout Atlanta and the surrounding towns that hold their pasts and traditions so near and dear.

In Atlanta and Marietta, you will be "charmed" with the famous Gone With the Wind Museum and Margaret Mitchell House and Museum. You will see the Jimmy Carter Presidential Library & Museum and the Martin Luther King, Jr. National Historic

Site, which commemorates the life and legacy of the famous Civil Rights Movement champion. Sports are definitely "major league" in Atlanta, where you can cheer on the Braves or see a Falcons' touchdown in the Georgia Dome.

South of Atlanta you can take time to smell all the roses, magnolias and peaches you possibly can. Then find the South's "musical roots" in the rhythm and blues of Macon, the hometown of Little Richard, the Godfather of Soul, and the unforgettable Otis Redding. Follow Union General William Tecumseh Sherman's "March to the Sea" through Milledgeville and the Heartland of the Confederacy. This city's warmth and beauty will amaze you with its "Capitals, Columns & Culture." Be sure to experience the "warmth" of Warm Springs and tour the Little White House where President Franklin D. Roosevelt spent summers in the healing warm waters of the land. And, of course, you must not leave this beautiful part of Georgia without a visit to the magnificent Callaway Gardens in Pine Mountain.

The Appalachian area north of Atlanta is a stunning land, blessed with glassy lakes and beautiful mountain vistas. You'll find toe-tapping bluegrass and folk music, a renaissance of notable Georgia wineries and unique Bavarian mountain communities. Enjoy awe-inspiring waterfalls, white-water rafting and fly-fishing. You can even tour a real gold mine and enjoy a "Moonshine Fest!" Take advantage of the limitless shopping opportunities, and then tour a Kangaroo sanctuary.

From Cabbage Patch Kids to NASCAR heroes, your entire family will find something exciting and memorable here. The magnolia-scented, moss-draped Atlanta and the wonderful small towns within her reach will wrap you in a loving embrace and serenade you with a soulful song that will stay forever on your mind.

"Georgia On My Mind"

Special People
Who Call Georgia Home

I have a dream . . .

Otis Redding

Born in Dawson, Otis Redding's father was a Baptist Minister, which may explain Otis' musical influence. When he was 5 years old, his family moved to Macon and he began his career as a singer in the church choir. Otis worked with Little Richard's former band, the Upsetters, sang at the Grand Duke Club, and joined Johnny Jenkins and the Pinetoppers. He appeared throughout the United States, Canada, Europe and the Caribbean. His concert tours were among the biggest box office successes of any touring performer during his time. Otis Redding's family still reside in Macon.

Martin Luther King, Jr.

Atlanta is the birthplace of famed civil rights leader, Martin Luther King, Jr. Known for his "I Have a Dream" speech, the African American clergyman, who advocated social change through non-violent means, was shot to death on April 4, 1968. However, his powerful writings and public appearances of the 1950s and 1960s, including his organized march on Washington, D.C., that drew 200,000 people demanding equal rights for minorities, won him the Nobel Peace Prize, and shaped the American civil rights movement. His influences on our society still live on today.

Ray Charles

Ray Charles, just the mere mention of his name sends a vision of the beloved blind pianist, cloaked in black sunglasses, bedecked in a savvy suit, rocking on the piano bench with head laid back belting out favored tunes from a mixed genre of jazz, R & B, Latin, blues, big band, country and gospel. The infamous singer, nicknamed "The Genius," helped make Pepsi popular with the slogan song, "You got the right one, Baby," and let the world know that he never forgot his

Georgia roots with one of his biggest hits, "Georgia On My Mind," which became the official state song in 1979.

Ray Charles, who was proud of his black heritage and the fact that he had been inducted into the Grammy Hall of Fame, won more than a dozen Grammy awards throughout his lifetime, including some awarded posthumously. After the singer's death, "Ray: The Movie," the story of his life, received several Oscar nominations, including best motion picture of the year.

Julia Roberts

Pretty woman Julia Roberts hails from Smyrna, where she is by far the most famous person to come from the quiet suburb of Atlanta. The multi-award winning actress is well known for her roles in "Erin Brockovich," "The Conspiracy Theory," "Steel Magnolias" and many more, but she will forever be associated with the popular film, "Pretty Woman" where she co-starred with Richard Gere.

Elton John

Maintaining a residence in Buckhead, and actively involved in many local organizations, the five-time Grammy award winner has adopted Atlanta as his hometown. As one of the world's greatest entertainers, this vocalist/pianist/songwriter, who won an Oscar and a Golden Globe for his musical contribution to "The Lion King," has recently had his image emblazoned on a fleet of Air Tran airplanes.

Whitney Houston

Atlanta resident, Whitney Houston, who was once referred to as America's sweetheart, has made an enormous contribution to American pop culture with hits such as "The Greatest Love of All," "I'm Every Woman," "I Wanna Dance with Somebody," and "Didn't We Almost Have it All." Her musical efforts have earned her several Grammy awards and over 20 American Music Awards.

Georgia's Peaches
– Its People

SONNY PERDUE

Born December 20, 1946 in Perry to a farmer and a classroom teacher, Governor Sonny Perdue had the seeds of servitude and Southern hospitality instilled deep within him.

Though at a young age he had vowed to become a veterinarian, and was well on his way to earning a doctorate in veterinary medicine from the University of Georgia, Perdue signed up to serve his country in the United States Air Force. Having served during Vietnam and reached the rank of Captain, Perdue received an honorable discharge in 1974.

Following a brief tenure as a practicing veterinarian in Raleigh, North Carolina, Perdue returned to his native Georgia where he became a successful businessman, starting two businesses in agribusiness and transportation. Today, those businesses have grown to include several locations across the Southeast.

Through the years, Perdue continued to serve the community as a Sunday school teacher, State Senator, Majority Leader and President Pro Tempore of the Georgia State Senate. Then on January 13, 2003, he was sworn in as the 81st Governor of Georgia.

Faith and family are at the heart of this Georgian Governor as he champions the cause of the New Georgia missions. He tackles tough issues like providing compassionate care for Georgia's children. He also works in making amendments to Georgia's Constitution for faith-based social service providers, allowing them to compete for government funding so they can maintain and improve services for all at-risk Georgians, especially children. Governor Perdue does not believe his state should discriminate against private, volunteer groups, merely because of connections to religious organizations.

In remembering that his position is one of public service, Governor Sonny Perdue personally initiated "Saturdays With Sonny," a program, which provides private one-on-one time with citizens from around the state of Georgia. Through these scheduled meetings with private citizens, Perdue listens as they share their thoughts, discuss issues, and ask questions.

True to his humble Southern-born, Southern-bred upbringing, the Governor says for all of his success in business and public service, he is proudest to hold the offices of devoted husband, loving father and proud grandfather.

The Georgia folks we had the pleasure to meet over the past year were very thankful to have Sonny Perdue as their Governor.

LINDA KERCE

Linda Kerce is one of the most amazing women you will ever have the pleasure to meet. This striking, energetic, exuberant Middle Georgian is one of the area's most successful businesswomen, with a passion for life that seems to touch everyone she meets. She is a mother, grandmother, community leader and the owner of four hugely successful businesses in Milledgeville.

"My life is centered around work and family," Linda says. "I wake up happy and go to bed happy."

Honestly, we can't believe she has time to sleep! Her energy and enthusiasm for everything she does radiates through her face in a beautiful smile, and in the way she lives her life.

Linda and her family have been in the construction and engineered truss business for many years, and she credits her father Johnny Kerce for her intuitive business sense. "I followed him around every job site from the time I was eight years old," she says, "and learned every part of the construction business."

Her father made her believe that a woman could be successful in a construction world that was dominated by men. Her mom, Dot, made sure this knowledge was coupled with a genteel Southern charm. Linda is still very much a part of that world with the family's engineered truss business, but she is also the owner of the beautiful and popular Serenity Wellness Spa in Milledgeville.

Spas have always been one of Linda's passions. In fact, she chooses her vacation destinations by the quality of the local spas. She visited the top spas in the country, drawing inspiration from her favorites in places like Las Vegas, New Mexico and Atlanta. Her desire in opening the spa was to bring the very best services and the purest comfort and serenity to the people of Milledgeville. Serenity Wellness Spa and Salon is a breathtaking combination of luxurious surroundings, tranquil music and calming fragrances. It is a full-service day spa, salon and gift boutique—the ultimate in pampering, fitness and beauty.

Linda and Bob Kerce have a beautiful home on Lake Sinclair, and absolutely love living on the lake. She recently became even more involved in the Lake Sinclair community when she purchased the long time local favorites, Choby's Restaurant and the Little River Park. This premier campground has long been a tradition on the lake, servicing fishermen and locals with gas, food and lodging space. She moved the popular Choby's Restaurant from across the street to the Little River Park, giving fishermen and customers a great place to relax and enjoy some of the best Southern food in the county.

We can't imagine what she runs on, but whatever it is, we want it! Linda's incredible energy and love for life is evident not only in the way she runs her businesses, but in the way she loves her family and friends. Holidays are the most special times at the Kerce home. In fact, you'll see the merry twinkling lights outlining her entire estate from across the lake. Her friends tease her that they can't stand still too long, or she'll hang lights on them! She entertains throughout the season with parties that are legendary, in a house that is decorated from floor to ceiling with bright and wonderful collected treasures.

When asked what drives her to keep going at such "get it done speed" Linda just laughs and says her energy comes from her love of friends, family, work, people, and the chance to share all that she has with others. You absolutely must meet this beautiful and special woman. She will dazzle you with her captivating smile and genuine love of life. Linda Kerce is indeed one of middle Georgia's most special people! *(See related stories pages 199, 204, 206)*

CHEF AUDREY GEORGE

Tucked into the mainstream of Warner Robins, amid the many chain restaurants and shops, beckons the uniquely different Chef Audrey's Bistro & Bakery. Brimming with culinary concoctions to tantalize the eyes and please the palate, the European-style eatery is the cache for celebrity chef Audrey George.

Chef Audrey, who is backed by a laundry list of degrees, certifications and expertise in the field of fine food, fulfills her life-long dreams as Executive and Pastry Chef of Chef Audrey's Bistro & Bakery, as well as host of middle-Georgia's "Now We're Cooking" cable show.

Whether donning her white chef's hat in front of cameras or the patrons of her self-named establishment, Chef Audrey is winning the affections of her followers. They've even made "Chef Audrey" the catchphrase in the Atlanta area.

However, Chef Audrey is quick to comment on her common cooking show quip, "It's all about me!" making it known that it's really not all about her.

"In the Scriptures it says, 'For surely I know the plans I have for you … Plans for your welfare and not for harm, to give you a future with hope.' — Jeremiah 29:11. That's my favorite verse and what keeps me grounded," Chef Audrey shared. "This restaurant, the television show, all that I am and all that I hope to become, is only by Him."

Once inside her eatery, it is easy to see her expressions of faith, from the beautiful landscape oil paintings, to the Christian literature intermittently dispersed throughout to the purposely placed prayer request boxes in the restrooms. And if that is not enough, even as the succulent scents of fine dining fills the air, so does the strains of Christian music.

"People know right away when they enter the restaurant that this is a Christian-oriented place," The Chef said.

Chef Audrey, who is accustomed to carrying on conversations with her dining guests, soon discovered many of the customers had a desire to see if she could cook up some Southern comfort food as well as she could flaunt her European fare. "My guests have requested that I offer a soul food fare, which, I guess, because I am African American, they assume I can do that well too," she said, adding a hearty laugh.

Recently, Chef Audrey's Bistro & Bakery added down-home menu items the third Thursday of every month. Items like black-eyed peas, collard greens, hearty meatloaf, three cheese macaroni and cheese, sliced tomatoes and onion, cornbread and biscuits are served up with a sermon, a side of soul-full singin' and a dollop of prayer. She calls it "Soul Food for the Soul." "This was something I felt God told me to do," she said. Packed with preachers o' plenty and songbirds of the soul, Chef Audrey hopes to feed her customers both body and soul. "I was nervous at first, thinking people would think I was strange ... but, I figure if I'm going soul, I'm going all the way. It's all about Him!"

Now, that's our "Chef of the South!" *(See related story page 307)*

BEVERLY BREMER
The Silver Lady on Peachtree Road

When standing inside the famous Beverly Bremer Silver Shop, a trove brimming with sterling silver treasures, one might find it hard to believe that Bremer's humble start was as unappealing as a tarnished silver spoon found in the back of Grandma's silverware drawer. Yet, her rags to riches story shines as brightly as all the polished silver in her shop.

At the very birth of the silver shop is the story of Beverly Bremer—a married, mother of three, and Buckhead volunteer.

Following her divorce, Bremer found herself responsible to support three children, one of whom had hospital bills over $30,000. Unfortunately, she had no means of income. Dumping her despair and swallowing her pride, Bremer took her prized possession, the *Burgundy* and *Francis I* sterling flatware trousseau her friends and relatives had given her as a wedding gift, and headed to a local flea market in hopes of hawking her goods to feed her children.

"I had to have money, and it was time to let my good grooming and my personal manners go. In short, I got over being a snob," Bremer recalled.

With her silver booth set up between a magician and a coin dealer, who later taught her about weights and measures, her first day at the flea market was a mixture of buying and selling silver.

Soon she found her niche.

"I began building my business one customer at a time," Bremer said.

With the added success of a simple black and white ad placed in national magazines that simply asked the question: "Missing a piece?" Silverware became her mainstay.

Her first year at the dank, rat-infested, very busy flea market proved profitable for Bremer. She earned $50,000 in sales. The next year she made $225,000, followed by third year sales of $500,000. With an eye for detail, a dogged determination and an ever-increasing list of famous flatware, her business continued to prosper from behind the secondhand counters and showcases at the month-to-month leased space.

"When I left the flea market (six years after her 1975 opening), I had $1 million in sales per year," Bremer said.

The savvy entrepreneur moved her silver business to her current Buckhead location, with the aid of a Brinks truck to haul the inventory.

Today, Bremer is known internationally as a connoisseur of countless collections of sterling flatware, hollowware, picture frames, jewelry, and is considered the Contessa of Table Settings. With an inventory of over 2,500 items on display and a customer base of well over 80,000, the Beverly Bremer Silver Shop is celebrating its 30th anniversary. And, offering silver with price tags from $20 to $40,000, there is surely something sterling for everyone.

If visiting the Buckhead area, stop in at the Beverly Bremer Silver Shop. Not only will you get your eyes full of some of the finest silver around, but you may even get a gregarious greeting from the "Silver Bell" of the shop. You can't miss her ... she's the tall, ageless blonde, dressed with impeccable taste and sporting a wonderful sense of humor. *(See related story page 43)*

JEAN KIDD

How would you like to have to tell your husband that you bought "half a town" while you were out shopping?!! That is exactly what Jean Kidd had to do in 1982. She and two friends had started out with their daughters to visit Callaway Gardens when they accidentally found the small rural community of Warm

Springs. This beautiful and historic town had been quite a thriving community in the past, drawing visitors from around the world to see the Little White House where President Franklin D. Roosevelt spent his summers. When President Roosevelt died there in 1945 the town suffered a downward spiral, and had little life left. Jean says she couldn't even find a cup of coffee while she was there.

As she and her friends sat on the curb in knee high grass, an idea began to formulate that would eventually bring life and vitality once again to Warm Springs. In the dilapidated and run down buildings she envisioned brightly painted walls and potted plants, charming signage and rocking chairs on the front porches, and shoppers with bags piled high. She saw the promise of what could be. As fate would have it, the man who owned the buildings happened by and saw Jean's interest. "Want to buy it?" he asked. She did!

Jean immediately began to contact business owners she knew about relocating to Warm Springs in her "half town," and found someone to buy the other side of the street. She found bed and breakfast owners, antique dealers, bakers and boutique owners who worked along side each other in rebuilding, redecorating and revitalizing the sleepy town. She added benches for brave husbands and landscaped the beautiful courtyard. Today people flock to Warm Springs to browse through the interesting and unique shops on Broad Street, to spend an afternoon in the Victorian Tea Room, or to once again tour President Roosevelt's Little White House. All because Jean Kidd happened by one day, looked past the weeds and peeling paint and saw the promise of the future in Warm Springs.

Jean Kidd is a woman of amazing character and strength. She is energetic, creative and insightful, and credits her challenging childhood for her never-say-never attitude. After living in an orphanage and then with a neglectful foster mother, Jean was finally adopted by Mrs. Acuff.

Jean's adoptive mother was an antique dealer who taught her the antique business at a very early age. Later, Jean used her trained eye and creative talent to renovate a 150-year-old farmhouse near Warm Springs with her husband. She loves this beautiful part of Georgia and says that it is like "stepping back in time." Thank you Jean Kidd for seeing all of the wonderful possibilities in historic Warm Springs. This charming town will be one of your favorite places to visit!

LISA NEWSOM

Have you ever picked up a magazine and found yourself so intrigued by the simple, yet sophisticated, cover you couldn't wait to take a peek inside? Then once inside, your eyes were so dazzled by each beautiful photo, and every article was so articulate and tastefully written that you absolutely devoured every word? If so, you might be one of the more than 435,000 readers of *VERANDA* magazine.

This celebrated magazine, distinguished by its artful photography of interiors, gardens, table settings and floral arrangements, as well as authoritative articles on decorative arts, books, collectibles, luxury goods and must-see art exhibitions, is the brainchild of Georgia native Lisa Beckwith Newsom.

Founder and editor-in-chief of the Atlanta-based publication, Lisa has been blessed with a discerning eye for detail, quality and beauty. These inspire her to dig deep within the world of professional journalism, cultivating top designers, photographers, editors, writers and stylists. Drawing upon the expertise of editors such as Miguel Flores-Vianna, formerly of *House Beautiful*, *Town & Country* and *Elle Decor*, and Tom Woodham, former contributor to the Chicago Tribune, The Atlanta Journal and American Horticulturist, as well as the skills of publisher Sims Bray, who oversees advertising and marketing, Newsom is clearly dedicated to excellence.

However, despite *VERANDA's* success, Lisa remains modest, inspiring loyalty and respect. She did not seek out fame and fortune in publishing. As a matter of fact, her first career choice was that of a medical technologist. It was during her work in that field that she met and married Neal Newsom, a much-admired, now-retired Atlanta physician. Supporting his career, she became the mother of four children. It wasn't until much later that she launched her unlikely career in the world of magazines.

It was "unlikely" because Lisa did not have a journalism background or training as a writer, nor did she possess skills in the field of advertising. Yet she had a passion to pursue that which she loved, upscale home publications.

It all started in 1976 when a company conducted a direct-mail campaign to see if there was sufficient public interest in a proposed Southern interiors magazine. The response was dismal. Lisa, who was trained in art and design, believed the concept was a good one and provided a new mailing list, pinpointing the right audience. This time, the response was overwhelmingly favorable. Lisa became a co-founder of *Southern Accents* and went on to serve as its editor-in-chief. She stayed with that magazine nearly 10 years until it was about to be bought out by an Alabama-based company.

Determined that she could create a new upscale home magazine that would expand on her ideas, Lisa, along with Chuck Ross, former art director of *Architectural Digest*, ventured out on their own. Soon, *VERANDA* made its debut in the South but rapidly expanded nationally and internationally. In 2002, The Hearst Corporation bought the magazine, and its founding editor continues to lead the staff. *VERANDA* showcases the country's leading designers and travels far and wide to bring its readers some of the most fascinating interiors of the world. And to think, it all started with a Southern belle who had a passion to preserve something she loved.

Discover Atlanta

Perhaps no city in the United States can rival Atlanta for its beauty, vibrancy and history. It is the capital of the "Peach State," a high-energy shopping mecca, and a beautiful "Gateway to the South." Atlanta has a rather brassy, Bohemian personality tempered with a sweeping Southern style and charm. You will stay busy from morning to night discovering all of Atlanta's exciting and historical attractions. Whether your love is roller coasters, cozy tea rooms, zoos or Armani, Atlanta is your city.

Atlanta began like many cities, with the coming of the railroad. In 1837, the Western & Atlantic Railroad decided that Atlanta would be its southern endpoint, and named the area Terminus. The name changed to Marthasville in 1843 and then finally to Atlanta in 1845. Within just a few years, the community became a major transportation city, linking the North to the South. It is still considered to be a center of transportation in the United States. Everyone has surely heard the saying, "No matter where you are traveling, you have to go through Atlanta." The Hartsfield-Jackson Atlanta International Airport is located just 10 miles south of downtown, and is currently the world's busiest airport. *The Atlanta and Georgia Tour Manual* notes that "80 percent of the nation's population lies within a two-hour flight of Atlanta."

It's easy to get here, and once you do, you will be swept up in this Southern city's bewitching glamour. It will charm you with its culture and class, and entertain you with everything from top-rated theater and art to superior shopping venues and world-class cuisine.

For a city whose history was indeed almost gone with the wind of Civil War, Atlanta has risen from the ashes to become a glorious testament to the strength of her inhabitants. It has become a dynamic cultural mix of old and new, a city with antebellum social graces and futuristic expectations. We know you will love discovering all of the fascinating areas of Atlanta metro and the charming outlying communities. We have found some of the most interesting boutiques, antique shops, tea rooms and galleries that attract visitors from across the world. We found places to rendezvous with the past, kick our heels up, and shop 'til we drop. Frankly my dear...Atlanta is absolutely incredible!

The Winds of War

As a small "rail terminus," Atlanta was said to have been a rather rough place to live—a frontier town built around the railroad depot and a far cry from the mint-juliped city it has become. By the time General Sherman marched through with his Union troops in 1864, the city had grown to be a beautiful and vibrant place, filled with stunning antebellum homes and thriving businesses. There were four rail lines, iron foundries, tanneries, banks and retail shops, and it was the shipping center of the Confederacy.

As depicted in the epic novel *"Gone with the Wind"* by Margaret Mitchell, much of the pre-war grandeur of Atlanta was destroyed during the Civil War. General William Tecumseh Sherman laid siege to Atlanta for an entire month until it surrendered on September 2, 1864. He ordered the city evacuated and everything burned. It is said that when Sherman began his "march to the sea" there were only 400 structures left standing. General Sherman's "Burning of Atlanta" forced the ghost town to rebuild everything.

The Areas of Atlanta—A Box of Chocolates

Affluent residents began building magnificent homes on lower Peachtree, Whitehall, Marietta, Broad and Washington Streets, and this "silk stocking" area became known as the **Buckhead** Community. Buckhead has remained the "shopping mecca of the Southeast" through the years with upscale shops, fine restaurants and beautiful people. *The Atlanta Journal-Constitution* calls Buckhead a place "where old money lives and new money parties!" History buffs love examining the Georgian and neoclassical architecture in the 1950s and 1960s mansions of Buckhead. The area is also home to the Governor's Mansion, the historic Swan House and the Atlanta History Center. You will find luxury hotels, swanky nightclubs, exclusive restaurants, art galleries and specialty boutiques. A visit to the Atlanta's famous Buckhead area is a definite must!

Chamblee also offers great shopping. Don't miss Atlanta's Chinatown Shopping Square, which features two restaurants, a grocery store, a bookstore, jewelers and many other retail shops.

Sandy Springs is a bit off the beaten path but well worth your time. Are you a history buff? Heritage Sandy Springs manages the Sandy Springs Historic Site and the Williams-Payne House at 6075 Sandy Springs Circle. The historical house is a museum with working gardens around the springs for which Sandy Springs was named.

Vinings has its own charm as well. From antique shops to darling boutiques, you'll get lost in the Southern beauty of it all. Don't miss the Vinings Jubilee Shopping Center on Paces Ferry Road.

Each area of Atlanta has its own charm and unique identity. You'll find great shopping, wonderful dining, historical sites, natural beauty and hot nightlife in every section. Our advice? Sample each area like fine chocolates and enjoy a little decadence!

Scarlett's Atlanta

Though the actual mansion called "Tara" didn't really exist, the incredibly beautiful land of this area was Margaret Mitchell's inspiration for the best-selling novel that defines our image of pre-war antebellum Atlanta. *"Gone with the Wind"* was one of the best-selling and adored novels of all time, and continues to mesmerize fans with its haunting memories of an antebellum South torn apart by war. Never will we forget Scarlett and Rhett, Ashley and Melanie, or the scene of the city of Atlanta as it burned to the ground. A visit to the Margaret Mitchell House & Museum features a documentary, photographs and exhibits that tell the story of author Margaret Mitchell's life. The brick house behind the main building is where Mitchell and her husband lived and where she wrote most of the novel.

Top Atlanta Attractions

The Jimmy Carter Presidential Library and Museum showcases important documents, President Carter's Nobel Peace Prize and a life-size replica of the Oval Office. The Atlanta History Center offers visitors a glimpse of the city's history, a Civil War display and changing exhibits through the year. Zoo Atlanta is located in historic Grant Park and is home to giant pandas named Lun Lun and Yang Yang. Midtown's Piedmont Park is one of the city's favorite destinations for walking, jogging and biking, and is the site for many of the city's seasonal festivals. Turner Field is home to the famous Atlanta Braves, one of America's favorite baseball teams. This downtown stadium also houses the Ivan Allen Jr. Braves Museum and Hall of Fame. Lennox Square and Phipps Plaza are two of the city's most prominent malls, located in the exclusive Buckhead community. Atlanta's Antique District includes Bennett Street, Miami Circle and Chamblee's Antique Row—fabulous places to shop for incredible antiques and collectibles. Historic Oakland Cemetery is the final resting place of many of the city's prominent citizens, including Margaret Mitchell, author of *"Gone with the Wind"*. It is a beautiful "green place" and an example of a Victorian-era, rural garden cemetery.

For more information about Atlanta, contact the Atlanta Convention and Visitors Bureau at 800-ATLANTA, 404-521-6600 or visit www.atlanta.net online.

Atlanta
Fairs Festivals & Fun

January
  Honda Battle of the Bands
  Power Plays, The Essential
    Theatre Festival

February
  Southeastern Flower Show

April
  Atlanta Dogwood Festival
  Blue Grass Festival
  Decorators' Show House
  Inman Park Festival and Tour of
    Homes

May
  Atlanta Jazz Festival
  Sweet Auburn Spring Festival
  Tour of Homes

June
  Atlanta Film Festival
  Atlanta Pride Festival
  Music Midtown
  The VIBE MusicFest
  Virginia-Highland Summer
    Festival

July
  Heritage Arts Festival
  National Black Arts Festival

August
  Latino Festival

September
  DragonCon Festival
  Montreux Atlanta
  Sandy Springs Festival
  Yellow Daisy Festival at Stone
    Mountain Park

October
  Atlanta Greek Festival
  Harvest Midtown Festival
  Pumpkin Festival at Stone
    Mountain Park
  Taste of Atlanta

November
  A Southern Christmas at Stone
    Mountain Park

December
  Christmas Parade Downtown
  Festival of Trees

MICHAEL GIBSON
ANTIQUES & DESIGN, INC.

Michael Gibson has always had a love for art, history and beautiful items, so he began his career in art and design when he was only 12! Michael studied in adult classes with Austrian artist Anton Weiss, and began selling his own paintings at the age of 16. On a buying trip to the Orient in 1985, Michael realized that

he could use his design talents in the production of fine quality furniture, using copies of 18th and 19th century French and English furniture. His beautiful Atlanta showroom, at 631 Miami Cir., is filled with his "Family Heirloom Collection"—exceptional mahogany reproduction furniture—and antique treasures. Stop by Monday-Saturday 10 am-6 pm and Sunday by appointment only. For more information, visit www.michaelgibsonantiques.com online or call 404-261-7161. *(Color photo featured in front section of book.)*

Jane J. Marsden
Antiques & Interiors

Looking for the "crème de la crème" in home décor? Everyone in Atlanta knows exactly where to shop. In fact, even the address gives it away. Jane Marsden Antiques & Interiors, 2300 Peachtree Rd. A-102 in Buckhead, is one of the most beautiful, elegant and remarkable places you will ever visit. The cobblestone entrance gives the allure of a castle gate, and the buildings appear to have been transported from another time and place. The complex is located in the Peachtree Battle area on the banks of Peachtree Creek, near the site of a famous Civil War battle, with Marsden's building as the anchor. Some of Atlanta's most distinctive antique dealers and designers have shops here—each unique and memorable.

The "Marsden Magic," as the business has been called, can be attributed to the talents of the entire Marsden family. Jane, her daughter Janie and her son-in-law Mike have built a hugely successful business. Jane lives above the store in an apartment that opens onto the patio gardens, while Janie and Mike are renovating an old apartment building adjacent to the property.

The entire store is bathed in brilliant light from antique crystal chandeliers, which illuminate the distinguished antiques and fine porcelains displayed throughout. Handsome English and French pieces hold porcelains, crystal, lamps, and objects d'art, and luxurious rugs cover the floor. The Marsden family scours the world for special pieces, knowing that "they bring authenticity and an Old World root to their clients' interiors." You must visit this incredible place to appreciate the beauty of the many special items inside. Jane Marsden Antiques & Interiors is open Monday-Friday 9 am-5 pm and Saturday 11 am-4 pm. Visit www.marsdenantiques.com or call 404-355-1288. *(Color photo featured in front section of book.)*

Luxury has never been more affordable! The Plantation Shop, 3193 Roswell Rd. is tucked into the heart of Atlanta's famous Buckhead area. It's all you will need to know for classic style and designs for your home. The Plantation Shop first opened its doors in 1979 in Florida, then in 1992 in the Buckhead area of Atlanta, and the newest location in North Carolina. All stores are family-owned-and-operated and have become local favorites. The Buckhead store features fine English and French antiques, reproductions and accessories, including a great mix of lamps and wall art. The store is beautifully decorated with elegant antiques displaying collections of china, silver, crystal and tabletop décor. The talented staff can assist you in decorating every room in your home with fine linens, original artwork, porcelains and so much more.

The Plantation Shop also is well known for its own line of classic children's clothing. The collection includes designs with finely appointed details in hand-selected fabrics and you will find beautifully smocked and embroidered pieces, as well as sister-brother coordinated outfits perfect for holidays and special occasions. Be sure to visit www.theplantationshop.com online to see some of the special pieces in the Children's Collection and shop for home accessories, gifts and furniture.

The Plantation Shop is a classic! It is unrivaled in its presentation of sophisticated antiques and accessories for the home. The wonderful staff is always there to greet and help you with any decorating need, making sure your shopping experience is unforgettable. Open Monday through Saturday 10 am-6 pm. For more information, call 404-239-1866. *(Color photo featured in front section of book.)*

CHAMBLEE'S ANTIQUE ROW DISTRICT

Chamblee's Antique Row District is a must stop for antique lovers. This great attraction of charming antique shops offers the unexpected in shopping and dining. If you haven't shopped Chamblee—you haven't shopped!

My Sister's Closet, 5350 Peachtree Rd., specializes in resale of nearly new and vintage apparel, along with accessories such as jewelry, hats, shoes and handbags. Items arrive weekly from private and estate collections. Visit www.mysistersclosetonline.com or call 770-458-8362.

Broad Street Antique Mall, 3550 Broad St., features selections of American and English furniture, Black Americana, paintings and prints, pottery and glassware, and vintage jewelry. Call 770-458-6316 or 877-645-4728.

Rust 'n' Dust Antiques, 5486 Peachtree Rd., has one of the South's largest collections of sports equipment, furniture, radios, luggage, western gear, phones, toys and Coca Cola memorabilia. Call 770-458-1614.

Faded Rose Tea Garden & Restaurant, 2201 American Industrial Way, serves lunch Monday-Saturday 11 am-2:30 pm, afternoon tea until 4 pm, and dinner Friday-Saturday 5-9 pm. Call 678-547-0273 or visit www.fadedroseteagarden.com.

For more information on all of the wonderful Antique Row businesses, visit www.antiquerow.com or call 770-458-1614.

 ## ATLANTA ANTIQUE GALLERY

Atlanta Antique Gallery, 3550-A Broad St. in Chamblee's Antique Row District, has 11,000 square feet, with 155 showcases and 50,000 antiques! Don't miss the costume jewelry, art deco, toys, glass, barware, pottery, porcelain, Victorian smalls, and so much more. Open Tuesday-Saturday 10 am-5 pm and Sunday 1-5 pm. Visit www.atlantaantiquegallery.com or call 770-457-7444.

Antiques of Vinings

Located at the foot of Historic Vinings Mountain on the outskirts of Atlanta, you'll find the charming Antiques of Vinings. Once a group of 13 individual antique shops, they consolidated in 1992 to form one upscale multi-dealer shop. As a result of their shopping trips abroad, the dealers at Antiques of Vinings offer a stunning variety of 18th and 19th century English, French and Continental furniture, porcelain and silver, as well as an assortment of American antiques, oriental rugs, paintings and prints. A shopping trip to beautiful Antiques of Vinings combined with a tasty lunch at one of the Jubilee's charming cafés will make for a delightful "Ladies Day Out." Located at 4300 Paces Ferry Rd. NW in the Jubilee Shopping Center, and is open Monday-Saturday 10 am-5 pm. Browsers are always welcome! Call 770-434-1228.

Bakeries

Beautiful cakes on pedestals fill the windows of the Little European Bakery, 334 Sandy Springs Cir. NE in Sandy Springs, luring you inside to a decadent selection of baked goods. Owners Mike, Vicki and Steve Rogers offer beautiful, tasty European-style breads, pastries, tortes, cookies and pies, which are baked daily. The bakery was featured in *Southern Living* in October 2004 for their unusual custom cakes for all occasions. The full-service delicatessen features delicious sandwiches on homemade bread, as well as a large selection of imported food items from Europe. This bakery is a shopper's delight offering unique gift items, from tabletop accessories to gifts for baby. Open Tuesday-Friday 8 am-6 pm and Saturday until 4 pm. Call 404-255-8200 or visit online www.littleeuropeanbakery.com. If in Alpharetta, stop by their second location at 3050-A Winward Plaza Dr. or call 678-319-9568.

Bridal & Weddings

A BRIDAL SALON

The most important decision a bride makes when planning her wedding is, of course, her wedding dress. That's why Joan Pillow is committed to helping each bride find the dress of her dreams. With Joan's background in high-end retail with stores like Neiman Marcus and Marshall Fields, the transition into the bridal industry was a natural step. She credits Stanley Marcus for instilling the vision, integrity and principals that have made her bridal boutique one of the most successful in the nation. Impressions is located at 99 W. Paces Ferry Rd. NW in the heart of Atlanta's upscale Buckhead district. Joan carries Vera Wang,

Christos, Monique Lhuillier, Ulla-Maija, Carolina Herrera, Peter Langner and Richard Glasgow. Open Monday-Saturday 10 am-5 pm, but appointments are always suggested. Call 404-841-6202 or visit www.impressionsbridalsalon.com online. *(Color photo featured in front section of book.)*

This long-time Atlanta favorite is located in a historic Buckhead residence that has been made into a fabulous designer women's clothing store. Susan Lee Fine Ladies Attire, 56 E. Andrews Dr. NW, is a beautiful place to shop for the finest in women's clothing from casual wear to the most formal gown. Because Susan Lee has been a part of the apparel markets in New York, the West Coast and abroad for many years, she carries many designers exclusive to Atlanta. Whether you are

looking for a mother-of-the-bride dress, something fabulous for a formal ball, or just something fun and casual for a special event, you must visit this charming shop. Mom and daughter run the store (along with the adorable Shitshu, She She Lee). Stop by Monday-Saturday 10 am-6 pm. Call 404-365-0693. *(Color photo featured in front section of book.)*

Children's

Visit just once and you'll see why Sweet Repeats, 321-B Pharr Rd., was previously voted "Atlanta's Best Consignment Shop" by *Atlanta Magazine*. Leigh-Ellen Fitzgerald is an energetic, very friendly owner who is committed to making Sweet Repeats your favorite and first place to shop. She takes only quality, gently used children's and maternity clothing. Hours are Monday-Saturday 10 am-5 pm. For consignment appointments, visit www.sweetrepeatsatlanta.com online or call 404-261-7519.

Fashion & Accessories

Considered one of Atlanta's best special occasion shops, Celebrity on Paces has been fulfilling its customers' needs for more than 20 years. This beautiful shop, located at 99 W. Paces Ferry Rd. in the distinguished Buckhead area of Atlanta, has achieved a discerning customer following from the Southeastern United States. The owners and experienced staff take pride in having their customers leave with the "perfect" garment for any occasion. They offer a wide variety of daytime, cocktail, eveningwear, and mother of the bride apparel, by quality designers, such as Baratelli and Tom & Linda Platt. Let Celebrity on Paces dress you for those very special occasions in your life. The store is open Monday-Saturday 10 am-5 pm. Call 404-237-5565. *(Color photo featured in front section of book.)*

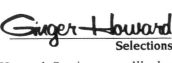

Not only will you find wonderful clothing and accessories at Ginger Howard Sections, you'll also be treated like a lifelong friend. The warm and friendly staff at 3164 Peachtree Rd. in Buckhead is so personable that many customers drop by just to say hi. The boutique is named Ginger Howard Selections because owner Ginger Howard personally selects the very best and latest in fine fashions for her customers. She carries Sara Campbell, an exclusive line of dresses and sportswear, as well as the trendiest in fashion accessories. Open Monday through Saturday 10 am-5 pm. To learn more, call 404-869-0115.

Makeup artist, fashion consultant, image-maker, Beth Ann does it all. Celebrated throughout Atlanta, Beth Ann has created a divine boutique consisting of makeup that adds spice and vigor with hot new colors, jewelry designed internationally and locally, and vintage accessories sought after for their innovative style. Beth Ann continues to captivate both the media and the Southeast region's fashion savvy women who have closely followed her lavish career from model to image maker. Stop by Beth Ann's, 47 Irby Ave., in Buckhead's West Village. Call 404-233-4424 or visit www.bethanninc.com online.

Transcending several generations and catering to people of all walks of life, this trendy ladies boutique has been "dazzling" Buckhead for more than 30 years. Razzle Dazzle, 49 Irby Ave., features lines like Juicy Couture, Da-Nang, Michael Stars, ABS, Raw 7 and Free People. You will love the great fitting jeans, embroidered novelty T-shirts and gorgeous sweaters. Stop by Monday-Saturday 10:30 am-5 pm. For more information, visit www.razzledazzleboutique.com online or call 404-233-6940.

Heart to Heart
for Kids, Inc.

When Pam Smart heard that several children at a local YMCA were sidelined from the pool because they didn't have the proper attire, she was moved to action. Pam established Heart to Heart for Kids, a non-profit organization that has helped make a difference in the lives of underprivileged children, "one hand and one heart at a time." In May 2003, Heart to Heart opened an upscale boutique in Buckhead to raise funds for the organization. Located at 3198 Paces Ferry Pl., the store carries both new and nearly new high-end designer clothing and accessories for women and children. And, one hundred percent of the proceeds go directly to serve underprivileged children. The boutique is open Monday-Friday 9 am-5 pm. For more information, call 404-949-0904 or visit www.hearttoheartforkids.org online.

ALEXIS MATERNITY COLLECTIONS

Alexis Maternity Collections is one of the finest maternity boutiques in the Sandy Springs area of Atlanta. Located in the Abernathy Shopping Center at 6631-G Roswell Rd. NE, the shop always has the latest fashions at great prices in casual, career and special occasion maternity clothing. The goal is to offer a variety of quality merchandise and a high level of service! Don't miss the other location at 1860 Duluth Hwy. in Lawrenceville. Open Monday-Saturday 10 am-6 pm and Sunday noon-5 pm. Call 404-236-0105 or visit www.alexismaternitycollections.com.

merci woman

Full-figured women of Atlanta have a friend in Merrideth Colwell-Shea, owner of Merci Woman, 4511 Olde Perimeter Way, #500. She carries wardrobe selections for special occasions, work, play and exercise, as well as jewelry and fashion accessories. Open Monday-Saturday 10 am - 7 pm and Sunday noon - 5 pm. Visit www.merciwoman.com or call 770-399-9899.

OH! FINE LINGERIE

This elegant lingerie boutique features hand-selected vintage clothing, jewelry and exquisite European fine-designer lingerie. Oh! Fine Lingerie, 3209 Paces Ferry Pl. in Buckhead. Open Tuesday-Saturday 11 am-6 pm. Don't miss this one! Call 404-949-9901.

Furniture

Savvy Snoot is a unique, upscale furniture consignment store neatly tucked to the back of Atlanta's chic Westside Urban Market at 1187 Howell Mill Rd. The name says it all...snooty brand furniture at savvy prices. Owner/operator Marty Mason has created a winning concept by cleverly mixing one-of-a-kind pieces with designer furniture in contemporary, traditional and retro styles. Savvy Snoot prides itself on using individual consignment pieces to fashion a certain "look." Customers also receive assistance in acquiring their look by using Savvy Snoot as a resource. If you are on the hunt for that special piece, the Savvy Snoot is just the place to find it—the hunt stops here! Stop by the Savvy Snoot Monday-Saturday 10 am-5 pm. For more information, visit www.savvysnoot.com or call 404-355-1399.

Andrea's
china cabinet, inc.

It is "a designer look at a discount," that will quickly become your favorite place to shop in Atlanta for unique home accessories, antiques and wonderful gifts. Andrea's China Cabinet, Inc., 764 Miami Cir. in Buckhead, has evolved over the last 30 years into one of the area's most respected stores, due mostly to the faces behind the counter! Judy Appel and daughter Andrea Davis have a definite flair for design and a discriminating eye for the latest trends, but they love a bargain. We found furniture, crystal, jewelry, vintage and reproduction Chinese porcelains, hand-painted Italian chests, framed art, beautiful lighting, French earthenware and more! It is the perfect place to shop! Open Monday - Saturday 10 am-5 pm. Call 404-869-1850 for information.

Fine Gifts
by Glass, Etc.

After a long and successful career with Anchor Hocking and Corning companies, Ed Sutter and his wife Shirley decided to open a retail store specializing in dinnerware and kitchen serving pieces. Glass Etc., 4135 La Vista Rd. (770-493-7936) in Tucker became their first store in 1983, and was successful, but they soon realized that there was even greater opportunity in the fast growing collectible market. They added collectibles to their merchandise and the business just exploded.

In 1995, with their daughter Cathy Seagraves they opened a store in Sandy Springs at 6623 C. Roswell Rd. (404-250-1010), and another location, in Woodstock at 1428 Towne Lake Pkwy. (678-445-0137). Now known as Fine Gifts by Glass Etc., these shops have become complete gift stores, making it easy for all of Atlanta to find exactly what they are looking for. The sparkling stores provide an ever-changing collection of wonderful lines, such as Hummel, Swarovski, Fenton Glass, Wee Forest Folk, Madam Alexander Dolls, and Dept. 56. You'll find gifts for every occasion and holiday from names like Arthur Court, Mariposa, The Thymes and Brighton.

This family-owned-and-operated collection of fine gift stores is committed to providing a warm and comfortable shopping atmosphere where experienced, dedicated, and friendly sales people will serve you. You will find wonderfully unique glass pieces that will transform any room in your home. For more information, visit www.finegifts.com online. Stop by Fine Gifts by Glass Etc. Monday-Friday 10 am-7 pm, Saturday until 6 pm and Sunday (Sept.-Dec.) 1-5 pm.

Boxwoods Gardens & Gifts, located at 100 E. Andrews Dr. in Atlanta, is one of the most popular shops in the Southeast due to its eclectic mix of affordable merchandise. Offering everything from unique gifts and home accessories to faux bois planters and antique furniture, Boxwoods has it all! Established in 1995 in a small English-style cottage, Boxwoods has steadily grown so that it now occupies two charming side-by-side houses, a connecting breezeway, two flower-filled conservatories, a large exterior courtyard, and an ever-changing outdoor garden area. Co-owners Dan Belman and Randy Korando go on quarterly buying trips to Europe, as well as frequent outings across the United States to keep their inventory at its overstocked best. This shop's unusual blend of merchandise has been featured in numerous national publications and cited in dozens of "best of" listings—it truly is a shopper's paradise! Stop by Monday-Saturday 10 am-6 pm. For more information, call 404-233-3400.

BREAD   BOOKS   GIFTS

Owner Carol Johnson, a Buckhead native, first began baking whole-grain bread for friends. The demand for her delicious, premium whole-wheat bread became so great, she felt led to open what she calls, "a market place ministry serving bread and The Word." All of Carol's baked goods are free from preservatives and processed flour and her selection includes a variety of breads, as well as cookies, granola, muffins and sandwiches. You will also find inspirational books and gifts, beautiful linens, jewelry and more! Full Cup Bread, Books & Gifts offers unique one-of-a-kind, high-end, inspiration gifts created by local artists. Located at 3188 Paces Ferry Pl. NW, Full Cup is open Monday-Friday 9 am-5:30 pm and Saturday 10 am-5 pm. For more information, call 404-848-1002 or visit www.fullcup.org online.

the Scarlet Tassel

UNCOMMON GIFTS & HOME ACCENTS

Since its opening, The Scarlet Tassel has established itself as a successful home décor and gift store in Sandy Springs. In fact, the highly regarded store was awarded the Bronze ASID 2004 Design Excellence Award. With close to 40 years of combined retail and catalog experience and innate style, owners Shelly Dozier-McKee and Deirdre Staab have

created an extraordinary showroom of wonderful gift items, home accessories and furnishings. You will find accent furniture, candles, lighting, wall décor, textiles, personal care items, wine/bar accessories and, of course, fabulous tassels. The Scarlet Tassel is located at 6235-A Roswell Rd. and is open Monday-Saturday 10 am - 6 pm and Sunday noon - 5 pm. Call 404-843-0387 or visit www.thescarlettassel.com online.

BELLES CHOSES

Though born and bred in Atlanta, Patricia Pennington enjoys all that is French. Her amazing store Belles Choses, 4300 Paces Ferry Rd. SE in the Vinings' Jubilee Shopping Center, is an incredible collection of beautiful gifts and home accessories, as well as elegant French antiques that will give your home a true "French accent." From hand-glazed pottery and crystal stemware to exquisite table and bed linens, Belles Choses is a cornucopia of inspired products from France and truly lives up to its name, which means, "beautiful things." You will also find a wonderful selection of children's clothing from Zutano, Amanda Remembered and Bailey Boys, as well as soft, cuddly stuffed animals. Don't miss the other location at City Walk in Sandy Springs at 227 Sandy Springs Pl. NE. Belles Choses is open Monday-Saturday 10 am-6 pm. For more information, call 770-435-8384 or visit www.belleschoses.com online.

Gifts and Home Decor

What a fun, fabulous place to shop! Felicity Gifts and Home Décor is located in a 1920s cozy cottage at 150 Hilderbrand Rd. in Sandy Springs. Decorated in warm colors and bright displays, Felicity offers a remarkable selection of fun, fashion accessories; beautiful jewelry and handbags; children's items; and artsy, elegant gifts for the home. You will love the delightful atmosphere and appreciate the tea and sweets while you shop. Be sure to ask about the beautiful complimentary giftwrap.

Owners Yvette and Tim Saker host Felicity's "Girls Day Out" once a month from 10 am-8 pm—where customers are treated to light fare, beverages, a gift with purchase, and, of course, great sales. The boutique is open Monday-Saturday 10 am-6 pm, with extended holiday hours. Call 404-843-6456 or visit www.felicitygifts.com online.

Buckhead
Ornamentals
Personal Style for
YOU, YOUR HOME & GARDEN

Buckhead Ornamentals is a personal-style store presenting a unique and eclectic product mix for your home, garden and gift giving needs. This store, located at 721 Miami Cir., #106 in Atlanta, offers more than 140 wonderfully expressive lines, focusing on color, with a high focus on quality. You will find beautiful furniture (even Asian antiques), divine tabletop collections, hand thrown ceramic dinnerware, gourmet foods, stationery and even personal care items. In addition, this store celebrates the talent of local artists. Open Monday-Saturday 10 am-5 pm. For more information, visit www.buckheadornamentals.com online or call 404-816-9338.

Hotels & Inns

WYNDHAM VININGS℠

Located in a wooded oasis in the Historic Vinings area of Atlanta, this striking, elegant hotel echoes the charm and Southern hospitality of a bygone era. Wyndham Hotel & Resort, 2857 Paces Ferry Rd., is a quiet, beautiful hotel that is just minutes from everything Atlanta has to offer. The rooms are handsomely decorated and furnished with your total comfort in mind. From the pillow top mattresses and shower massagers to the designer bath and body products, you will love being pampered. Business travelers will appreciate the cordless and speakerphones, modem/data port, and work desk in each room. And, the Overlook Room at the Wyndham is the perfect place for memorable occasions. For information or reservations, call 770-432-5555 or visit www.wyndham.com online.

Whether you are traveling just for pleasure or on business, you will find the Fairfield Inn & Suites all that you have come to expect from Marriott Hotels. This outstanding seven-story hotel is located in the Vinings area of Atlanta—2450 Paces Ferry Road—just minutes from Six Flags, Turner Field, Georgia Dome, Buckhead and downtown. The guest rooms are full of thoughtful amenities such as, cable television, refrigerator, coffee maker, pull-out sofa bed and a crib, if needed. Some rooms have beautiful panoramic views of the Atlanta skyline.

Guests are treated to a complimentary breakfast buffet, high-speed Internet access, a newspaper, and the coffee pot in the lobby is always on. For more information, call 770-435-4500, 800-455-7007 or visit www.marriott.com online.

Atlanta Perimeter's newest all-suite hotel allows guests to feel more comfortable than ever before. Atlanta's Staybridge Suites at 4601 Ridgeview Rd. is committed to being your "home away from home." There are three floor plans including a two bedroom, two-bathroom suite, and you can stay connected with voice mail, data port and high speed Internet service. The hotel offers a daily hot breakfast and evening receptions Tuesday-Thursday. Visit www.staybridge.com/atlanta-pr or call 800-238-8000 or 678-320-0111.

ᔑ WAN ℋOUSE

From its early pioneer beginnings to its influence on the Civil Rights Movement and its hosting of the 1996 Olympic Games, Atlanta has profoundly influenced America's history. A visit to the wonderful Atlanta History Center allows you to appreciate this influence in all its beauty. The Atlanta History Center began in 1926 when a group of 14 civic-minded individuals decided to found a place that would celebrate Atlanta and "arouse in the citizens and friends of Atlanta an interest in history." This slice of Americana is set on 33 acres in the heart of Atlanta's Buckhead district. Today, it serves as a primary source of history for the city, region and nation.

One of the most memorable points of interest is the classically designed Swan House. Built in 1928, this home was designed by famed architect Philip Trammell Shutze. It received its name from the noticeable swan motif found throughout the interior. You'll love touring this newly restored lovely home, which still contains most of its original furnishings of 18th century antiques to 20th century objects. It was added to the National Register of Historic Places in 1977, and has become one of Atlanta's most recognized landmarks. You'll, also find acres of enchanting gardens and nature trails, as well as the 1845 Tullie Smith Farm, and exhibits like "Turning Point: The American Civil War;" "Shaping Traditions: Folk Arts in a Changing South;" and "Down the Fairway with Bobby Jones." Stroll across the lawn to the Swan Coach House for some enchanting shopping and divine dinning (see page 41.) The Atlanta History Center is located at 130 W. Paces Ferry Rd. NW, and is open Monday-Saturday 10 am-5:30 pm and Sunday noon-5:30 pm. For more information, call 404-814-4000 or visit www.altantahistorycenter.com.

(Featured on front cover of book.)

Restaurants & Tearooms

dish

Sexy ambiance and friendly service come second only to the exquisite cuisine prepared by chef-owner Sheri Davis at her restaurant "Dish," 870 N. Highland Ave. in Atlanta. Dish opened in 1998 and features only the freshest seafood and seasonal organic vegetables in its "Globally Inspired/Contemporary American" menu. With 20 years of experience, Sheri moved from New York to Atlanta in 1994 to help open Brasserie La Coz in Buckhead. There, she also met her husband, another talented chef, Vando Davis. Stop by Dish for Sunday brunch 9:30 am-2:30 pm or dinner Sunday-Thursday 5:30-10 pm, and Friday and Saturday 5:30-11pm, followed by a special "After Hours Session" featuring music and cocktails until 2:30 am. For more information and reservations, call 404-897-3463 or visit www.dish-atlanta.com online.

SWAN COACH HOUSE
RESTAURANT · GIFT SHOP · GALLERY

Whether you are intrigued by American history, breathtaking artwork, natural settings, or interesting architecture, you'll want to visit the Swan Coach House. Located on the grounds of the Atlanta History Center at 130 W. Paces Ferry Rd. NW, the Swan Coach House is just steps away from the Swan House. Inside you'll find a tearoom that serves up the best the South has to offer—fine cuisine, warm ambiance and welcoming hospitality. Complimentary valet parking is available and reservations are accepted. This charming tearoom is open Monday-Saturday 11 am-2:30 pm. If you're looking for the perfect setting for a reception, dinner or party, you won't be disappointed. You can reserve this space for a small, intimate affair or for a larger group up to 175 people.

The Swan Coach House also has a gift shop that offers a special selection of antiques, baby and children's clothing, toys and more. The staff will not only help you find just the perfect gift, but they'll wrap it up beautifully for you. The gift shop is open Monday-Saturday 10 am-4 pm.

As you tour this magical place, you won't want to miss the Swan Coach House's gallery, which displays beautiful artwork by Southern artists, 19th century European and American paintings, and contemporary art that reflects Atlanta's artistic tradition. The gallery is open Tuesday-Saturday 10 am-4 pm. For more information, visit www.swancoachhouse.com or call 404-261-0636.

STANMILTON ⚜ SALON

"Treat Your Hair to Magnificent Care" is the motto at Stan Milton Salon, 250 Pharr Rd. in Atlanta. Stan Milton's greatest inspiration is his mother—an incredibly artistic hairdresser. She taught him to treat everyone like they were glamorous superstars. You will definitely be in "glamorous company," because many of their clients are well-known local celebrities, television personalities, and gorgeous catwalk models! The Salon's highly trained and well-respected stylists are experts in fashion-forward hair care, and known for their iconic cuts. Stan Milton Salon is also the exclusive salon of choice for both Neiman Marcus and Saks Fifth Avenue fashion shows. Every client is treated to the highest level of personalized care possible with wonderful products. For salon hours, contact owners Stan Milton or Johnny Cowart at 404-233-6242 or visit www.stanmiltonsalon.com online.

Beverly Bremer
SILVER SHOP

From "Southern Belle" to "Silver Bell," Beverly Bremer has been the silver queen of Atlanta for more than 30 years. As with many great success stories, Beverly's road to success was paved with adversity. In 1972, she was left alone with three children to raise, and a huge hospital bill. Without even blinking an eye, she gathered together all of her "wedding silver" and rented a booth at a flea market. Customers soon began bringing their own silver to her to sell, and her incredible business was born. Soon after, she moved her inventory to her Buckhead location at 3164 Peachtree Rd. Whether you are looking to fill in gaps of missing silver flatware or even adding to a collection of antique baskets, you will find it all in this gleaming silver paradise. Stop by Monday-Saturday 10 am-5 pm or visit www.beverlybremer.com online. For more information, call 800-270-4009 or 404-261-009. *(Color photo featured in front section of book.)*

Discover Macon

It is called the "Song and Soul of the South," the "Heart of Georgia," and the "Cherry Blossom Capital of the World." Macon boasts a rich cultural, historical and musical heritage that will satisfy your soul with the "slow-moving rhythm of an old sweet song," You'll find a "heapin helpin" of wonderful Southern hospitality, breathtaking scenery, delicious Southern food, Civil War and African American history and of course, soulful rock n' roll. Macon has emerged through the years as one of the great historic cities of the South. From its prehistoric burial mounds and magnificent antebellum mansions to its worldwide musical impact, Macon has it all. Richard Moe, President of the National Trust for Historic Preservation says, "All travelers who want a unique vacation experience full of history, scenery, music, food and great Southern hospitality should put Macon at the top of their must-see list." Plan to spend as much time possible in this beautiful "blooming" city enjoying historical tours, internationally recognized festivals, world class museums, lively nightlife, theatre, antiques, boutiques and dining. It's no surprise Macon was named one of America's "Dozen Distinctive Destinations." Take a tip from Macon's Good Will Ambassador Little Richard, who says, "Tell 'em that the Architect of Rock 'n' Roll sent ya' and told you to have a good time!"

Historical Macon
(From Prehistoric Rocks to Rock 'n' Roll)

When Hernando DeSoto first traveled to this area in 1540, it had already been inhabited for more than 12,000 years by the

Moundbuilders and Hitchiti Indians. Theses two tribes later became part of the Creek Indian Confederacy. They lived along the Fall Line Plateau and the Ocmulgee River. DeSoto recorded the first Christian baptism on the new continent when priests in his expedition baptized two Native Americans in the nearby Ocmulgee River.

The first documented account of the Ocmulgee Old Fields was made by James Oglethorpe and a group of Georgia Guards in 1739. The trading post that was opened a few years later is protected today as part of the Ocmulgee National Monument. The frontier outpost, U.S. Fort Hawkins, was built on the hill overlooking Ocmulgee Fields in 1806 and hosted General Andrew Jackson. In fact, Macon is one of the only cities in the state to grow out of a real frontier fort. You can visit a replica of Fort Hawkins' 1806 Blockhouse on Emery Highway near the Macon Centreplex.

In 1822, Bibb County was created by the Georgia legislature and the following year Macon was established near Fort Hawkins. The town was named in honor of Nathaniel Macon, an anti-Federalist North Carolinian who was Speaker of the House and President Pro Tempore of the Senate. The city's first founders planned it with large squares of garden parks and wide avenues. You still see this design today as you tour the attractive business district. Macon was once called the "Queen Inland City of the South" because of its booming trade on the river and railroad. Elaborate houses and charming cottages were built by wealthy planters during the pre-Civil War days, and many of these have been preserved as a tribute to Macon's colorful antebellum past.

During the Civil War, Macon served as a hospital for wounded Confederate soldiers and a prison for Union soldiers. It was attacked by General George Stoneman's Calvary in 1864 and captured by General James H. Wilson at the end of the war. It was actually named the state capital by Governor Joseph E. Brown for a few months during 1865. As you can imagine, Civil War buffs will love Macon.

This city definitely felt the hard times of the Great Depression, experiencing severe crop failures, drought and economic uncertainty. However, during the 1950s and the 1960s, the city began to produce quite a few talented musicians, including Otis Redding, James Brown and "Little Richard" Penniman. With such an impact on American music, it was no surprise that Macon was chosen as the location for the Georgia Music Hall of Fame. For a city with such an incredible historic heritage, Macon also has a strong vision for the future. Visitors are treated to entertaining and enlightening historical tours, museums, theatre, art and music as this beautiful and soulful city celebrates its colorful tapestry of history and life.

Antebellum Macon

You might want to start your day with a visit to the city's very beginning—the Ocmulgee National Monument, where you will actually walk through one of the prehistoric mounds. There were five distinct Indian tribes that occupied these mounds, from the Paleolithic Ice Age to the Creeks. You will see a ceremonial earthlodge, and several platform mounds, as well as the fascinating museum.

You can get lost in time, as you tour Macon's beautiful, Historic District. More than 5,500 individual structures in 11 districts are listed on the National Register of Historic Places. The city also has more acreage listed on this Register than any other in the state. Included in a tour of Macon is a visit to the 1860 Hay House, known as the "Palace of the South." This Italian Renaissance Villa is now owned and operated by the Georgia Trust for Historic Preservation, with daily public tours. It is considered the most advanced antebellum building in America because of its craftsmanship and technological innovations. The extraordinary seven-level mansion features beautiful 18th century furnishings, Italian Carerra marble fireplaces, marbleized and trompe l'oeil finishes, a 30-foot clerestory ceiling, 24-karat gold leafing, a beautiful music room, and magnificent stained glass. It has been featured on A&E's "America's Castles."

You will also have a chance to tour the famous "Cannonball House," a building that earned its name because it was struck by a cannonball during a Federal attack on Macon in 1864. Two rooms in the house recreate the original meeting rooms of the first two secret societies for college women in the world; Alpha Delta Pi and Phi Mu. These two sororities began at Wesleyan College in 1831 and 1852. The kitchen and servants' quarters now serve as a Civil War Museum and Museum Shop.

The best way to view many of the magnificent historic homes and museums of Macon is to hop on board the "Around Town

Tours." Explore scenic boulevards, interactive museums, and extraordinary antebellum homes with a packaged tour discount program. You should also take advantage of the incredible "Lights On Macon," a self-guided tour of the Historic Intown Neighborhood that features 30 architectural gems, each dramatically illuminated to highlight its antebellum beauty.

Song and Soul

Get ready to "rock" when you roll into Macon. Here you'll hear everything from Native American rhythms to Southern rock and classic R&B. It is called the Song and Soul of the South for many reasons, and as such, it was chosen as the location for Georgia's Music Hall of Fame. This facility creates a never-ending music festival of great Georgia tunes—from jazz, R&B, Southern rock, blues, country, gospel, classical and of course, rock 'n' roll. It honors great Georgian born or raised legends, such as Little Richard, James Brown, Otis Redding, the Allman Brothers, Ray Charles, Brenda Lee, Gladys Knight, Alan Jackson and the B-52's. In fact, Southern rock was born in Macon at Capricorn Records. The Allman Brothers Band, Lynyrd Skynyrd, Wet Willie, and the Marshall Tucker Band all recorded at Capricorn.

Little Richard" Penniman was born and raised in Macon's Pleasant Hill neighborhood and later performed in the Douglass Theatre. He has been named Macon's "Good Will Ambassador for Tourism**." Otis Redding, Jr**. lived in Macon and was discovered at the Douglass Theatre. Otis was killed in a plane crash in 1967, but his widow and children still reside in this great city. (Sons Otis III and Dexter continue their father's musical legacy.) You can actually "watch the tide roll away," next to a life-size bronze statue of Otis Redding sitting on the dock of the bay at the Ocmulgee Heritage Trail**. James Brown** came to Macon because the radio station WIBB was playing R&B music long before it became mainstream. His hit single, "Please, Please, Please" was recorded here. **Duane Allman**, one of the greatest guitar players in history lived in Macon and recorded at Phil Walden's Capricorn Studios with the Allman Brothers Band. Duane was killed in a motorcycle accident and is buried in Macon next to his fellow Allman Brother **Berry Oakley**. **Chuck Leavell**, formerly with the Allman Brothers Band, is the current Rolling Stones keyboardist. Apart from being famous as a member of the Stones, Chuck is a nationally recognized tree farmer in Dry Branch, near Macon.

The Cherry Blossom Capital of the World

We cannot tell a lie! When it comes to cherry trees, Macon blooms supreme. In fact, Macon has more cherry blossoms than any other city in the world, including Washington, D.C. and even cities in Japan. Each year an additional 10,000 flowering Yoshino cherry trees are planted in Macon, which is one reason why it was named The Cherry Blossom Capital of the World by the Japanese Consul General. Celebrating the spirit of spring, the "Macon, Georgia's International Cherry Blossom Festival" in March is a 10-day celebration of events, performances, exhibits, and great food amidst thousands of beautiful cherry trees.

Girlfriends' Getaway

Every now and then, women deserve to indulge in guilty pleasures…sleeping late, massages, girl talk, shopping and leisurely meals. For a wickedly luxurious time, schedule a Girlfriends' Getaway in Macon, and let the Macon-Bibb County Convention and Visitors Bureau help plan the itinerary. Choose from spas that offer relaxing massages and soothing facials, boutiques that carry contemporary fashions and shoes galore, antique and outdoor gardening shops, and art galleries. Enjoy bistro dining, wine dinners and soulful nightlife. Take a trolley ride through the Historic District and visit antebellum homes and fascinating museums.

Family Fun

Journey to outer space in the planetarium, touch live animals, hike nature trails, and experience the hands-on beauty of art and science at the Museum of Arts and Sciences. Travel the 10-mile Ocmulgee Heritage Trail from the primeval Bond Swamp to the ancient mounds to historic Rose Hill Cemetery. The trail includes river walks, heritage trails and riverside parks. If you happen to be there during September, you'll have the privilege of attending the Ocmulgee Indian Celebration. You can stomp your feet to a primitive beat as Creeks, Cherokees, Chickasaws, Choctaws and Seminoles perform ceremonial dances in colorful dress. If your family loves theme parks, don't miss Tune Town, a musical streetscape at the Georgia Music Hall of Fame. The 43,000-square-foot facility features the music and costumes of more than 450 artists in permanent and changing exhibits. Children will love the Music Factory Children's Wing, where they can explore the world of music through hands-on exhibits. The Tubman African American Museum offers a soulful journey from Africa to America. Dynamic exhibits allow all ages to experience African American art, history and culture. Georgia's athletic heritage is spotlighted at the Georgia Sports Hall of Fame, where educational and interactive exhibits honor state heroes such as Henry "Hank" Aaron. Finally, outdoorsmen will love the fishing, camping, boating and swimming opportunities at Lake Tobesofkee. There are three white sand beaches with picnic pavilions, tennis courts and playgrounds.

If it's shopping and dining you love, don't worry, we've found some of the most wonderful little places in town you won't want to miss. The people of Macon are friendly and warm, and they open their doors to visitors with a welcome as warm as the Georgia sun.

For more information about Macon, contact the Macon-Bibb County Convention and Visitor's Bureau at 800-768-3401, 478-743-3401 or visit www.maconga.org online.

Macon
Fairs Festivals & Fun

January
Downtown Macon (first Friday every month Jan-Dec)

March
Cherry Blossom Fesitval

April
Dodge Tour de Georgia
Pan African Festival of Georgia
Earth Day

May
Mansions, Moonlight and Garden Tours

June
Mid-Summer Macon Music & Arts Festival

July
Bragg Jam

September
Ocmulgee Indian Festival
Georgia Music Week
Georgia State Fair
Macon Music & Heritage Festival

October
Pumpkin Pops

November
Festival of Trees at Museum of Arts & Sciences

December
Christmas in Olde Macon
Nutcracker
Kwanzaa Celebration

MACON-BIBB CVB
Song & Soul of the South

Named one of America's "Dozen Distinctive Destinations" by the National Trust for Historic Preservation, Macon is a remarkable place to visit. Experience captivating architecture, interactive museums, seasonal festivals, wonderful music, charming boutiques and antique shops, delightful local restaurants, and much more. The Macon-Bibb County CVB Around Town Tours offer the best-packaged deal to see "The Song and Soul of the South." Choose from two exciting itineraries or a combination ticket and receive up to a 25% savings. Hop aboard the trolley for the Intown Tour, which includes the Hay House, Sidney Lanier Cottage, the Cannonball House and a bonus stop at St. Joseph's Catholic Church. The Downtown Tour will take you to the Georgia Sports Hall of Fame, Tubman African American Museum, the Georgia Music Hall of Fame and the historic Douglass Theatre. For more information or reservations on the Around Town Tours, call 800-768-3401, 478-743-3401, or visit www.maconga.org, or stop by the Macon-Bibb County CVB's Downtown Welcome Center at 200 Cherry St. Monday-Saturday 9 am-5 pm.

HISTORIC MACON GA TOURS

Georgia™

georgia.org

Antiques

Mike and June Pennington moved from England in 1994 to follow their dream of opening an antique store and bringing quality English antiques to America. That dream soon became reality! Since 1995 they have been hosting antique buying tours to England, for both serious collectors and interested amateurs.

Mike and June devote themselves to bringing quality European and American antiques, and designer merchandise to their loyal customers in a comfortable environment. In 2003 they opened their newest store, Ingleside Village Antique Centre, located at 2340 Ingleside Ave. in Macon's Historic District of Ingleside. Stop by Tuesday-Saturday 10 am-5:30 pm, visit www.inglesideantiques.com online or call 478-743-7110 for more information. Visit www.oldenglandtours for tour information.

Payne Mill Village Antique Mall is located at 121 Rose Ave. in the old Bibb Cotton Mill in Payne City—the perfect location for an antique mall. The mill was built in 1899 and lends a great historic impact to the many antiques and treasures you'll find inside. From furniture, collectibles and glassware to garden items, vintage clothing and jewelry, you will love shopping in this interesting old mill. Open Monday-Thursday 10 am-5 pm, Friday-Saturday until 6 pm and Sunday 2-5 pm. Call 478-741-3821.

After working in the antiques industry for ten years, two friends teamed up to open an antique and gift shop in Macon, and the result was phenomenal. The Columns, 2356 Ingleside Ave., carries an amazing collection of fine antiques, luxurious rugs, breathtaking chandeliers and one-of-a-kind treasures from around the world. They specialize in unique Dutch antiques. The Columns is open Monday-Saturday 10 am-5 pm. For more information, call 478-741-4466.

COTTAGE HILL ANTIQUES

Jake and Michele Ferro have loved and collected antiques for years, so it was a natural progression for them to open Cottage Hill Antiques, 2186 Ingleside Ave in Macon. They travel extensively to keep their inventory of English and Continental pieces high. Jake and Michele are committed to finding the perfect treasures for their customers. They'll even make "house calls" to help them arrange their homes. Stop by Tuesday-Friday 11 am-5 pm, Saturday noon-4 pm or call 478-746-1223.

Artists, Art Galleries, Framing & Photography

Greg Lanterman's family knew at a very early age that he was destined to be a great artist. He began winning awards for his creative designs and musical talent in the third grade! His eclectic style is evident throughout his fun and beautiful gallery called Dreamscape, 2372 Ingleside Ave. in Macon. The shop is a collection of stunning home décor, unique gifts and incredible pieces of original art work. You will also  find extraordinary garden sculptures and hard to find Asian and African art and décor. Greg travels across the Southeast completing custom and mural display work for homes and businesses. View his work and this beautiful shop at www.dreamscapeartandgifts.com. Dreamscape is open Monday-Friday 10 am-5 pm and Saturday until 4 pm. For more information, call 478-750-8588.

m a c o n A r t s

Macon Arts, 414 Cherry St., is the single organization that represents all of the arts in Macon and Bibb County. Macon Arts was formed in 1985 and its mission is to "actively promote involvement in and access to the arts through funding, advocacy, coordination and education." The gallery showcases original art by regional artists in all mediums, so remember Macon Arts when you need that special birthday, wedding or anniversary gift. The Gallery has one-of-a-kind sculpture, ceramics, pottery, paintings, photography, as well as jewelry. Macon Arts is open Monday through Friday 11 am-5 pm and by appointment on Saturday. For more information, visit www.maconarts.org online or call 478-743-6940.

OCMULGEE ARTS, INC.

A family's love of art and the desire to work together resulted in the creation of Ocmulgee Arts, Inc., 2242 Ingleside Ave. Lou Warren, Louise Burkhalter and Sissie Maffeo love helping their customers find the perfect piece of art in this beautiful 7,000 square foot gallery. You'll find original art, antique prints, posters, works by Southern artists and wonderful gifts. Ocmulgee Arts has earned the reputation as Macon's premiere framing business, which eventually led to the creation of Multicut USA. This secondary business imports handmade marbled papers and rice paper, which is marketed internationally. Open Monday-Friday 9 am-5:30 pm and Saturday 9:30 am-5 pm. For more information, call 478-746-3541 or visit www.ocmulgeearts.com or www.multicutusa.com.

Attractions & Entertainment

DOUGLASS THEATRE

African-American entrepreneur Charles H. Douglass, son of a former slave, founded the Douglass Theatre at 355 Martin Luther King, Jr. Blvd. in 1921. It was the premier movie theatre and vaudeville hall open to African-American citizens in Macon, and it hosted jazz and blues greats like Ida Cox, Cab Calloway, Duke Ellington, Bessie Smith and Ma Rainey. During the 1960s the theatre showcased Little Richard, Otis Redding and James Brown. This famous theatre reopened in 1997, serving all races and cultures with events, films, and performances. For more information, call 478-742-2000 or visit www.douglasstheatre.org online.

Bakeries

Owners Jon and Emily Haygood set out to create unique and delectable confections that taste as good as they look. From hand-dipped truffles to gourmet petit fours and custom specialty cakes, Petit Sweets is sure to make you the star of the party—or just make you happy. Petit Sweets, 4123 Forsyth Rd. in Macon, makes everything from scratch with high-quality ingredients like real butter, Neilsen-Massey vanilla and Venezuelan chocolate. Stop by Tuesday-Friday 10 am-6 pm or Saturday until 5 pm, call 478-471-9822, or visit online at www.AtTheConfectionery.com.

Cream of the Crop

Moms, moms-to-be and grandmothers love this adorable children's clothing boutique at 3256 Vineville Ave. in Macon. Cream of the Crop is a delightful collection of children's clothing, accessories, as well as baby and shower gifts. Owner Heather Neal carries well-known lines such as Eland, Rosalina, Wills River, and many more—from preemie to size 12 boys and junior girls. Cream of the Crop is open Tuesday-Friday 10 am-5 pm and Saturday until 4 pm. Call 478-477-7045.

Tina's SHOES

"If the shoe fits, it must be from Tina's" is Tina Foreman's motto. A perfect fit is one of the things she takes great pride in as owner of Tina's Shoes, 3259 Vineville Ave. in Macon. Tina has been selling children's shoes for more than 19 years and has owned the store since 1995. She sells specialty and European children's shoes from Aster-Faro and Deasu—shoes you won't find in department stores. The store is open Tuesday-Friday 10 am-5 pm and Saturday until 4 pm. Call 478-476-8333.

The Barnes House

The Barnes House, in downtown Macon, would be at home on any of the world's great shopping streets like Rodeo Drive or Worth Avenue. It has been described as the store you never want to leave! Housed in a Victorian treasure built in 1895, downstairs and upstairs are a rare combination of distinctive gifts, items for the home, and anything to indulge a woman's senses—spectacular jewelry, fine coffees and one of the largest selections of furs in the South. There are fur fashions and accessories for all ages; vests, jackets, fur trimmed leather or denim—hats, purses and scarves—anything fur! You won't know what you're missing until you visit The Barnes House, with more than 5,000 items from BBQ sauce to Barguzin sable. Stop by The Barnes House at 807 Cherry St. Monday-Friday 9:30 am-5:30 pm and Saturday until 4:30 pm. Visit www.barneshousemacon.com online or call 478-743-1909.

JOYCINE'S

Joycine's, where Georgia's New York award-winning designer/artist Barbara Joyce Barry-Nishanian, recipient of the Southern Women's Achievement Award, showcases her talents and those of other artists. Established in 1945, Joycine's dishes out an eclectic mix of local art, rare "Virgin Vintage" jewelry, clip earrings, one-of-a-kind handbags, hats, jackets, gifts and jewelry, jewelry, jewelry.

This delightful little shop is a place where customers drop in as much for advice, a dose of attitude or a hug, as they do to buy Barbara's Signature cosmetics, unique fragrance or Karma Sutra products.

Barbara believes that "individuality is the very essence of an unforgettable woman" and uses her training and talents to carry on her mother's legacy. Assisting women—from conservative to those with a funky arty edge—to enhance their style and appearance at reasonable prices. Stop by 613 Cherry St. in Macon Tuesday-Saturday 10 am-5:30 pm. Call 478-743-3144 or visit www.joycines.com for "1st Friday" artist receptions information. Joycine's Art, Attitude and Accessory Gallery, more than a destination...it's an experience!

DREAMS

Zelma Redding, the widow of legendary Otis Redding, has worked hard to make her "dreams" come true in Macon. In her beautiful boutique called Dreams, Zelma has set a standard for excellence in ladies' clothing and accessories. Dreams is located at 339 Cotton Ave. in Historic Downtown Macon. Just look for the most beautiful and impressive window display of fabulous designer clothing and fashion accessories. Dreams carries distinguished lines such as Garfield Marks, Isda & Co., and Drama. Dreams has been described as a "chic and sophisticated boutique for the mature lady." You won't want to miss this fabulous store! Dreams is open Monday-Friday 10 am-5:30 and Saturday 10 am- 4 pm. For more information, call 478-742-5737.

shoe boutique

Can a girl ever have too many shoes? Of course not! Karla's Shoe Boutique, 603 Cherry St., is a Macon favorite for shopping for the most fabulous shoes you can imagine. Owners Zelma Redding and Karla Redding-Andrews, mother and daughter to the legendary Otis Redding, are so helpful and fun that your shopping experience will never be forgotten "We sell fine shoes," says Karla, "But we also sell customer service." You will find great lines such as Donald J Pilner, Anne Klein, Vaneli, and more—in sizes 5-12, including narrow widths. This should definitely be your first choice for great shoes and handbags, but also stop by just to say hello. Karla's Shoe Boutique is open Monday through Friday 10 am-5:30 pm and Saturday until 4 pm. For more information, call 478-741-2066.

A woman is like a tea bag…you don't know how strong she is until you put her in hot water.

— Eleanor Roosevelt

Creter's

Mother/daughter team Barbara Every and Patsy Knott are third and fourth generation owners of one of the most well-loved and respected gift shops in Macon. Creter's first opened its doors in 1947 in downtown Macon. Creter's is now located at 2374 Ingleside Ave. in Macon's first and oldest shopping center, and

has continued to live up to its reputation for always having the most wonderful selection of fine gifts and outstanding customer service. In fact, Creter's was featured in *Southern Living,* and in *Southern Living Special Edition* as the number "7" favorite place to shop in 2003! Creter's also carries Hallmark cards, jewelry, baby gifts, holiday décor, Vera Bradley items and decorative accessories, such as needlepoint pillows and framed art. Creter's is open Monday-Friday 10 am-6 pm and Saturday until 5 pm. Call 478-745-6709.

GEORGIA MARKET HOUSE

The Georgia Market House, 612 Poplar St., began more than 60 years ago as a full-scale meat market and grocery store. It was the very first business in the area to make fruit baskets. This family-owned-and-operated market has changed just a little through the years. It is no longer a meat market, but a wonderful flower shop that specializes in gift baskets. Mother and son, Pam and John Paul Pearson carry gourmet items like jam and jellies, salad dressing, cookies, candy, and of course, Georgia's famous Vidalia onions. They create beautiful and delicious gift baskets for clients across the country that include a stunning assortment of flowers and those great Georgia treats. For information on baskets and delivery, call 478-742-3053. Open Monday-Friday 9 am-5 pm and Saturday during the holiday season only.

Furniture

Enchanted Pieces We know that you will be as "enchanted" as we were with this amazing furniture and home décor boutique in Macon. Enchanted Pieces, 415 Cherry St., is just that—a magnificent collection of "enchanting pieces" that will wow you with the impact they make in your home. Tony and Beverly Dillard carry hand-carved, wood pieces in cherry and mahogany with gold inlay. You'll find beautiful contemporary and traditional items that will make great conversation or anchor pieces in your home. They call their niche "fine and unique home furnishings at reasonable prices," with the emphasis on unique. You'll find "picture-n-picture" art embossed in enchanting frames, tall vases, handsome Bombays, elegant chaises and accent chairs. Enchanted Pieces is a treasure trove of tastefully elegant and unusual furniture. Open Monday-Friday 10 am-6 pm and Saturday 11:30 am-6 pm. Call 478-743-4435.

Gardens & Nurseries

Located in Ingleside Village—Macon's oldest shopping center—The Society Gardener is a below street level outdoor shop, specializing in perennials, herbs, topiaries and garden accessories. The iron gate at 2389-B Ingleside Ave. invites visitors down the steps to an aromatic world of flowers and herbs. You'll love the selection of cast iron, concrete and terra cotta containers, as well as imported antiques and gifts from around the world. The Society Gardener is open Monday-Friday 10 am-5 pm and Saturday until 4 pm. Call 478-744-2402.

CROWNE PLAZA®

MACON

Look for the tallest building in Macon to find absolutely great Southern comfort and hospitality. The upscale Crowne Plaza Hotel, 108 First St., is located right in the very heart of Historic Downtown Macon, just minutes from all the astonishing museums and the first-rate shopping this soulful musical city has to offer. The 16-story hotel boasts a beautiful lobby and mezzanine, spacious guestrooms, an elegant ballroom, an executive boardroom, banquet rooms, and a top-rated restaurant and lounge.

There are 297 attractive guest rooms and eight suites. The rooms feature in-room movies, personal coffee service, wireless Internet, work desks, and direct dial telephones with data ports. Business travelers will appreciate the copy and courier service, executive floors and suites, and the private limousine service. The Crowne Plaza Club Executive Level offers guests access to a private lounge with evening cocktails and hors d'oeurves, and a continental breakfast. The ballroom, boardroom, and conference rooms can accommodate groups up to 900 for special meetings or receptions.

Leisure travelers rave about the luxurious rooms and suites, and the personal attention they receive from the friendly staff. From the quality bedding to the complimentary morning newspaper, you will feel pampered during your entire visit. Delicious food and drink is served in the hotel restaurant during breakfast, lunch or dinner. Of course, if you've had a long day enjoying Macon's many wonderful attractions, you may want to have a quiet dinner delivered to your room. Call 478-746-1461, 800-227-6963, or take a virtual tour at www.crowneplaza.com. *(Color photo featured in front section of book.)*

The beautiful Atrium La Quinta Inn & Suites is conveniently located in residential north Macon at 3944 River Place Dr. It is within walking distance to dining and shopping and only a short drive to historical homes and museums in downtown Macon. This home-away-from-home does "whatever it takes" to make your stay perfect and considers its guests to be friends and neighbors. A beautifully landscaped courtyard lends to a cheerful atmosphere and you can utilize an on-site workout room, enjoy the beautiful-outdoor pool and spa, or visit with friends in the gazebo. You may also start your day in the two-story glass lobby for a full breakfast while listening to the tranquil sound of cascading water. There are deluxe two-room suites with separate sitting and sleeping areas, and king-size suites with microwaves and refrigerators for guests looking for extended stays. All rooms are equipped with free high-speed Internet. For more information or reservations, call 800-531-5900, 478-475-0206 or visit www.laquintamacon.com online.

The first thing you'll notice during your stay at the Wingate Inn in Macon will be the pride the staff has for their "soulful Southern city." They welcome visitors with true Southern kindness and treat them like family. Wingate Inn, 100 Northcrest Blvd., features 80 oversized deluxe rooms and two executive suites. Free high-speed Internet access is available in every room, and a business center with computer, fax, copier and printer is open 24-hours a day. A hospitality breakfast bar is offered each weekend and a hot breakfast on weekdays. Guests can make themselves right at home because each room has a refrigerator, microwave, coffee maker and safe. You'll enjoy the fitness room, large outdoor heated pool and indoor heated whirlpool. Located near many attractions—including the famous Cherry Blossom Festival—the Wingate Inn is a perfect "home base" during your visit. For information or reservations, call 478-476-8100, 800-228-1000 or visit www.wingateinns.com.

C.R. RADER
J E W E L E R S

As timeless as the original cast iron street clock on the front sidewalk, C.R. Rader Jewelers has held a tradition of excellence since 1914. They maintain an exquisite selection of loose diamonds, cultured and South Sea pearls, and quality gold jewelry. If you can't find exactly what you're looking for, then they'll help you create it.  This store offers gold and platinum mountings and semi-mounts so that you can design your perfect "something special." You will also find porcelains, watches, sterling and silver-plated hollowware, and estate jewelry. And, to help you prepare for your special day, they offer a premier bridal registry. They are members of the American Gem Society and offer a repair service that is known for prompt attention and excellent workmanship. Stop by Monday-Friday 10 am-5:30 pm at 667 Cherry St. in Macon. Call 478-742-6494.

Museums

GEORGIA MUSIC HALL OF FAME AND MUSEUM

Over the years, Georgia has produced a dynasty of music legends, from Dr. Thomas Andrew Dorsey and Gertrude "Ma" Rainey, to James Brown and Trisha Yearwood. Commemorating the lives and musical contributions of the state's songbirds, the Georgia Music Hall of Fame has become a beloved treasure, attracting visitors from more than 40 countries. The Georgia Music Hall of Fame is a 40,000 square foot, three-story building featuring permanent and changing exhibits that include music, video, memorabilia, instruments and performance costumes that honor the works of more than 450 artists. Don't miss the music store for that special souvenir. Located in Macon at 200 Martin Luther King, Jr. Blvd., and open Monday-Saturday 9 am-5 pm and Sunday 1-5 pm. For more information, call 888-GA-ROCKS, 478-751-3334 or visit www.gamusichall.com.

The Georgia Sports Hall of Fame resembles a turn-of-the-century ballpark with a red-brick exterior, green roof and old style ticket booths. It not only portrays Georgia's history of sports, but is itself making history. This remarkable facility is the largest state sports hall of fame in America with 14,000 square feet of exhibit space, a 205-seat theater, and an interactive area that includes football, basketball, NASCAR, and several sports-based computer programs. This exciting facility at 301 Cherry St. in Macon opened to the public in 1999 and is available for a variety of events including receptions, dinners, birthday parties and business meetings.

There are more than 3,000 pieces of memorabilia on a rotating display in the building, and interactive programs that pay tribute to more than 300 Hall of Fame inductees. An entire floor of the building is dedicated to High School, Collegiate, Olympic, Paralympic, Professional Sports, and Great Moments in Georgia sports history. You'll see special tributes to Hank Aaron, baseball's "Home Run King," who played in Atlanta from 1966-1974; Jackie Robinson, who broke the color barrier in baseball; and Bobby Jones, who many consider the greatest golfer to ever play the game. You'll also see the largest display of 1996 Atlanta Paralympic Games memorabilia anywhere in the country. You can drive against NASCAR's best in a Riverside Ford NASCAR simulator, kick the winning field goal on the football field, or stuff the ball on the basketball court.

Stop by the Georgia Sports Hall of Fame Monday-Saturday 9 am-5 pm or Sunday 1-5 pm. For more information, visit www.gshf.org online or call 478-752-1585.

In 1980, Father Richard Keil sought to build a cultural center in Macon that would celebrate the tribulations and accomplishments by African Americans. The Harriet Tubman Center for Spiritual and Cultural Awareness opened its doors at 340 Walnut St. in 1985, educating people about African American art, history and culture. Now called the Tubman African American Museum, it houses 14 galleries, including the world class Noel Collection of African Art, 2,000-year-old Nok figures, beaded Yoruba wall panels, and Benin bronzes. The Tubman Museum

Store carries an array of items from unusual jewelry and masks to pottery and musical instruments. The Museum is open Monday-Saturday 9 am-5 pm and Sunday 2-5 pm. Visit www.tubmanmuseum.com or call 478-743-8544.

HAY HOUSE
A PROPERTY OF THE GEORGIA TRUST

In the mid 1800s, William B. Johnston was a keeper of the Confederate treasury, but the mansion he built is the real treasure he left behind. Noted for its Italian Renaissance Revival architecture and advanced technology in 1859, the National Historic Landmark Hay House in Macon is filled with world renowned decorative finishes, exquisite stained glass, and 18th and 19th century furnishings. Hay House is con-

sidered one of America's finest antebellum homes, and has been featured on "America's Castles" on the A&E Channel. Located at 934 Georgia Ave. and open seven days a week for tours. Call 478-742-8155 or visit www.hayhouse.org.

MUSEUM
ARTS AND
SCIENCES

Whether it is an exotic bird, a work of fine art or a shooting star, your imagination will soar at the Museum of Arts and Sciences, 4182 Forsythe Rd. in Macon. This magical place will engage and excite visitors of all ages. From the Planetarium and Mini-Zoo to the Art and Science Exhibitions and Discovery House, you will be lost in the wonder of discovery. Open Monday 9 am-8 pm, Tuesday-Saturday 9 am-5 pm and Sunday 1-5 pm. Visit www.masmacon.com or call 478-477-3232.

The Cannonball House at 856 Mulberry St., is a stately Greek Revival built in 1853 and struck by a cannonball during Stoneman's Raid on Macon in 1864. This mansion has been restored and furnished to the period's glory and is listed on the National Register of Historic Places. Tours of The Cannonball House, grounds, original brick kitchen and servants' quarters are available Monday-Saturday 10 am-5 pm. Stop by the gift shop where you will find Georgia memorabilia and specialty foods. Visit www.cannonballhouse.org or call 478-745-5982.

Quilts, Needlework & Stitchery

Me & Thee

Needleworkers of all ages and all walks of life will find just what they are looking for at Me & Thee, located in Historic Ingleside Village at 2360 Ingleside Ave. in Macon. Me & Thee carries bright, festive yarns, needlepoint canvases, patterns and accessories for each project. You can feel the yarn, search for the perfect pattern and visit with other "stitchers" that share your love of needlework. Open Monday-Friday 10 am-5 pm and Saturday until 3 pm. Call 478-746-2223.

Restaurants

Gerard and Karen Andre own and operate Eden'z, 617 Poplar St., Macon's only true vegetarian restaurant. All meals are vegan, plant-based foods, made without meat, eggs, milk or cheese. You'll want to try their delicious "cheeseless" cheesecakes, refreshing fruit smoothies and eggless desserts. Gerard and Karen also teach vegetarian cooking and health classes. Open Monday-Thursday 11 am-7 pm, Friday until 3 pm and Sunday 11 am-4 pm. Call 478-745-3336.

Owner Phillip Rossini has more than 30 years experience in the restaurant and catering business. His journey began in Italy, then off to New York and South Carolina, and now he impresses Macon with an exciting menu at Adrianna's Café, 359 Third St. Try the Sun-Dried Tomato soup—it's the best, the Italian Hero or Adriatic Salad. But, be sure to savor an authentic cappuccino or a cup of gourmet coffee. Everything is delicious! Open Monday-Saturday 9 am-5 pm, with dinner served Friday-Saturday 5:30-10:30 pm. Call 478-742-2255.

Bert's Customers love this charming Macon restaurant for many reasons. Bert's, 442 Cherry St., is known for its delicious food and wine tastings. Owner Allan Bass opens six or eight different reds and whites every weekend, inviting guests to try complimentary samples. This allows everyone to find their favorite wine! Also, be sure to try the wonderful Bistro Salad. Bert's is open for lunch Monday-Friday 11:30 am-2 pm, and for dinner Thursday-Saturday 5:30 -9 pm. Call 478-742-9100.

The Back Burner Restaurant

As one of the most respected eateries in Macon, The Back Burner Restaurant, 2242 Ingleside Ave., continues to satisfy locals and entice visitors with its superb menu and wine list. Owner/Chef Christian J.P. Losito is a trained food professional from Nice, France, who adds a European flair to specialties such as Chilean sea bass and rack of lamb. The restaurant's ambiance is warm and cozy; the service is top-notch; and the food is delicious. In addition, a private party room can seat up to 40 for lunch or dinner, and up to 65 for cocktails and hors d'oervres. Open Tuesday through Saturday for lunch 11:30 am-2:30 pm, for dinner 6-9 pm and Friday through Saturday until 9:30 pm. Call 478-746-3336.

Ingleside Village Pizza

Hand-tossed, New York style pizza with homemade dough and only the freshest toppings—if this makes your mouth water, we've found just the place for you. Ingleside Village Pizza, 2396 Ingleside Ave., is a favorite Macon pizzeria with one of the best beer selections in town. Your kids will also love getting their own little piece of dough while they watch the pizzas being tossed. Try the "White Pizza"—absolutely delicious! For more information and hours, call 478-750-8488.

WILLOW ON FIFTH

Fried green tomatoes, crispy fried chicken, chicken and dumplings, and homemade peach cobbler…mmm—sounds like the perfect Southern meal. Willow on Fifth will be one of your favorite places to eat in downtown Macon at 325 Fifth St. Delicious Southern buffets are served daily for lunch and dinner Monday-Saturday and Sunday lunch only. For more information and hours, visit www.willowonfifth.com or call 478-745-9007.

Discover
Athens / Watkinsville

ATHENS

Just below the foothills of the magnificent Blue Ridge Mountains, among the rolling red clay hills of North Georgia, you'll find the beautiful city of Athens. It is a unique blend of Southern heritage and contemporary entertainment. It is also a vibrant city whose upbeat energy echoes through the red and black halls of the University of Georgia (UGA), the quaint downtown boutiques and galleries, and its music, arts and entertainment. Athens has even earned the title, "One of America's Top 25 Arts Destinations." It offers visitors attractions and activities that will excite every member of the family. The restored downtown area is filled with wonderful shops and restaurants, and the top-rated Georgia Bulldogs live and play near downtown at the historic UGA campus. Even the city's nightlife is a spectacular event. Outdoor recreational opportunities abound in Athens with botanical gardens, state parks, top-rated golf courses, and of course exciting football games!

A Little History

Clarke County was enacted in 1801. It was named for Elijah Clarke who came to Georgia in 1774 to help fight battles with the Cherokee and Creek tribes. The tiny settlement of Athens sprang up near Cedar Shoals, a place where an ancient Cherokee trail crossed the Oconee River. It was incorporated in 1806, and named in honor of the center for higher learning that had flourished in ancient Greece. UGA had already been established in 1785, and was chartered as America's first state college. The histories of Athens and the University have been entwined from the earliest days—from the founding of the city, through the Civil War and Reconstruction of the South, to present day where more than 30,000 students each year discover all that classic Athens has to offer.

How 'Bout Them Dogs?!

UGA is home to the Georgia Bulldogs football team (1980 National Champions) and the Sanford Stadium. In fact, the entire city of Athens will be painted red and black through the football season, and bulldogs become treasured creatures. The stadium is the fifth-largest on-campus stadium in the United States and can accommodate 92,746 fans. As evidence of the almost rabid passion of UGA fans, you will read in our book about a new concept called Gameday Centers, which allow fans from across the country to stay and play near their alma mater. Needless to say, this quaint city takes on an entirely different hue during football season. Old-timers will tell you that Georgia selected the name "Bulldogs" because of its strong ties with Yale University, whose nickname was "Bulldogs." The first university president, Abraham Baldwin was a Yale man and had many of the buildings on campus designed from blueprints of Yale. Uga, the Georgia Bulldog, is one of the best-known mascots in the country. Perhaps the most famous Uga was Uga V, who had a cameo role in the movie "Midnight in the Garden of Good and Evil," and was featured on the cover of *Sports Illustrated*. As you can imagine, history and tradition play a big part in the lives of UGA students.

Artistic Athens

It is said, "No community of comparable size in the Southeast can boast richer cultural resources than Athens." From Athens' remarkable symphony orchestra and theatre companies to the exciting headline entertainers and Broadway productions, Athens offers visitors a myriad of top-quality entertainment. Visitors to Athens in June will enjoy the AthFest Music and Arts Festival and Concerts on the Lawn. *RollingStone* magazine has dubbed Athens the #1 Music Mecca/College Music Scene in America, and *New York Times* calls it "Live Music Central." It is the birthplace of the B-52's, REM and hundreds of other well-known bands. With everything from jazz, classical, country, blues, hip-hop and, of course, rock and roll, Athens is one of the most diverse music scenes in the country.

Shopping, Dining and Day Trips

Listed in the National Register of Historic Places, the Victorian buildings in downtown Athens hold a plethora of fabulous shopping opportunities. Quaint antique shops, fine restaurants, cozy coffee shops, fun collegiate stores, and outstanding art galleries offer visitors the finest in fashion, gifts, jewelry and art. Athens has many wonderful shopping areas. Five Points, a one-of-a-kind shopping community, is drenched in Southern charm and hospitality. Most of the businesses are housed in original 1920s and 1930s homes on tree-lined streets and sidewalks. From home furnishings and antiques to flowers and ice cream cones, you will love exploring this charming part of Athens. You will also be very impressed with the variety of wonderful dining opportunities in Athens. From a cup of gourmet coffee at a sidewalk café to nouveau Southern cuisine at a top-rated restaurant, you will be treated by some of the great chefs of the South.

WATKINSVILLE

The charming community of Watkinsville is a must-see for any visitor to Athens. Just minutes from Athens, Watkinsville was incorporated as a town in 1815, and today has a population just over 2,100. This lovely little Oconee County town is overflowing with wonderful shopping, family entertainment and art. No visit is complete without a trip to Chappelle Gallery, Happy Valley Pottery or Georgia Originals.

Watkinsville is also home to the Elder Mill Covered Bridge, one of only a few remaining covered bridges in Georgia. It was built during the late 1800s and was recently restored—one of the last wooden bridges still being used on a public road.

For more information about Athens and Watkinsville, contact the Athens Convention and Visitors Bureau at 706-357-4430, 800-653-0603 or visit www.visitathensga.com online.

Athens/Watkinsville Fairs Festivals & Fun

January
Georgia Bridal Show

February
Taste of Athens

March
Robert Osborne's Classic Film
Festival

April
Athens Twilight Criterium and
Festival
Piedmont Gardeners' Garden
Tour
UGA International Street
Festival

May
Ashford Manor Concerts on the
Lawn (May-Oct)
Athens Heritage Antiques Show
and Sale
Memorial Day in Memorial Park

June
AthFest Music and Arts Festival
Sunflower Music Series (June-
Aug)

July
Star Spangled Classic

September
Insectival

October
Conifer Weekend
Halloween, Athens Style
North Georgia Folk Festival

November
Athens Holiday Lights
Chocolate Lovers' Auction
Holiday Craft Fair
Holiday Open House Happy
Valley Pottery, Chappelle
Gallery & Georgia Originals
(Watkinsville)

December
Downtown Athens Christmas
Parade of Lights
Watkinsville Christmas Parade

ATHENS
INTERIORS MARKET

With more than 30 dealers shopping the country for the finest antiques, collectibles and home décor, you are sure to find the perfect treasure for your home here. The Athens Interiors Market, 250 Old Epps Bridge Rd. in Athens, has a reputation as a premier antique destination. You will find everything from a fine antique to a unique teacher's gift. Linda Cook found the location for the market when her lamp business outgrew its original space. After talking with interior designers and antique collectors, she made the decision to turn it into a multi-dealer store. You will find an incredible selection of fine antiques, art, silver, porcelain, children's items, and of course, Linda's lamps and lampshades. Athens Interiors Market is open Monday-Saturday 10 am-5 pm. Call 706-583-4095.

APPOINTMENTS AT FIVE

Appointments at Five specializes in English and French antiques, decorative accessories, bridal registry, and a wide variety of gift items. It's a shop where old and new coexist beautifully, where English and French country antiques live in perfect harmony with today's sparkle.

Since 1987, Appointments at Five has been an Athens tradition. Longtime friends and co-owners Kitty Culpepper and Jenny Sligh turned this early 1900s house into a specialty shop that offers almost everything. In 2000, they expanded to include the 1920s cottage next door—making room for the growing French country collection. The two houses are joined by an outdoor garden filled with ever-blooming flowers and unique garden statuaries purchased abroad.

Kitty and Jenny have traveled throughout England and France for many years. They know how and where to find the best buys these countries have to offer.

A rare treat, Appointments is an old-fashioned store where service is spontaneous, the selection is unsurpassed, and customer satisfaction is the raison d'etre. You'll leisurely browse through each room of this quaint shop and want to return again and again to see what's new. And for a virtual tour, visit www.appointmentsatfive.com. After all, it's the little things that make a house a home.

Though the displays change often, the theme is constant—gracious living with a timeless flair. Visit 1730 S. Lumpkin St., Monday-Saturday 10 am-5:30 pm. Call 706-353-8251.

CIRCA ANTIQUES & GARDENS

As a recent "empty nester," Delores Schofill found the time to grow her passions for collecting antiques and gardening. Circa Antiques & Gardens, 13 N. Main St., is a great collection of primitives, 19th century furniture, Southern pottery and estate jewelry. Watkinsville's longtime residents fondly refer to the building as "Ms. Edward's Store," built in 1902 it was the only drygoods store in the area. Stop by and see true Americana and unique garden accessories Tuesday-Saturday 10 am-6 pm. Call 706-769-1212 or visit www.circantiquesandgardens.com.

Athens Antique Mall

With 10,000 square feet of floor space, you're sure to find something fabulous at Athens Antique Mall. We did! Located on the western edge of Athens at 4615 Atlanta Hwy. in Bogart, it has been an institution for more than 20 years. The dealers are friendly, knowledgeable and helpful. You'll find primitives, Federal, Empire and Victorian antiques, plus 20th century furniture, collectibles and estate jewelry. Open Monday through Saturday 10 am-6 pm and Sunday 12:30-5:30 pm. Call 706-354-0108.

Ann Reynolds began her business in 1999, selling artwork by local artists. Now she has a 2,500-square-foot showroom for unique pieces of art, antiques, home accents and jewelry at Sunshine Village, Ltd., 11 N. Main St. The citizens of Watkinsville will remember this building as a grocery store and even a gas station before being transformed into this lovely gallery. You will definitely experience the warmth at Sunshine Village, open Tuesday-Saturday 11:30 am-5 pm. Call 706-769-2223.

Artists & Art Galleries

Within minutes of each other in Watkinsville, we found three wonderful art and pottery galleries. They are all the result of Jerry and Kathy Chappelle's lifelong passion for art. Since 1970, they have headed a thriving community of artists on a bucolic farm

near Watkinsville. They purchased the farm when Jerry came to teach art at the University of Georgia.

As you wander down the country road to **Happy Valley Pottery,** 1210 Carson Graves Rd., you'll see the artistic works of numerous artists. Visitors can roam from one studio to the next, meeting and watching the resident artists. They'll see artists throwing pots, blowing hot glass, and painting in a variety of styles. Open daily 9 am-4 pm. Call 706-769-5922.

The Chappelles also own **Chappelle Gallery,** 25 S. Main St. It is located in the historic Haygood House, which was built in 1827. After the restoration, the Chappelles opened the Gallery to showcase the work of about 65 local and national artists.

Chappelle Gallery

Open Monday-Saturday 10 am-5:30 pm. Call 706-310-0985.

Just a short walk away, you'll find **Georgia Originals,** 2 S. Main St. It is a wonderful collection of items handmade or produced in Georgia—pottery, blown glass, fibers, music, food and bath products. Open Monday-Saturday 10 am-8 pm. Call 706-310-0030.

Children's

$Southern$ $Belles$ and $Beaus$ Ladies, you must bring your little ones to Southern Belles and Beaus, 40 N. Main St. in Watkinsville. A love for children is Marjorie Ross' reason for creating this enchanting and whimsical boutique. A grandmother of nine, Marjorie offers all children an environment where they can play dress up, sit and have a classic tea party, craft a work of art through pottery painting, play with blocks, or watch a movie. Her specialty shop also offers brands found only in boutiques including shoes to match many of the outfits. While dressing up for tea parties may be best suited for the little ones, people of all ages can enjoy the pottery painting or have a gift personalized with monogramming. Stop by Monday thru Friday 10 am-5 pm and Saturday 10 am-4 pm. For more information, call 706-769-5375.

 The craftsman bungalow at 1676 S. Lumpkin St. features an English garden filled with blossoms, butterflies and honeybees. Inside Homeplace Gifts & Toys you will find Crabtree & Evelyn products, as well as handcrafted pottery, jewelry, apparel, and more. For more than 20 years, owners Lane and Jim Norton have stocked an amazing selection of children's books, Playmobil, Folkmanis puppets and wooden toys by Brio. Homeplace is open Monday-Friday 9:30 am-6 pm and Saturday 10 am-5:30 pm. Call 706-549-0829.

Condominiums, Resorts & Rentals

If you're a sports fan, you'll love this innovative and fascinating concept! Luxury condominiums located within close proximity to college athletic facilities offer sports enthusiasts the perfect place for socializing, lodging and investing in profitable real estate. Gameday Centers, Luxury Sports Condominiums have been built in Auburn, Tuscaloosa, Lexington, College Station, and Tallahassee and now in "Bulldawg country," Athens. The center opened in all of its "red and black glory" in 2004, and in no time was completely "Sold Out." The condos—ranging from a small Tailgate Suite to a three-bedroom, three-bath penthouse—are furnished with everything from bedding to barware to reflect the spirit of the University of Georgia.

Some owners occupy their condo year-round, and others only use them on game days and special events. The rest of the year, they list them in a rental pool. They are conveniently located to the stadium with private parking, so your day can be practi-

cally hassle free. Guests of Georgia Gameday Center have access to high-speed Internet, a conference room and an exercise room, and the building has gated security. You'll feel as though you are investing in a home-away-from-home, just minutes away from the activities at UGA.

Many owners have condominiums at beach or mountain resorts, and use them only a week or two out of the year. This is the same idea, except even better. You'll be able to focus on cheering for your team during each home game. No more worrying about hotel reservations or game day parking fiascos. Now, you'll have the ease and convenience of a home and what's even better is you'll be able to share your new home with fellow fans that love the game as much as you do. The Georgia Gameday Center is located at 250 W. Broad St., within walking distance to downtown restaurants, shopping and the UGA Sanford Stadium. Call 706-583-4500 or 800-693-8204 for information or reservations, or visit www.gamedaycenters.com. "Go Dawgs!"

Stiles Properties

Conveniently located in the heart of Athens' Five Points, you'll find a unique group of historic apartment buildings that reflect the charm and quiet ambiance of the 1920s. With a Gatsby-like feel and charm, you'll almost expect to hear the sounds of a jazz band playing. The hardwood floors, brass hardware, glass doorknobs and classic black and white tiled bathrooms add a nostalgic element to the Milledge Park, Milledge Circle and Henrietta Apartments. A new generation is discovering the elegance of the past in these "close to campus" apartments. For more information, stop by 1660 S. Lumpkin St. Monday-Friday 9 am-5 pm, visit www.stilesproperties.com online, or call 706-549-9600.

Fashion & Accessories

SHOES ✱ ACCESSORIES ✱ HANDBAGS

With one visit to the fabulous shoe boutique Slippers, you will agree with *Southern Living* in voting it one of their "Favorite Shops of the South." It is located at 1696 S. Lumpkin St. in Athens' charming 1930s Five Points district. Owner Amy Bray is unique, in that she tries to select unusual items that are not found in other stores. Amy carries shoes from designers like Donald J. Pliner, Claudia Ciuti and Anne Klein. She also has a great selection of extraordinary jewelry, handbags, clothing and fun accessories. Amy says, "Slippers—dresses you from the bottom up," and you will love her fun, funky style. Slippers has amazing items for every age, along with superb customer service. Stop by Monday-Friday 10 am-5:30 pm and Saturday until 5 pm. Call 706-548-3179.

Opulence

Opulence, a ladies' clothing boutique, is located in the popular Five Points district. The shop carries exclusive lines and prides itself in helping its clients feel beautiful and confident. It's "An Experience in Fashion"—fine clothing for the young and the young-at-heart woman. Located at 1719 S. Lumpkin St. in Athens. Stop by Monday-Saturday 10 am-5:30 pm. Call 706-543-6850 or visit www.opulencefashion.com.

Jean and Chelle Pujol are a delightful mother/daughter team—they are "The Cat's Pajamas!" Their unique gift boutique at 1664 S. Lumpkin St. has emerged over the years as a favorite Athens place to shop for extraordinary things. You'll find a wide selection of jewelry and purses, girlfriend gifts, fun gifts for the bride and groom, and great sorority items for the UGA girls. They have become "The Niche You've Been Looking For." Stop by Monday-Saturday 10 am-5:30 pm for great gifts and great atmosphere! Call 706-208-1075 or 877-228-7757.

For more than 17 years, Frontier has been one of Athens' most unique shopping experiences. Frontier features local items and gifts with an international flair including French soaps, Danish tapers, primitive antiques, handcrafted jewelry, and handmade ceramic tableware. It is also home to the lovely Honeypot® by Bee Natural®, a locally crafted beeswax candle accented with natural botanicals. Open Monday through Thursday 10:30 am-6 pm and Friday through Saturday 10 am-6 pm. Call 706-369-8079. Stop by 193 E. Clayton and enjoy warm friendly service.

Gifts, cards, candles, antiques, jewelry, flowers, balloons...Jingles, 1737 S. Lumpkin St. in Athens is filled top to bottom with treasures you will love. Owner Linda Ford and her very friendly staff will help you choose from an outstanding selection of fine gifts like Tyler Candles, Department 56 collectibles, and many more. Jingles is open Monday-Friday 10 am-5:30 pm and Saturday until 5 pm. For more information, call 706-549-6843 or visit www.jinglesatfivepoints.com.

Southern Comforts, at 1658 S. Lumpkin St. in the Five Points area of Athens, is a decorative arts consignment shop. Specializing in estate silver, elegant furnishings, exceptional antiques, vintage linens and original art—things to make your home uniquely yours. Open Tuesday-Saturday 10 am-4 pm. Call 706-543-8130 or 800-431-6560.

HOUSE TO HOUSE
Furnishings Consignment

When this shop owner tired of the "high-heel corporate world" of Dallas, she returned to her hometown of Athens, and opened House to House Furnishings Consignment. Here you will find a unique selection of quality gently used furniture and home decor. Drop in often and browse slowly...treasures abound in this wonderful shop, and inventory changes daily! Stop by 10 Huntington Rd., Tuesday-Saturday 10 am-6 pm. Call 706-548-7800 or visit www.h2hconsignment.com. Look for a larger location soon!

MAIN STREET YARN AND FIBERS

Whether you are a seasoned knitter or don't even know how to "knit one, purl two," you will feel right at home at Main Street Yarns and Fibers, 16 N. Main St. in Watkinsville. Owner Ruth Barrow carries the most beautiful yarns from top designers, as well as the latest patterns, books, magazines and accessories. Classes are held for every age and ability, and there are weekly "spin-ins" if you want to bring your wheel or drop spindle. For more information and hours, visit www.mainstreetyarns.com or call 706-769-5531.

Restaurants

GAUTREAU'S

CAJUN CAFÉ

You will only need one taste of Kenny Gautreau's spicy gumbo to believe him when he says he is "Cajun through and through." Kenny and wife Taffy create fantastic dishes from family recipes passed down for generations—and trust us the gumbo is the best! Taffy's bread pudding is also legendary, and it is the perfect ending to a meal at Gautreau's Cajun Café, 2 Main St. in Watkinsville's Town Center. Open Tuesday-Thursday 11 am-9:30 pm, Friday-Saturday until 10:30 pm, and Sunday brunch 11:30 am-2:30 pm. Call 706-769-4177.

The University of Georgia

Georgia Center for Continuing Education

The Georgia Center for Continuing Education opened in 1957 on the historic University of Georgia campus, 1197 S. Lumpkin St. in Athens. It is the world's largest university-based adult education center, serving more than 100,000 adults each year. The Center boasts 28 conference rooms, two auditoriums, 200 hotel rooms and suites, and banquet halls serving up to 500. It's also popular among locals for its two restaurants, the cafeteria-style Courtyard Café and the Savannah Room, which serves delicious Southern cuisine. Visit www.gactr.uga.edu or call 706-542-2654.

Specialty Shops

Dory's

HEARTH & HOME

Dory and Steve Brown say, "From Season to Season . . . Indoors & Out . . . we have everything you need for a cozy fire!" From exclusive designs of gas logs and wood stoves to chimneys, fireplace accessories and Big Green Egg grills, you'll find it all at Dory's, 1222 Greensboro Hwy. in Watkinsville. If you love everything about a wood fire except the mess of wood, you will find quality, clean burning Direct-Vent appliances and many styles of superior Peterson Real-Frye gas logs. They also carry freestanding stoves and fireplace inserts in a variety of sizes and styles. You'll be able to express your personal style with traditional or contemporary fireplace accessories. Dory's is open Tuesday through Friday 10 am-6 pm and Saturday until 2 pm. Visit www.doryshearthandhome.com or call 706-769-7997.

Discover Blue Ridge

You will learn more than three "Rs" when it comes to discovering Blue Ridge. You can ride, ramble, retreat, roam, rock, relax and enjoy all that this enchanting mountain town has to offer. The town of Blue Ridge was once considered a "retreat for the elite," because of its pure mineral waters. Tourists would ride the train to town to enjoy the mineral springs, and maybe have dinner at the Blue Ridge Hotel. Not much has changed here since the first railroad tracks were laid in 1886.

The first thing we noticed when we rolled into town was the sweet sounds of mountain music from volunteer musicians and that time seems to have almost stopped here. The railroad depot has remained a focus in downtown Blue Ridge, a meeting place for friends, and the hub of activity. The Blue Ridge Scenic Railway starts at the charming depot and takes its passengers not only through the winding trails of the Mountains, but almost back in time.

Blue Ridge was founded in 1886 with the arrival of the Marietta and North Georgia Railroad. Businesses and homes began to build up around the depot, and in 1895 Fannin County seat was moved from Morganton to Blue Ridge. The Blue Ridge Mountains meant a form of wealth for the early settlers. Agriculture was the major industry in the area, but lumber and mining in the mountains meant a significant income to the settlers. As the lumber began to be harvested, the federal government bought all of the mountain land and created the Chattahoochee-Oconee National Forests. These forests have more than 500 developed campsites, 200 picnic sites, developed recreation areas and swim beaches, and the crystal clear aquamarine waters of Lake Blue Ridge make it one of the state's most beautiful mountain lakes.

Blue Ridge "R & R"

The first thing folks usually want to do in Blue Ridge is hop aboard the Blue Ridge Scenic Railway. It departs from the old downtown depot and chugs all the way to downtown McCaysville alongside the beautiful Toccoa River. Walk just across the "Blue Line" and you'll be in Tennessee! The view is breathtaking in every season; wildflowers and rhododendron in red, orange and golden foliage, and lots of holiday red and green during December. Jolly Old St. Nick even boards the train with his elves for a special holiday ride! During the early years of the railway, visitors journeyed to Blue Ridge to take advantage of its pure mineral waters. Today tourists can still ride the train and enjoy all of the wonderful shopping experiences Blue Ridge has to offer. The Blue Ridge Railway is a 26-mile roundtrip ride and active from March through December.

Shop Till You Drop

Appalachian arts and crafts, handmade quilts, hand-painted pottery, antiques, and unique mountain home furnishings are just a few of the remarkable treasures you will find in this "mountain town." Artists have been attracted to Blue Ridge for many years because of its natural beauty, peaceful ambiance, mist covered mountains and clear starry nights. They have used the quiet beauty of the mountain as inspiration in creating extraordinary art like paintings and sculpture. You will see artists at work on their crafts, including blacksmiths, potters, glassblowers and painters.

You will love all of the wonderful and unique mountain folk art in the shops around town, and the hand-spun sweaters and shawls made from alpaca wool produced at Sugar Creek Farm.

If antiques are your passion, plan to spend hours snooping through eclectic antique shops around Blue Ridge. Main Street is filled with specialty shops, galleries and boutiques from end to end, so you'll be pretty busy!

Feast and Slumber

You must stop to eat sometime! When you do, you'll find a smorgasbord of delicious Southern specialties. From Main Street eateries and mountain cafés to Mercier Orchards, you'll be satisfied with everything from smoky trout to apple fritters and a glass of sweet tea!

At the end of a long fun day, you'll find no shortage of wonderful mountain retreats, bed and breakfasts and great hotels. Whether you want to stay a weekend, a week or a lifetime, there are beautiful mountain cabins, and country homes to rent or buy. There are magnificent golf courses in the high mountain valleys and beautiful parks and campgrounds. Whether you come to white water raft, hike or bike the mountain trails, or (like us) browse through every unique shop, you'll find Blue Ridge ready to welcome you with wonderful lodging and entertainment.

For more information about Blue Ridge, contact the Fannin County Chamber of Commerce at 706-632-5680, 800-899-6867 or visit online at www.blueridgemountains.com.

Blue Ridge Fairs Festivals & Fun

April
  Blue Ridge Mountain Adventure
    Race

May
  Arts in the Park
  Cinco de Mayo Festival

July
  Concerts in the Park (July-August)
  Old Timers Day

August
  Kiwanis Rodeo

September
  Family Fishing Festival
  Labor Day Barbeque
  Ocoee River Days
  Wildlife Festival of Arts

October
  Halloween Safe Zone
  Mountain Harvest Sale
  Smokey Bear's Birthday

November
  Holiday Art Show (Nov-Dec)
  Light Up Blue Ridge

December
  Festival of Trees
  Hometown Christmas
  Scenic Railway Christmas
    Express

Antiques

Timeless Reflections

When visiting the Blue Ridge Mountains, you must experience Blue Ridge's Historic Antique District on Main St. Begin with **Timeless Reflections** at 661 E. Main St. It is a unique antique shop that blends yonder year's treasures with gift ideas of today. You will also find lovely home décor items and other treasures. Call 706-632-0425.

If the treasure hunt leaves you hungry, go next door to 657 E. Main St. for delicious homemade menu items for breakfast, lunch or dinner. At **Serenity Garden Café** you'll find soups, salads and sandwiches, as well as homemade desserts. Call 706-258-4949 or visit www.serenitygardencafe.com.

Still have a sweet tooth? **Three Sisters Fudge** offers more than 26 varieties of fudge well worth your review. Located within Timeless Reflections. Call 706-258-4574.

BLUE RIDGE

ANTIQUES & MALL

Enjoy a 25-cent cup of delicious gourmet coffee and spend time browsing this charming antique mall. Blue Ridge Antiques & Mall is located at 733 E. Main St. in what was once the old Gartrell Hotel. Today, each room houses a different vendor with unique presentations of quality antiques. Owners Robert and Liz Sanchez are second-generation owners and the entire family is involved. Stop by Monday through Friday 10 am-5 pm, Saturday until 5:30 pm, and Sunday 1-5 pm. Call 706-632-7871.

HIGH COUNTRY
ART & ANTIQUE

When they married, Michelle and Patrick Bright developed a "five-year plan," to own a business in the beautiful Blue Ridge Mountains they loved so much. Their plan really worked—it only took six months! High Country Art & Antique, 715 E. Main St. in Blue Ridge, is home to almost 1,000 pieces of original artwork from more than 65 local and regional artists. The works range from oil paintings, pottery and wood bowls to photography, metal art and jewelry. Stop by Monday and Wednesday-Saturday 10:30 am-5:30 pm and Sunday noon-5 pm. Call 706-632-6882 or visit www.highcountryart.com for upcoming events.

Dan and Gayle Barton spent a week each year visiting the breathtaking mountains of Blue Ridge and loved it so much they finally decided to build their own cabin. Using the cabin as a rental property proved so successful that this Atlanta couple decided to build another. They finally gave up busy careers, moved north, and started First Class Cabin Rentals, 3980 E. 1st St. Each property offers an up-scale "lodge style" décor, a hot tub, at least one fireplace, and a fully equipped kitchen. You'll enjoy a mountain lodge fantasy in a luxurious rustic setting. Dan and Gayle consider their guests to be more than just customers or clients, they treat them like family. It's no wonder much of their clientele is based on repeat and referral customers. For more information or reservations, visit www.firstclasscabins.com or call 877-277-5409 or 706-258-3018.

The friendly folks at My Mountain Cabin Rentals have a theory: "If you are lucky enough to be in the mountains—you are lucky enough!" Especially if you are fortunate enough to stay in one of their wonderful luxury mountain cabins! "My Mountain" is a private, 1,500-acre mountaintop neighborhood, just minutes from Blue Ridge at 3945 Old Loving Rd. in Morganton. Choose from two to four bedroom cabins with hot tubs, rock hearth fireplaces, game rooms, satellite TV, barbecue grills, fully equipped kitchens, and washers and dryers.

No need to leave your favorite four-legger behind; pets are very welcome! For more information, visit www.1MyMountain.com on-line or call 706-374-4111 or 800-844-4939.

Blue Ridge Inn Bed & Breakfast

Built in 1890, this stately, three-story Victorian inn is nestled in the beautiful Blue Ridge Mountains. The Blue Ridge Inn Bed & Breakfast, 477 W. First St., features 14 rooms, eight fireplaces, 12-foot ceilings, original hand-carved woodwork, heart-pine floors and claw-foot tubs. Experience charming rooms decorated in unique themes, such as the Marilyn Monroe Room, the Rose Room and Grandpa's Suite. Your stay includes a delicious full country breakfast served with homemade bread, biscuits and seasonal fresh fruit, all elegantly placed on

beautiful linens. The Blue Ridge Inn is located within walking distance of the top-ranked Victorian House Restaurant and the many downtown antique shops. For more information or reservations, call 706-632-0222 or visit online www.blueridgeinnbandb.com.

Coffee

L&L Beanery

The aroma of freshly brewed coffee is not the only reason customers love L & L Beanery. Located in a 1920s bank building at 260-A W. Main St., the original vault houses wonderful gifts and gourmet foods, and the fireplace and piano create a cozy setting to linger over a cup of coffee. Stop by Monday-Thursday 7:30 am-5 pm, Friday until 9:30 pm, Saturday 7 am-5 pm, and Sunday noon-5 pm. Don't miss the local entertainment on the weekends, call 706-632-3242 for times.

N & N Florist

Shopping at N & N Florist is always an experience. Becky Howard's customers love watching from a special entertainment chair as their floral arrangements are being created. N & N Florist, 4084 E. First St. in Blue Ridge, is a bright, colorful store filled with beautiful fresh and silk flowers.

Situated in what was once the first Kentucky Fried Chicken building in town, N & N Florist is as special as its gifted owner. Becky attributes her success as a florist to the grace of God and the encouragement of her family. You will love Becky's warmth and sense of humor, and appreciate her creative ability and talent. The shop is open Monday-Friday 8:30 am-5 pm, Wednesday until 3 pm and Saturday until 1 pm. For more information, call 706-632-2446.

Furniture

HIGHRIDGE GALLERY

The names Dellon Ash, II and Highridge Gallery are known and respected throughout the southeastern United States. Dellon's work as an interior designer takes him as far south as Florida, but he always returns to the beautiful area of Blue Ridge. Highridge Gallery, 636 E. Main St., features classic furniture, decorator pieces, and more. Stop by Tuesday-Saturday 10 am-4 pm. For information or consultation, call 706-632-6116.

Betty's Vintage Boutique

Betty's Vintage Boutique, 611 E. Main St. in Blue Ridge, is a delightful store filled with beautiful treasures for your home and office. Owner Betty Waters carries high-quality bed linens by Waverly and Thomasville, quilts by Patch Magic, as well as distinctive lamps and accessories. She also offers a line of beautiful specialty linens, hand-crafted from the fabrics and styles you choose. From fascinating sterling silver and beaded jewelry to unique fan pulls and pillows, extraordinary items are available to transform your style and space. You'll also find Vera Bradley handbags and accessories, Crabtree & Evelyn Bath and Body products, plus Ganz "Time & Again" candles. Stop by Monday-Saturday 10 am-5 pm. For more information, visit www.distinctivelinens.com online or call 706-632-7631.

BRITISH BITS & BOBS

When Judena Burt moved from England to Blue Ridge, she missed the teas, candies and cookies she had grown up with. "I wanted to bring a little part of England to y'all Americans," she says. She opened British Bits & Bobs, 661 E. Main St. to do just that. You will love the fascinating selection of British candies, cookies, drinks, jellies, teapots, cups and saucers. Judena will even take special orders for things an "ex-Brit" may miss. The store is open daily 9:30 am-5 pm. Call 770-841-8862.

ANASAZI

'Lil Sis Hart' often said to her first born, "Al Jr., you sure do have good taste!" As an applications engineer, Al didn't have much opportunity for creative expression, but retirement from the chemical industry brought the opening of Anasazi in Blue Ridge, and with this new-found passion, he is having the time of his life. Through Anasazi, at 641 E. Main St., Al introduces clients and visitors to Southwestern lodge furniture and home accessories. You will find beautiful hardwoods from the West, gloriously "charactered" aspen from Colorado, worm wood pine from Old Mexico, bars and mirrors created from pecky cypress dating to the Antebellum period, and accent pieces from Arizona, New Mexico and Montana.

Al characterizes his "Gift Gallery" as a presentation of "crafts, serving bars, rugs, dinnerware, lamps, jewelry and unique gift items in a wonderfully open space." You will love the atmosphere and have plenty of room to shop without the mass merchandising claustrophobia. The "Furniture Gallery" offers a broad range of leather sofas, aspen beds and tables, worm wood furniture, leather game tables, and magnificent bars crafted from cypress wood more than 150 years old. These are perfect furnishings for a mountain home, but the extraordinary furniture and home accessories will add a unique style and flair to any room. Al personally selects each piece of his collection—some with particular clients in mind—so if you are looking

for something special, be sure to let him know. Stop by Anasazi Monday-Saturday 10 am-5 pm and Sunday noon-5 pm or call 706-632-7661. One visit will have you convinced that 'Lil Sis Hart' was right! Al really does have good taste!

Whether you are planning a vacation, a business trip, or a fun weekend with "the girls" in the beautiful Blue Ridge Mountains, you will have an enjoyable, relaxing stay at Douglas Inn & Suites, 1192 Windy Ridge Rd. The affordable accommodations offer all of the comforts of home in one-or-two-bedroom suites, the two-bedroom can comfortably sleep up to eight individuals. The suites include a full kitchen with range, refrigerator, microwave, cookware, dishes and a coffee maker— perfect for families wanting to prepare their own breakfast or lunch. All rooms include a private phone with data port, so business travelers are set—the rooms also offer cable television. The management is friendly and helpful, and will work with churches on discount rates. For information or reservations, call 877-778-3600, 706-258-3600 or visit www.douglasinn.com. Play hard in Blue Ridge, then sleep well at Douglas Inn & Suites.

Kick back in the beauty and comfort of the Ramada Limited of Blue Ridge at 30 Overview Dr. This Gold Key Award Winning hotel offers an indoor heated pool and an outdoor deck overlooking the beautiful Blue Ridge Mountains. Enjoy all the perks, including a free continental breakfast. Call 800-272-6232, 706-632-4444 or visit www.ramada.com online.

They are called, "The Prime Team in the North Georgia Mountains," and they will make your real estate experience a true pleasure. Dedicated to matching their clients with the perfect permanent or vacation home, Georgia Prime Real Estate is a team of 15 full-time real estate professionals who know and love this beautiful section of the Blue Ridge Mountains. You, too, will fall in love with Blue Ridge, which has become one of the top 10 retirement communities in the United States. Georgia Prime Real Estate has two locations—11 Overview Dr. and downtown, just across from the historic Blue Ridge Train Depot at 709 E. Main St. Stop by Monday thru Saturday

9 am-5 pm and Sunday noon-5 pm. Call 877-632-1192, 706-632-8555 or visit www.georgiaprime.com for a free color brochure.

After living in the Atlanta area for many years, June Slusser moved to the Blue Ridge Mountains for the beauty and relaxation. She became familiar with the Coldwell Banker High Country Realty group while looking for her own home, and purchased the company in 2003. The company focuses on real estate services in North Georgia, Tennessee and North Carolina, with a slogan, "Life's a Mountain, Not a Beach." Thirty-three professional agents in three offices specialize in lake properties, cabins, land, investment properties and commercial real estate. The Blue Ridge office is located at 10156 Blue Ridge Dr. and is open Monday-Friday 9 am-5:30 pm, Saturday until 5 pm, and Sunday 1-5 pm. For more information, contact June at 800-307-0777, 706-632-7311 or visit www.cbhighcountry.com online.

VICTORIAN HOUSE RESTAURANT

Beautiful china, antique table linens and gleaming crystal compliment a delicious meal and perfect Victorian experience at the Victorian House Restaurant, 224 W. Main St. in Blue Ridge. Not only has this restaurant been called, "North Georgia's most elegant dining atmosphere of yesteryear," it is also recommended by *Southern Living* magazine. We loved the Wild Mushroom Soup!

Doreen Borgemeister and parents Milt and Irene Darden own and operate Victorian House Restaurant, and consider their work "play" because they have so much fun. The décor is true 1900 circa, with fun, vintage hats, fur pieces and costume jewelry for all to enjoy. You may even see a few "Red Hat" ladies enjoying their day out. Doreen says, "Young girls dress up and become very sophisticated and dignified, while ladies dress up, giggle, and become child-like!" Visit www.victorian-tea-room.com online or call 706-258-2275 for more information..

Discover
Bolingbroke / Juliette

BOLINGBROKE

If you are looking for quaint shops and quality antiques, then Bolingbroke is a must-see! A former railroad and farming town, Bolingbroke has become an antique lover's dream come true. Take a stroll through the many shops and art galleries, where you will find something for everyone. And, if all that shopping has left you hungry, be sure to visit one of the delicious restaurants or stop and enjoy an afternoon tea or a root beer float at the soda fountain. No matter what brings you to Bolingbroke, the Southern charm will keep you coming back for more!

JULIETTE

The sleepy little town of Juliette was heading for demise until 1991 when Hollywood producers discovered the quaint community. The historic cottages and buildings, the railroad, the river and the rural atmosphere of the city were the perfect location for their movie, *"Fried Green Tomatoes at the Whistlestop Café,"* based on the book by Fannie Flagg. Today, Juliette enjoys a booming tourist business, with a "Green Tomato Festival" that is the place to be in October. Besides the famous café and gift shop, you'll find a delightful collection of wonderful little antique stores and places to eat. Visit the Juliette Gristmill, which was built in 1927, and the

Piedmont National Refuge. You will be "starstruck" by the natural charm of this sweet Georgia town, and of course you will love feasting on the famous "fried green tomatoes!"

For more information about Bolingbroke and Juliette, contact the Forsyth-Monroe County Chamber of Commerce at 888-642-4628, 478-994-9239 or visit www.forsyth-monroechamber.com online.

Juliette Fairs Festivals & Fun

July
Independence Day Festivities

September
Labor Day Celebration

October
Annual Green Tomato Festival

November
Christmas Lights & Decorations

December
Christmas Lights & Decorations

Antiques

Henry's of Bolingbroke This customer-friendly antique and home décor store is located under massive shade trees in a two-story 1920s Georgia farmhouse. Henry's of Bolingbroke, 6009 Hwy. 41 S., is owned-and-operated by 12 women with retail and design experience. The owners individually select each item, and merchandise arrives daily—so the inventory is always changing. Since 1997 area shoppers have returned for Period to 1930s American, Continental, and English Country antiques made from pine, oak and mahogany. In addition, the collections at Henry's include estate pieces, home and garden accessories, a large selection of oil paintings, children's

items, unique gifts, and vintage books. Henry's is a wonderland during the holiday season. Stop by Monday through Saturday 10 am-5 pm or call 478-992-9878.

Realtors

RE/MAX® Properties Plus Since Bobby Lee and Vicki Smith opened RE/MAX Properties Plus in 2000, it has grown from just the two of them to more than 15 realtors. It has become the first choice for hundreds of Middle

Georgians for their real estate needs. Located at 6241 Hwy. 41 S. in Bolingbroke, and is open Monday-Friday 9 am-5 pm or by appointment. Call 478-474-7320 or visit www.remax-midga.com.

The Red Tomato

He studied at Johnson & Wales in Charleston, S.C., apprenticed at Maxim's in Paris, and worked with French Chef André Rochat and food superstar Emeril Lagasse. Chef Michael Falduti and his lovely wife Sara then came home to the South. His wonderful restaurant The Red Tomato, 7248 N. Alexander Ct. in Bolingbroke, continues to garner rave reviews from customers and food critics who consider his cuisine some of the most innovative and delicious in the South. The white farmhouse with the large front porch is perfect for both inside and outside dining, and the shabby chic décor is beautiful. Because Chef Falduti only uses fresh ingredients bought each day, the menu is everchanging. The Red Tomato is open for lunch Tuesday-Saturday 11 am-2 pm and for dinner Thursday-Saturday 5:30-9:30 pm. Call 478-994-6336.

There is absolutely no way you can visit this part of Georgia without a stop at one of the state's most famous cafés. The Whistle Stop Café, 443 McCrakin St., is the original café featured in one of the all time favorite movies, "Fried Green Tomatoes" Originally built in 1929 as a general merchandise store by Mr. Edward L. Williams Sr., it closed in 1972, and re-opened by Robert Williams after the filming of the movie in 1991. Elizabeth Bryant purchased The Whistle Stop in 2002 and continues the tradition and reputation for the best "fried green tomatoes" in the land.

A sampling of the "countrified" menu includes of course Fried Green Tomatoes, served with Ranch or radish sauce, Homestyle Onion Rings, Sweet Root Sticks—country fried sweet potatoes dusted with cinnamon and sugar, Rooster Strips, and Country French Fries topped with cheese and bacon bits. One of the most popular salads is the Fried Green Tomato Salad—a delicious salad including Vidalia onions, topped with a sizzling hot fried green tomato slice. Of course, barbecue is on the menu, as well as burgers, chicken strips, and Big Lee's Peach Cobbler! If a meal at The Whistlestop Café doesn't satisfy your hungry soul, honey, you Ain't Southern!

Elizabeth has renovated and "revitalized" the Whistle Stop in Juliette to its original historic beauty. She invites customers to BYOB from the Habersham Winery for evening events, and she can cater for parties for more than 400. If you are lucky enough to be visiting during October, you can be part of the Fried Green Tomato Festival. The Whistle Stop Café is open Tuesday-Sunday 11 am-4 pm. Call 478-992-8886 or visit www.thewhistlestopcafe.com.

Discover Covington

With a wealth of treasures old and new, Covington will be a delightful experience. It is a small community just outside the Atlanta metropolitan area that is almost perfect. Its laid-back lifestyle, timeless Southern charm and evident sense of community draws new residents and visitors from across the country. Covington's Downtown Square is the heart of this enchanting vibrant town, and is framed with quaint shops, restaurants and historical buildings.

Antebellum History

During the 1700s the entire county belonged to the Creek Indian Nation until the first white settlers began arriving in the early 1800s. The Creeks were forced to relinquish their claim to the land in 1813, and Newton County was officially formed in 1821. The county was named for Sergeant John Newton, a Revolutionary War soldier. The first building to be erected here was "The Brick Store," a general store, stagecoach stop and location of the first court session. The Brick Store is still standing today with the title of "Historical Marker Number 1." The town of Covington was named for General Leonard Covington, who served in the Revolutionary War, the Indian Wars and the War of 1812. The history of Covington resembles that of most early towns in that the railroad ushered in progress and growth. Until the Civil War, cotton, textile and pulpwood industries flourished in the county. Fortunately, not many of the beautiful homes or plantations were burned during Garrard's raid, and this precious legacy is today one of Covington's most remarkable attractions. The antebellum homes have been carefully and beautifully preserved and maintained. The Newton County Courthouse, which was built in 1884, is one of only five in the state built in the Second Empire style. This unique style was inspired by the architecture of France under Napoleon III. Covington is part of several regional tourism organizations including Georgia's Historic Heartland, and Georgia's Treasures Along 1-20. The citizens have shown a passion in making their historic district one of Georgia's largest National Register Districts.

"Hollywood of the South"

If Covington's Downtown Square and tree-lined neighborhoods seem a little familiar, it's because this charming town has been used in many movies and television shows. The most famous of these, "In the Heat of the Night," starring the late Carroll O'Connor, was filmed in and around the Downtown Square for seven years during the late 1980s and early 1990s. Covington was also the setting for several episodes of the original "Dukes of Hazard" series. Many fans still flock to the Courthouse to see the filming location. There is even an annual convention of Heat of the Night fans. Covington and Newton County have become a "Mecca" for television and movie production. It can be transformed into a Civil War Village or a 1950s town with ease, and the list of film credits is impressive. Some of the productions you will recognize include "Cannonball Run" (1980), "A Father's Homecoming" (1988), "I'll Fly Away" (1991-92), "My Cousin Vinny" (1991), "Savannah" (1996-97), and "Remember the Titans" (2000).

Enjoy Covington!

You will absolutely love shopping in Historic Downtown Covington. It is a delightful blend of old and new, from wonderful antique stores to fabulous restaurants—many in wonderfully restored historic surroundings. You will find apparel boutiques, gift shops, florists and even a beautiful day spa. When you must stop to eat, you will be satisfied with a choice of everything from traditional Italian to subtly spiced New Orleans fare, all within walking distance from the Square. The Square is even host to occasional outdoor luncheon concerts. "The Market" is open from the first Saturday in May through the last Saturday in October, with organically grown vegetables, fruits, flowers, handmade items, soaps, and homemade bakery goods.

Covington is a town that is as much fun in one season as the next because there is always something exciting planned. The entire town seems to glow with the spirit of holidays past and the citizens' passionate pride in their historic city!

For more information about Covington, contact Main Street Covington at www.downtowncovington.org or call 770-385-2077. Or, contact the Covington Convention and Visitors Bureau at 800-616-8626, 770-787-3868 or visit www.newtonchamber.com online.

Covington Fairs Festivals & Fun

March
 Eggstraodinary Eggs Display

May
 Thursday Luncheon Concert
  Series

June
 Summer Concert Series (2nd &
  4th Friday Nights)

July
 July 4th Concert
 Summer Concert Series (2nd &
  4th Friday Nights)

September
 Thursday Luncheon Concert
  Series

October
 Annual Parade of Scarecrows
 Harvest Weekend and Classic
  Car Show
 Newton County Literacy
  Festival

November
 Holiday Season Preview
 Lighting of the Historic
  Courthouse & the Arrival
  of Santa on the Square

December
 Lion's Club & Main Street
  Covington's Holiday Parade

Main Street
COVINGTON

Did you know that the town of Covington is fondly known as the "Hollywood of the South?" More than 25 movies and television shows have been filmed on the downtown tree-shaded square, using the Historic Newton County Courthouse and the turn-of-the-century storefronts as a backdrop. To promote the economic development and preservation of the downtown, Main Street Covington encourages visitors to take advantage of the fascinating downtown events throughout the year. Enjoy art exhibits, luncheons, concerts, festivals and parades in this beautiful and charming Southern city. For more information, visit www.downtowncovington.org or call 770-385- 2077.

Artists, Art Galleries, Framing & Photography

SOUTHERN HEARTLAND ART GALLERY

Credited with helping to bring the visual arts to the community of Covington, the Southern Heartland Art Gallery continues to garner accolades for its beautiful collections. The gallery is a product of the Southern Heartland Art Guild, and operates as a co-op in which the participating artists take turns working in the gallery. The artists' works include a variety of mediums and styles, and an artist is always on hand to consult for custom framing. The Gallery, located on the Historic Square at 1132 Monticello St., is open Tuesday-Thursday 10 am-6 pm and Friday-Saturday until 7 pm. Visit www.southernheartlandart.com online or call 770-788-8799.

Bakeries

Man cannot live by bread alone—unless, of course, its bread from Town Center Breads! Located in a beautiful turn-of-the-century building at 1153 Monticello St., Town Center Breads has been enticing customers with its wonderful aroma since opening day. The delicious smell of fresh-baked baguettes, kalamata olive and rosemary potato breads, and many more, quite often bring back childhood memories.

President and chief baker Charles Skrobot (who with his wife Linda live above the bakery) along with sons Evan and Drew, guarantee that, "Every loaf of bread is hand-formed from organic flour and fresh ingredients and never sold as day old." We loved the unforgettable cinnamon raisin walnut swirl bread, which is now famous locally. This wonderful Historic Downtown Covington bakery is open Tuesday-Friday 7 am-6 pm, Saturday 7 am-1 pm. For more information, call 678-342-8774.

MERLE NORMAN*
Cosmetics Studio

Emily Rankin and Elizabeth Holcombe are more than business partners; they are family. Elizabeth is Emily's niece, and both share a love of beauty, makeup and people. After extensive training in Los Angeles with the Merle Norman experts, they decided to make a long-time dream come true. Their elegant Merle Norman boutique is located in the retail space under The Lofts, 1112 College Ave. They say that they chose that location in Covington because the class and style of the space reflects the product they sell. Customers love the fact that they can "try before they buy" with a complimentary makeover, which is one thing that makes all Merle Norman products so popular. Every purchase is personalized, from skin type to color. Although the boutique specializes in the signature Merle Norman skin products, Emily and Elizabeth also offer ear piercing and special gifts like jewelry, purses, potpourri, candles and gourmet food. They will soon bring in an aesthetician for facials and spa-related services. Open Monday-Friday 10 am-6 pm and Saturday until 5 pm. Emily and Elizabeth are always there, so stop by, say hi, and "try before you buy!" For more information, call 678-625-0052 or visit www.merlenorman.com.

Utopia Day Spa is a full-service day spa located at 1149 Washington St., in the heart of charming, Historic Downtown Covington. Utopia's owner Heather Braswell is a working mother who knows the importance of taking care of ourselves, so that we can take on life with the energy and vitality that is needed. Utopia's many services include therapy treatments from head to toe. Experience several different and invigorating body treatments and wraps—all focused on specific body needs. Utopia also has several massage therapists on staff, trained to relax and renew your body and spirit. At Utopia, standard services as ordinary as manicures, pedicures and waxing are transformed into experiences that will leave you refreshed. Utopia also offers many different and unique facials formulated to meet each client's needs. You can also experience Microdermabrasion, Intensive Pulse Light Therapy and Endermologie. In addition, Utopia has recently expanded and opened a retail area downstairs, that is full of many unique, specialty gift items for all ages. Utopia also has gift certificates and gift packages perfect for any holiday or occasion. For more information or to schedule a time to renew your spirit, call 770-786-2299.

Ramsey's FURNITURE

Ramsey's Furniture, 1145 Clark St., opened its doors back in 1919, and the company has remained Ramsey-owned-and-operated ever since. From great grandfather Ramsey to the present owner Sam Ramsey, the family name and stellar quality have remained constant. Ramsey's Furniture continues to offer its customers beautiful furniture and accessories at great savings, as well as friendly, personal customer service. Ramsey's Furniture is the headquarters for La-Z-Boy sofas and recliners, and Simmons Beautyrest mattresses. The Ramseys are extremely knowledgeable, helpful, and committed to giving back to their community. In fact, Sam is presently the mayor of Covington! Stop by Monday-Saturday 9 am-6 pm and Wednesday until noon. For more information, call 770-786-2635.

A TOUCH OF COUNTRY

Harold and Dianne Duren have a motto, "We are the store of times remembered." The old-fashioned soda fountain in this downtown Covington store at 1105 Church St. does indeed lend a charming feel of yesteryear to this wonderful furniture, eatery and home-accent shop. Harold has been building fine furniture for more than 30 years, and specializes in oak and pine reproductions. At A Touch of Country enjoy a hand-dipped milkshake with their famous homemade chili and cornbread. Also, visit "The Dukes of Hazzard" and "In the Heat of the Night" museum and souvenir shop within the store. Open Monday-Saturday 10:30 am-5 pm. Call 770-786-1098.

Gifts & Home Décor

SPIRES INTERIORS & GIFTS

Denise Spires had worked as an interior decorator since 1982 and as a Display Designer for Rhodes and Haverty's for several years before opening her own gift and home décor boutique in 2000. Her years of experience served her well. Spires Interiors & Gifts was such a huge success, that in just a few exciting years, Denise moved her small shop to its present location on Covington's town square, 1114 and 1116 Monticello St. Both historical buildings are more than 100 years old and lend a gracious charm to the beautiful accessories within. Specializing in accessories, Denise selects the finest lines for her customers, including furniture, oil paintings, lamps, mirrors, china, silver and crystal. She is the largest Peggy Karr Glass dealer in the state, as well as an authorized Lampe Berger dealer. You will find extraordinary gifts for ladies, men, teens and children and recognize top names such as Vera Bradley, Lady Primrose, Lenox, Christopher Radko, Sedgefield and Bob Timberlake. Spires Interiors & Gifts is open Monday through Saturday 10 am-5 pm. For more information, call 770-787-9001.

Trinkets

The best way to describe this store is to say "it makes you smile!" Fleeta Baggett and Gretchen Hughes are a wonderful combination of creativity and personality, and each brings a unique flair to Trinkets, 1137 Church St. Fleeta is a seventh generation Covington native and lives above the shop with her daughter Madelyn. Gretchen hails from Louisiana and lends an engaging mix of Creole flair to the business. Their eclectic taste for the unusual, along with their love for home and garden, ensures a lovely and fun experience every time you shop. A bucket of sidewalk chalk by the door allows budding young artists to leave their mark, and there is always a lollipop or Popsicle for little ones. Gretchen travels to Mexico several times a year for one-of-a-kind wrought iron and pewter items, while Fleeta scours the countryside for delicious candles and beautiful jewelry from names like La Contessa and BB Becker. You will find treasures galore at Trinkets, and absolutely love getting to know these two charming Southern girls. The store is open Tuesday through Saturday 10:30 am-5:30 pm and "by appointment only" on Sunday and Monday. For more information, call 770-788-6722 or visit www.downtowncovington.org/trinkets.htm online.

 Owners Kevin Newell and Chris Torino have been friends since their college days at the University of Georgia more than 20 years ago. Together, they have created wonderful restaurants and a very successful catering company, employing dozens of family members and friends in their venture. Amici Italian Café is now located in three other towns throughout the state, including Madison, Milledgeville and Athens, and all are centrally located in the downtown areas of these charming towns. While in Covington, visit Amici Italian Café at 1116 College St. SE, to enjoy some of the most delicious Italian dishes ever prepared. The piled-high pizzas are hand tossed and baked in a brick oven, and the calzones are wonderful. The chef has created a menu of exciting pasta dishes and salads, as well as a low-carb menu for their diet-conscious diners. You will love the inviting, casual setting of this family friendly café where you will be treated to outstanding Italian dishes with perfect Southern hospitality. Stop by Monday-Thursday 11:30 am-9:30 pm, Friday-Saturday until 10:30 pm and Sunday noon-9 pm. Call 678-625-3000 for more information.

 Robert "R.L." Holmes trained with Chef Paul Prudhomme in New Orleans for 18 years before becoming the head chef in restaurants in Washington, DC and Kansas City, Mo. His exciting restaurant in Covington is located on the Historic Square at 1113 Floyd St. featuring his classic New Orleans selections—you'll love the spicy Jambalaya, Etouffe and barbecue shrimp. For those of you with healthy appetites, try the Shrimp Boil or Fried Seafood Platter. You will also find delicious steaks, chicken and ribs on the menu, as well as pastas, sandwiches, and vegetarian delights. R.L. puts his own spin on everything for a yummy outcome. He has cooked for celebrities such as Billy Crystal, Rob Reiner, Stevie Wonder, Kathleen Turner and Presidents Reagan and Clinton. R.L.'s Off the Square is open for lunch Tuesday-Friday 11 am-2 pm, dinner Tuesday-Thursday 5-9 pm, and Fridays-Saturdays until 10 pm. Call 770-385-5045.

Specialty Shops

SCRAPPIN' SISTERS

Lisa Joyce and Heather Braswell are more than sisters; they are "Scrappin' Sisters," and two of the friendliest women you will meet in the South. They both grew up in Covington, and are now raising their own families in this wonderful town. Their love of scrapbooking and preserving memories for their children resulted in this fun and very popular store—Scrappin' Sisters, 1120 Monticello St. This captivating store offers customers a wide variety of scrapbook supplies including unique papers, fun stickers and quality scrapbooks. Lisa and Heather also offer classes for beginner scrapbookers, spreading their love of scrapbooking with others. They insist it is never too late to begin documenting and preserving the special moments in your life. And, it's never too early. Many children fall in love with this fascinating hobby. In addition to the wonderful scrapbooking supplies, you will also find a large selection of special occasion invitations, thank-you notes and unique gifts. Scrappin' Sisters is open Monday-Saturday 10 am-6 pm. For more information on scrapbooking sessions, call 770-385-7197.

Discover Dahlonega

The charming mountain town of Dahlonega will be one of your favorite places in Georgia. Even the name is enchanting. The town was named Dahlonega in 1833 for the Cherokee Indian word "Tahlonega, (Ta-lo-ne-ga)," which means "yellow or golden." It was also once called Licklog, because it had salt licks for the early settlers' cattle. It is a town rich in history, adventure, natural beauty and mountain charm. In one visit, you can sample some of the best cuisine in the state, browse remarkable shops and boutiques, kick up your clogging heels at a fabulous festival and even step back in time to the nation's first "gold rush" era. There are wildlife preserves to visit, trails to hike or bike, history to explore and some of the most pleasant and friendly mountain folk to befriend. Although the gold rush history takes center stage in town, Dahlonega is fast becoming known as a "Mecca for mountain bluegrass and old-time music." There are performances almost every weekend somewhere around the city, including the Historic Town Square, which is the center of attention in town, beckoning visitors to shop, play, eat and enjoy the best of Dahlonega.

A "Golden" History

Dahlonega is located in the foothills of the Blue Ridge Mountains, just one hour north of Atlanta. In fact, Dahlonega was a boom town when Atlanta was just a tiny village. Its earliest inhabitants could date as far back as 1,000 B.C. An archeologist discovered a woodland period site one mile east of town in 1990 that verified the first life in Dahlonega. The Cherokee Indians occupied several million acres of North Georgia, but with the coming of "gold" they were eventually removed from the land. A man named Benjamin

Parks was deer hunting in 1828 when he overturned a gold-flecked rock. This discovery of gold led to the very first major gold rush in the United States, and created the overnight boom town. In just four years there were more than 10,000 prospectors and their family members in the mining town. The discovery mine was called the "Calhoun," and was later operated by Senator John C. Calhoun of South Carolina. It is estimated that between 1829 and 1849 more than $36,000,000 in gold was mined in the county. It was at this time that the California Gold Rush began to entice the miners westward, and by 1906 Dahlonega's Consolidated Mining Company closed. Of course, everyone knows that there is still "gold in them thar hills!"

The Lumpkin County Courthouse, which was built in 1836, now serves as the Dahlonega Gold Museum. It was built of locally made bricks that held traces of gold. The courthouse served as the Lumpkin County Seat from 1836-1965 and is the oldest public building in this part of Georgia. The Gold Museum is incredible! It features local and area history that tells the amazing story of the first U.S. Gold Rush, and was voted the "Most Outstanding Historic Site in 2001."

To commemorate Dahlonega's exciting gold rush history, an incredible festival is held each year in October. The Dahlonega Jaycees Gold Rush Days is a wonderful event that draws tens of thousands of visitors to this historic town. It has been described as a "cross between a country fair and a rock concert!" Food vendors offer everything from cotton candy and candy apples to barbecue, hotdogs and hamburgers. The townspeople (and a few brave visitors) compete in contests, such as Buffalo Chip Throwing, Clogging and Hog Calling. The highlight of the festival is the crowning of the Gold Rush King and Queen and parade.

Another historic attraction in the downtown square includes the "Old Jail," which was built in 1884. Bars still cover the windows of the jail, which now houses the Lumpkin County Historical Society.

Appalachian Treasures

Dahlonega hosted famous "fiddling conventions" during the early 1900s, and gained the reputation though the years for attracting wonderful mountain music. At any given time, the early residents gathered round a group of old-time mountain musicians in the Square to enjoy the best Bluegrass in the hills. Not much has changed through the years. Appalachian Jams are held on Saturday afternoons from spring through fall right on the Public Square.

Live theatre also thrives in Dahlonega, and the works of many local and regional artisans are displayed throughout the city. Studios, galleries and cafes showcase local art. Visitors are even able to watch artists at work in the charming town square.

Lumpkin County has been recognized as the "epicenter" of the Georgia wine country. You will find some of the most outstanding wineries right here in Dahlonega. The mountainous elevations seem to provide the perfect conditions for "grape growing."

We just can't seem to say enough about the charm and beauty of Dahlonega. Many of its quaint shops and restaurants are located in buildings that are more than 100 years old. They are filled with antiques, collectibles, regional art, homemade foods and more. Dahlonega's golden heritage is celebrated throughout the year in ways that welcome visitors with open arms.

For more information about Dahlonega, contact the Dahlonega-Lumpkin County Chamber of Commerce and Visitors Bureau at 800-231-5543, 706-864-3711 or visit www.dahlonega.org online.

Dahlonega
Fairs Festivals & Fun

February
Literary Festival

April
Bear on the Square Festival
Gold Panning Championship
Tour De Georgia

May
Wildflower Festival of the Arts

June
Mountain Top Rodeo
Wine Country Festival

July
Family Independence Day
Celebration

September
AutumnFest
Six Gap Century and Three Gap
Fifty Bike Ride & Expo

October
Gold Rush Days

November
Dahlonega Wine and Food
Experience

December
Old Fashioned Christmas
Celebration

A Child's Garden is blooming with beautiful clothes, shoes, dolls and books. Susan Barefoot took a leap of faith when she purchased this wonderful children's store at 51 Grove St. N. in Dahlonega, and she loves every minute of it. A colorful teepee is a favorite hiding place for little ones to read while mom shops. Susan hosts monthly American Girl Club meetings and carries lines like English Rose, Capezio, Robeez, Will'Beth, and more. Open Tuesday through Saturday 10 am-5 pm and Thursday until 6 pm. For more information on special occasion parties, call 706-864-0222.

❀Cranberry Corners❀

Since 1995 Cranberry Corners, one of "North Georgia's Most Eclectic Mercantile," has been a cornerstone at 44 N. Park St. on Dahlonega's Historic Square. This family-run store is where to shop for unique gifts, collectibles, antiques, handcrafted items and custom gift baskets. The year-round Christmas section features an enormous selection. Their motto? "At Cranberry Corners, there are no strangers...Just friends we've yet to meet!" Open Monday through Saturday 10 am-5:30 pm and Sunday 11 am-5:30 pm. Visit www.cranberrycorners.com or call 706-864-6577.

GOLDEN CLASSICS
COLLECTABLES • GIFTS • AUTOS

Golden Classics has been featured in the *Atlanta Journal-Constitution* and is an incredible store that has been called "a gift shop for people who don't like gift shops." Owners Tim and Leigh O'Brien carry gifts for every occasion and occupation—something for everyone. Golden Classics, 16 Public Sq. in Dahlonega, is open Monday-Thursday 10 am-6 pm, Friday-Saturday until 8 pm and Sunday 11 am-6 pm. Call 706-864-0158 or visit www.goldenclassics.net.

Golf

Nestled in the breathtaking Blue Ridge Mountains in Historic Dahlonega, the Nicklaus Golf Club at Birch River blends harmoniously with its beautiful surroundings. Located at 639 Birch River Dr., this 6,955-yard, par 72 course was designed by renowned golfer and course architect Jack Nicklaus. It actually plays across the beautiful Chestatee River seven times. The fourth green, the fifth hole and the sixth tee play on an island in the river—you have to see it to truly appreciate it! The club offers private membership, as well as daily fees for guests with practice facility, chipping and putting greens. Guests can choose to dine in the dining room, lounge grill or outdoor covered patio, and the gorgeous mountain valley surroundings make the club a great choice for weddings, rehearsal dinners and receptions. Be sure to ask about the special packages. Call 706-867-7900 or visit online www.nicklausgolfbirchriver.com.

Resorts, Rentals, Spas & Indulgence

Your perfect getaway ... Pura Vida USA, associated with the famous Pura Vida Spas in Costa Rica and Maya Tulum, Mexico, is a premier yoga and wellness spa dedicated to rejuvenating you—body, mind and spirit. Whether you want a cozy bed and breakfast or a healing spa experience, Pura Vida USA, 400 Blueberry Hill in Dahlonega, is just what you're looking for. The main house is a replica of a 1920s farmhouse and includes 10 charming guest rooms. Its wraparound porch offers a breathtaking view of the Blue Ridge Mountains. Or for a more secluded retreat, you can take advantage of one of its eight private cabins. Co-managers Rakesh and Lou-Ann Goswami's mission is to "celebrate wellness through nature." Call 866-345-4900, 706-865-7678, or visit www.puravidausa.com. *(Color photo featured in front section of book.)*

Bordered by the Chattahoochee National Forest at the foothills of the beautiful Blue Ridge Mountains, this extraordinary mountain hideaway is known as "The Ultimate North Georgia Experience." Forrest Hills Mountain Resort & Conference Center, 135 Forrest Hills Rd. in Dahlonega, is too beautiful for words. Whether you are having a girlfriend getaway, a family reunion, a corporate retreat or a romantic weekend for two, relax in a rustic cabin, a contemporary room, or a romantic Victorian cottage. All are nestled in secluded wooded areas and filled with everything you will need for an unforgettable experience. While there, you can ride horses through the beautiful scenery, enjoy your own whirlpool spa, glowing fire, and a private deck, take a romantic carriage ride, or hop aboard the horse drawn wagon to the River House for a good old-fashioned cookout. You may also relax and unwind in the day spa with a therapeutic massage. Forrest Hills is also a perfect choice for wedding events and honeymooners. For information or reservations, visit www.forresthillsresort.com or call 706-864-6456, 770-534-3244 or 800-654-6313.

Caruso's is home of the Dahlonega Brewing Company and one of the best Italian restaurants you'll ever have the pleasure to visit. Its walls are wrapped in beautiful murals, which only add to the lovely ambiance, and its staff goes the extra mile to make your dining experience special. Located just off Dahlonega's Downtown Square at 19 E. Main St., Caruso's is an elegant dining restaurant. Along with great food, Caruso's is also a microbrewery with a separate bar area for relaxing and tasting their brew. Chef Reginald and Axa Hughey go above and beyond to insure their customers' complete satisfaction. Delicious starters include Fried Ravioli, Calamari with Parmesan Peppercorn, and Spinach Artichoke Dip. Their bread is baked fresh daily for Stromboli and Calzones, and the hand-tossed pizzas are perfect. Don't miss Caruso's White Pizza. Caruso's is open daily 11 am-1 am. Call 706-864-4664.

While shopping in Historic Dahlonega, you will discover a delightful eatery at 84 N. Public Sq.—Dante's on the Square is an outstanding luncheon experience. Signature sandwiches, like the Hickory Smoked BBQ Pork, Cajun Andouille Sausage and the Cubano, will satisfy the heartiest appetites. Or, for a lighter lunch, try an appetizer like the Smoked Chicken Quesadillas—we loved the Veggie Frittata. Reginald and Axa Hughey are hands on owners and chefs who guarantee the finest, freshest ingredients in all of their selections. You will love the variety on the menu and its cozy atmosphere. So, if you are looking for a cozy place where you can relax with a glass of wine and enjoy a scrumptious meal, visit Dante's on the Square. Open daily 10 am-3 pm. Call 706-864-4091.

Tucked among the trees along the Chestatee River, The Oar House, 3072 E. Hwy. 52 in Dahlonega, was voted one of the most romantic places for dinner and featured in *Southern Living*. Owners Tim and Leigh O'Brien offer delicious dishes—you'll have a difficult time choosing from their signature prime rib or the fresh fish of the day. You must save room for their famous, made from scratch desserts—like chocolate chip rum cake. Open Monday-Thursday 11 am-9 pm and Friday-Saturday until 10 pm. Call 706-864-9938 or visit www.theoarhouse.com.

PIAZZA ITALIAN RESTAURANT

How does Spinach and Walnut Ravioli sound? Trust us, it's wonderful. In fact, it is hard to choose from the extensive menu of familiar and specialty items at Piazza Italian Restaurant, 24 E. Main St. in Dahlonega and 24 Wolfscratch Village in Big Canoe. Owner/Chef David Meyer draws from his culinary degree from the Art Institute of Atlanta and his 11 years experience to create the upscale Italian cuisine at his two wonderful restaurants. Open Monday-Thursday 11 am-9 pm, Friday-Saturday until 10 pm, and Sunday noon-9 pm. Call 706-867-9881.

THE McGUIRE HOUSE

Built in the late 1800s, and listed on the National Historic Registry, The McGuire House Restaurant, 135 N. Chestatee St., specializes in succulent seafood and scrumptious steaks. You can dine inside the house or on the enclosed porch with a view of the Historic Square. Fireplaces in the dining room and on the porch make every meal romantic and memorable. You can also enjoy a glass of wine upstairs overlooking downtown Dahlonega. Hours are Monday-Thursday 4-9 pm and Friday-Saturday until 10 pm. Call 706-864-6829 or visit www.themcguirehouse.com.

Wines & Wineries

WOLF
MOUNTAIN VINEYARDS

The Boegner family is proud to introduce Wolf Mountain Vineyards & Winery. The pastoral-hillside vineyards, fieldstone-encased winery and hospitality facility overlook the foothills of the Blue Ridge Mountains, offering a beautiful setting for special events in Dahlonega. Located at 180 Wolf Mountain Tr., this 25-acre family-owned vineyard is home to plantings of Cabernet Sauvignon, Syrah, Mourvedre and Touriga. Wolf Mountain is proud of their award-winning handcrafted wines, which are aged in French oak barrels in the Old World ambiance of the cask room. The Winery is open Friday-Sunday noon-5 pm.

And, at the Vineyard Café you can choose from the gourmet menu on Saturday noon-3 pm or the elaborate buffet on Sunday. For calendar of events, winery tours, weddings or private events, visit www.wolfmountainvineyards.com or call 706-867-9862.

FROGTOWN CELLARS

Craig and Cydney Kritzer chose a beautiful 57-acre estate at the foot of the Blue Ridge Mountains for their remarkable Frogtown Cellars, 3300 Damascus Church Rd. in Dahlonega. They have a 30-acre vineyard with 15 different grapevines, and produce their award-winning wines under the "Frogtown" and "Thirteenth Colony" labels. You won't believe the quality of the wines and will love a bistro lunch, served Saturday and Sunday noon-4 pm. The wine taster and winemaker dinners are the ultimate experience. Frogtown Cellars has become a favorite for weddings and special events—accommodating up to 300 guests. This mortise and tenon cypress timber frame structure with Brazilian cherry floors, hand-carved Tennessee flagstone walls, and cathedral ceilings, has a wrap-around porch and decks with breath-taking views of the vineyard and mountains. Stop by Saturday noon-6 pm and Sunday noon-5 pm, and on Fridays in 2006. Call 706-865-0687 or visit www.frogtownwine.com.

DAHLONEGA TASTING ROOM

Representing the oldest and most celebrated wines in Georgia for more than 15 years, Dahlonega Tasting Room, 16 N. Park St., is one of the best places to visit on your trip to this charming town. It is located in the original 1914 Dahlonega Post Office building and filled with unique wine-themed gifts for aficionados, as well as home décor and gifts for non-wine drinkers alike. The Tasting Room allows customers to enjoy samples of more than 20 Habersham wines, some of which have won the Atlanta International Wine Summit "Magnolia Award." We're sure you'll find a favorite! Hours are Monday-Saturday 10 am-6 pm and Sunday 12:30-6 pm. Call 706-864-8275.

Discover Dawsonville

Spend just one day in Dawsonville and you will see why it is called the place "Where the Mountains Meet the Lakes." It is beautiful! From Amicalola Falls to Lake Lanier you will find adventure and fun for the entire family. It is an area whose history is filled with stories of Native Americans, a gold rush and exciting racing heroes. The magnificent Amicalola Falls is located in the 1,500-acre Amicalola Falls State Park, which is adjacent to the Chattahoochee National Forest. Here you'll find camping accommodations and cozy cottages perfect for an extended stay. Just so you'll know, Amicalola is a Cherokee word that means, "tumbling waters." The white falls drop 729 feet in seven cascades and it is the tallest waterfall east of the Mississippi River.

Historic Dawsonville

Although 1857 is recorded as the founding date for Dawson County, the Cherokee Indians settled the mountains and valleys during the earlier 1800s. In 1832 the nation's first gold rush began to bring settlers to the area and the Cherokee were moved from the land to Oklahoma along the Trail of Tears. There are still remnants of many of the original gold mines throughout the county. These mines continued operating well into the late 1880s.

Two of the first buildings built in Dawsonville were the log courthouse and jail. The first courthouse was replaced in 1860 with a stately red brick structure that holds the record as "Georgia's Oldest Working Courthouse." The Dawson County Chamber of Commerce and Welcome Center now occupy the old jailhouse. The Dawson County Chamber calls their city "Atlanta's Favorite Backyard Getaway!"

Racing Stripes and Kangaroos?

One of Dawsonville's favorite sons has "raced" into fame, and the city loves him. Bill Elliott has won more than 40 NASCAR races and is the most famous name in Georgia racing history. In fact, around town he is lovingly referred to as "Awesome Bill from Dawsonville." The Georgia legislature has even named October 8th "Bill Elliott Day." Dawsonville's racing history is documented at the Georgia Racing Hall of Fame Museum in the Dawsonville Municipal Complex. It is a collection of memorabilia, history and even a few retired stockcars. You can get a good taste of Elliott mania at the local Dawsonville Pool Room. This local grill and pool hall is almost a shrine to Elliott, with a huge collection of memorabilia in the Daytona Room. Owner Gordon Pirkle even sounds a siren every time Elliott wins a race. There have been many Dawsonville natives who have put the city on the racing map, including Bernard Hall, Roy Hall, Lloyd Seay, Gober Sosobee, Raymond Parks, and of course Bill Elliott. While you're there, be sure to try the world famous "Bully Burger," and ask about its story.

One of the most unique and fascinating attractions in Dawsonville is the Kangaroo Conservation Center. It is the largest Kangaroo collection this side of Australia! Spread over 87 acres of a privately owned wildlife sanctuary, the center is home to more than 200 kangaroos. Guides will take you on an "Outback" safari and introduce you to the gentle and fun loving kangas. Tours are offered from spring through fall and reservations are required.

There is an abundance of other exciting outdoor adventures and special events that make Dawsonville a great place to visit any time of the year. One of the most anticipated events of the year is the Annual Mountain Moonshine Festival in October. Sounds rather interesting, doesn't it? This festival commemorates the very beginnings of stockcar racing itself. Legend has it that the sport has its earliest roots in Dawsonville during the 1930s prohibition era, when bootleggers hustled illegal moonshine through the mountains in "fast" cars. The three-day festival is held each October, with a parade of vintage cars, music, Southern food and more!

You will find acres and acres of hiking trails, swimming holes and campsites, perfectly groomed golf courses and upscale shopping. Dawsonville is as diverse a city as its beautiful terrain.

For more information about Dawsonville, contact the Dawson County Chamber of Commerce at 706-265-6278 or visit www.dawson.org online.

Dawsonville
Fairs Festivals & Fun

May
  Dawsonville Days

September
  Chamber Golf Tournament

October
  Mountain Moonshine Festival
  U.S. Open Stock Dog
    Championship & Farm
  Festival

Dawson County
Chamber of Commerce

From Springer Mountain and the start of the Appalachian Trail to the shores of Lake Lanier and the 729-foot waterfall at Amicalola Falls State Park, Dawson County is as diverse as its terrain. The best way to discover all of the county's wonderful attractions is through the Dawson County Chamber of Commerce, 54 Hwy. 53 W. in Dawsonville. Here you will receive information and brochures on the many wonderful Dawson County adventures. Ask about our lake, rivers, waterfall, premium shopping and kangaroos! Stop by Monday-Friday 8 am-5 pm. For more information, call 706-265-6278 or visit www.dawson.org.

Antiques

Upon entering Endless Treasures you will immediately get a feeling of coziness. As you browse through this quaint shop, you will see how the eclectic, cottage-style mix of Primitive and vintage antique furniture and accessories, linens, architectural and garden elements, and "feel good" treasures can create a unique and inviting home. Endless Treasures also carries seasonal florals, home décor, whimsical folk art and personalized gift baskets. Owner Terri Winans will come to your home with her imagination and unique treasures to create a warm, comfortable feeling that's just right for you. Endless Treasures is located at 8399 Hwy. 53 E. in Dawsonville, just two miles from North Georgia Premium Outlet Mall. The shop is open Tuesday-Saturday 10:30 am-5:30 pm. 706-216-4913.

Bed & Breakfasts, Cabins & Cottages

Lily Creek Lodge
A Bed & Breakfast

The best way to describe this remarkable mountain retreat is "rustic elegance." Lily Creek Lodge, 2608 Auraria Rd., is located in the middle of a wildlife sanctuary between Dawsonville and Dahlonega. Built in European Chalet style, the Lodge rooms are furnished with antiques, collectibles, artwork and exquisite linens. A gourmet continental breakfast is served each morning on the deck, in the gazebo or in the dining room. Don't miss the secluded swimming pool and hot tub. Call 706-864-6848, 888-844-2694 or visit www.lilycreeklodge.com.

Books, Health & Beauty Products

NATURE'S HEALTH & CHRISTIAN BOOKSTORE

Linda Benson invites you to browse through her outstanding store for the latest in natural herbs, vitamins and body products. Nature's Health & Christian Bookstore, 3688 Hwy. 53 E., is filled with gifts, books, music, as well as a full line of natural products for total well-being. Linda's goal is to help her customers find their way to both physical and spiritual health. She carries natural products like Nature's Sunshine and NOW, and she can help you design the right health program for your specific needs. Nature's Health & Christian Bookstore is open Monday-Friday 10 am-4 pm and Saturday until 2 pm. Call 706-216-6062. And, if you are looking to add beauty to your home or business, be sure to ask Linda about her husband's business, Builder's Choice Stone Work, Inc. He has been doing custom stonework for more than 30 years.

GATHERING PLACE CAFÉ & EVENTS

"Where Friends Gather." Gathering Place Café & Events, 436 Academy Ave., is Dawsonville's most charming event facility. You can plan a lunch, dinner, reception or special wedding event here—all while enjoying a lovely lunch at the Café. Cathie Waddell is a fabulous cook, caterer and party planner who will work with you to create a most memorable occasion. Cathie has built her reputation by exceeding expectations. The Café is open Monday-Friday 11 am-3 pm and Sunday 11 am-2 pm. Call 706-216-8703.

Made famous by hometown racing hero Bill Elliott, the Dawsonville Pool Room on E. First St. is home to the world famous "Bully Burger." Gordon Pirkle has owned the Pool Room for almost 40 years and his nostalgic collection of automobile racing memorabilia has made it a favorite place for locals and visitors. Enjoy racing history exhibits along with great food, and don't miss Gordon's other eatery—Champion's Café. For more information and hours, call 706-265-2792.

Furniture, Gifts, Home Décor & Interior Design

From distinct lines of quality furniture, mirrors and framed art to handsome clocks, pottery and lamps, you will find exclusive accessories for your home at the Chocolate Moose. Located at 4055 Hwy. 53 E. in Dawsonville, this is a specialty furniture and accessory store with a reputation for the unusual. Owner Diane Cowart scouts out-of-the-way markets for furniture, accessories and gifts. Also available are items by Bob Timberlake, Habersham Plantation, Flat Rock, Zimmerman and many others. Diane says that Chocolate Moose is a place where you will find "casual, elegant furniture and accessories for lodge, lake or traditional homes."

She carries several lines of wonderful bedding and many exclusive items. You must see it to truly appreciate this fabulous store. Open Monday-Saturday 10 am-6 pm. Call 706-265-1990.

Lavender reigns in this delightful Dawsonville boutique. From Crabtree & Evelyn body products, beautiful tableware and Trapp Candles, to the soothing color on the walls, the entire store is kissed with a hint of Judy and Jennifer Martin's favorite color. We loved the dazzling jewelry by Emily Ray and the unusual gifts by Mud Pie. Lavender Loft is located at 276 Hwy. 400 N., and is open Monday, Tuesday, Thursday-Saturday 10 am-6 pm, and Sunday noon-4 pm. Visit www.lavenderloft.com or call 706-265-9878.

Design Finds

FABRIC SUPER STORE

Owners Barbara Cavender and Lara Eddleman approach a design dilemma with their philosophy of "two generations—two points of view!" This mother/daughter team of Design Finds, 671 Lumpkin Campground Rd., is known as the Design Divas of Dawsonville, and the store is one of Georgia's premier fabric and design stores. The selection is astonishing in this 14,000-square-foot showroom—filled with name-brand fabrics, trims, furnishings, home décor—and everything is at the lowest prices possible. The helpful staff will assist you in the store, or you can have

an in-home consultation with Barbara and Lara. The "Divas" are also featured in the local cable television series, "Design Finds," where they offer decorating advice to show you how you can turn your house into your dream home—for less. For hours, call 706-216-4125 or visit www.design-finds.com.

SIMPLY SOPHIE

Antiques Gifts & Home Decor

Jeannie Richey wanted her store to reflect the simple sophistication she had always loved in her grandmother. That's why she chose to name her outstanding antique and gift shop in Dawsonville Simply Sophie. Located at 837 Hwy. 400 S., Simply Sophie is a remarkable collection of fine European antiques and reproductions, amazing gifts, and unique home furnishings. In addition to the beautiful furniture and home accessories, Jeannie has the popular lines you are looking for such as, Vera Bradley handbags, Vietri, Spode, Casafina, Arthur Court and Peggy Karr dinnerware, and Peacock Alley and Pine Cone Hill bedding. You can also visit her newest location at 5530 Windward Pkwy. in Alpharetta. Simply Sophie is open Monday-Saturday 10 am-6 pm. Visit www.simplysophie.net or call 706-216-3900.

Quilts, Needlework & Stitchery

Just a hop, a skip and a stitch (that's about 10 minutes) from the North Georgia Premium Outlet Mall—Sew Memorable is the place to go for beautiful fabric, quilting patterns, supplies, and "bolts" of fun. Check out www.sewmemorable.net online or call 706-265-2121 for more information on classes and activities that await you. Have "Sew Much Fun" at 4055 Hwy. 53 E. in Dawsonville. Stop by Monday-Saturday 10 am-6 pm.

Spas & Indulgence

Serenity Medical Health & Beauty Spa offers a full menu of day and medical spa services in a luxurious and serene setting—just what every lady longs for when planning a special day out! Services include: massage, facials, body treatments, Botox, chemical peels, mineral makeup, and more! Serenity offers custom packages and delightful spa parties for your special group occasion. The Spa boutique delights the senses with exquisite handmade organic soap, original gemstone jewelry creations, and Eric Javits hats and bags. An outing to beautiful Dawson County is not complete without a visit to Serenity Medical Health & Beauty Spa, where you bring your stress and emerge with renewed beauty and a sense of serenity. Located at 5983 Hwy. 53 E. in Dawsonville. For more information and hours, call 706-265-6467 or visit www.serenity-spa.biz

Discover Decatur

Tucked between Atlanta and Stone Mountain, you'll find the delightful town of Decatur. It has the sophistication and excitement of a college town, the benefits of a metropolitan area, it's a stone's throw from the heart of Atlanta, and a wonderful, warm, small town atmosphere. Almost storybook in appearance, the tree-lined streets of downtown are filled with charming shops and eateries that will satisfy all. You will see parks and playing fields, libraries, colleges and art galleries. Decatur is a vibrant city, rich in history, heritage and culture.

Historical Decatur

Founded in 1823, Decatur is the second oldest municipality in the Atlanta metro and the county seat of DeKalb County. It was named after Stephen Decatur, a 19th century U.S. Naval hero, and retains a strong connection to its early history. The Historic Downtown Courthouse Square is located on a hill—a rise where two Indian trails once crossed. It was originally the community gathering place, and continues to be the focus of special events and Decatur festivals. During its early history Decatur had the chance to be a major stop for the Western and Atlantic Railroad, but the citizens voted against the noise and smoke it would bring. In 1843, the railroad moved seven miles west to a settlement that was eventually renamed "Atlanta." Decatur's Welcome Center and the DeKalb History Center are located inside the Old Courthouse building. There you will find helpful information on all of the wonderful attractions and opportunities of DeKalb County. The courthouse is itself an amazing piece of early history. It was built of granite from Stone Mountain, and was the site of a major Civil War battle. The historic Decatur Cemetery also provides insight into the city's past.

When popular shopping malls and strip centers found their way to Decatur during the early 1970s, the once vibrant downtown area was greatly affected. It lost a lot of retail business and had little activity. City leaders worked hard to revitalize the area by bringing in new restaurants, shops and galleries, and even expanding new trendy residential areas. Today, the charming shops and outside cafes display the community's pride and offer a warm welcome to visitors. In fact, the city has been called Atlanta's shopping "mallternative." Decatur has even been asked to be a member of the Sister Cities International, a program that partners cities with other American or foreign cities to foster vitality, self-awareness and cultural exchange. This program was launched in 1956 when President Eisenhower sought exchanges between American cities and cities from other countries.

Shopping, Art, Lunch!

We loved exploring all of the little tucked away shopping areas of Decatur. They are scattered along W. Ponce de Leon Avenue, Church Street and in the charming neighborhood of Oakhurst. From wine rooms and jewelry stores to needle shops and clothing boutiques, you'll love browsing the retail area and meeting the owners and locals. When you are hungry you'll have plenty of wonderful cafés, tearooms and restaurants to visit. It is great fun to sit outside at one of the cafés with sidewalk service and enjoy the people and city of Decatur.

Dance, drama and music come alive in Decatur with wonderful theatres, dance companies and art studios. There is always something exciting to do in Decatur.

For more information about Decatur, visit www.decaturga.com online or contact the Decatur Downtown Development Authority at 404-371-8386. Or, contact the DeKalb County Convention and Visitors Bureau at 800-999-6055, 770-492-5000 or visit www.atlantasdekalb.org online.

Decatur
Fairs Festivals & Fun

February
Big Chill Benefit Dance
Wine Crawl

March
Easter Egg Hunt

May
Arts Festival and Garden Tour
Blue Sky Concerts
Concerts on the Square

June
Beach Party

July
Pied Piper Parade, Concert &
Fireworks

August
BBQ, Blues & Bluegrass
Festival

September
Blue Sky Concerts
Concerts on the Square

October
Beer Tasting Festival

November
Terrific Thursdays
Wine Tasting Festival

December
Breakfast with Santa
Holiday Bonfire &
Marshmallow Roast
Holiday Candlelight Tour of
Homes
Terrific Thursdays

DECATUR ARTS FESTIVAL & GARDEN TOUR AND TERRIFIC THURSDAYS

The Decatur Arts Alliance is "a nonprofit partnership of artists, business owners, residents and government dedicated to supporting and enhancing the arts in the city of Decatur." Each May it sponsors the spectacular Decatur Arts Festival & Garden Tour. The annual Arts Festival poster is unveiled early in May, and then the fun begins. Artists of all ages literally "paint the town" with removable paints during Paint Decatur. Enjoy performances by the Decatur Civic Chorus, try your hand at acting in an exciting theatre workshop or shop at the popular juried Artists Market. Also in May be sure to attend the Film Festival, which features a reception with notable filmmakers, and enjoy the ArtWalk, with more than 28 participating galleries and shops. Finish with a beautiful tour of some of the most breath-taking gardens in town.

In November and December, Decatur businesses offer special events once a week—known as Terrific Thursdays. Look for book signings, holiday open houses, receptions and even Santa during the month of December. For more information, call Decatur Downtown Development Authority at 404-371-8386, visit www.decaturga.com, or the Decatur Arts Alliance at 404-371-9583 or www.decaturartsalliance.org online.

Art Galleries, Framing, Gifts & Home Décor

When owner Angela Atkinson opened Jolie Home, 252 W. Ponce de Leon Ave. in Decatur, it was a dream come true. Angela's love for intriguing design and beautiful things, coupled with her love of people, makes Jolie Home a favorite place to shop. As you enter the store, Angela and her friendly staff invite you to look through the amazing selection of gorgeous gift items and unique home décor that can best be described as elegant to whimsical. Enjoy the wonderful aroma of "Trimmings"—a fragrance exclusive to Jolie Home—available in candles, potpourri and bath products. Not only are there gifts for every occasion but for every age group. Be sure to check out the fabulous children's section! Customers proclaim, "We love this store." And we did too! Shipping or delivery is available on some items, and prices are great! Visit Tuesday-Saturday 11 am-7 pm and Sunday until 4 pm. Call 404-270-9224. *(Color photo featured in front section of book.)*

Rue de Leon

Experience a delightful taste of Europe right here in Decatur at Rue de Leon, 131 E. Ponce de Leon Ave. The store is located in a converted gas station that has been at the heart of downtown Decatur for more than 50 years. This charming gift boutique is a collection of old and new, including interior décor and garden accents, antiques, reproduction furniture from British Traditions, custom framing, and original paintings from local and European artists. Owner Leslie Joseph is herself an accomplished and talented photographer, with an artist's eye. She offers a full range of wonderful gifts, including Votivo and Pre de Provence products, as well as Turkish pottery, Parisian stationery, liquid flower candles from Magnolia Lane, and one-of-a-kind jewelry designs by Atlanta's own Christa Burton. Rue de Leon is open Monday-Thursday 11 am-7 pm, Friday until 10 pm, Saturday 10 am-10 pm, and Sunday noon-6 pm. Call 404-373-6200.

The Seen Gallery, 321 W. Hill St., is housed in the West Ward of the original Scottish Rite Hospital in Decatur. This premier art gallery was founded by photographer and CDC Microbiologist Bill Bibb in 2002. Artist Amy Bradford, who was trained at Parsons School of Art & Design in Paris/New York, joins Bill in managing this amazing collection of artwork and one-of-a-kind gifts. The historic building's Georgian Revival architecture and natural light create the perfect setting for the displays. Bill and Amy schedule artist showings and receptions and more than 40 artists are showcased in the gallery. Stop by Tuesday-Saturday noon-9 pm, Sunday until 5 pm or by appointment. Visit at www.theseengallery.com or call 404-377-0733.

Bed & Breakfasts, Cabins & Cottages

Garden House Bed & Breakfast

For "six-star" treatment in true Southern style, the Garden House Bed & Breakfast gets rave reviews. In fact, guests return again and again to this charming B&B, due in most part to the warmth and kindness of Doug and Rhoda Joyner. The 1950s bungalow is located at 135 Garden Ln. in a quiet Decatur neighborhood. The beautifully decorated second-story suite features a carved queen bed, a sitting room with desk and worktable, and a private bath. A spacious screened-in porch overlooks a beautiful perennial garden and is a restful, quiet setting in the midst of a busy city. A scrumptious breakfast is served each morning and sweet Southern hospitality all day long. Call 404-377-3057 or visit http://home.earthlink.net/~gardenhouse135/ online.

Children's

fun stuff for kids

Hoopla, an eclectic children's store at 123 E. Ponce de Leon Ave. in Historic Decatur, started as a seed of friendship. Sabrina Lilly and Linda Beckstein crossed paths as fellow "retailers." Jobs changed but the friendship grew with dreams of opening a store. Finally, that dream came true! Children's apparel, books and retro toys have combined to create a store for shopping and playing. Sabrina and Linda have added services like story time, monogramming and gift registry, too! For more information and times, call 404-377-6914 or visit hooplakids.com online.

Fashion & Accessories

"TO LOOK AT BEAUTY THROUGH FORM"

Camille Wright has created an amazing "Kaleidoscope" of colors, patterns, textures and style in her very popular Decatur boutique. Kaleidoscope, 225 E. Ponce de Leon Ave., is a fabulous place to shop for the very latest styles from top designers, such as BCBG, Nougat, Alexia Admor, Yyigal, Basil and Maude and Debbie Schuchat. A visit to the Web site www.kscopeboutique.com will give you just a hint at the flair of "Camille's Closet." Her fun fashion shows portray both women and men in fine and casual sportswear, timeless denim, and exciting party wear. One thing that makes Kaleidoscope such a special store is the staff's attention to detail and their emphasis on top-notch customer service. Discover your individual style at Kaleidoscope, open Monday noon-6 pm, Tuesday-Thursday 10 am-7 pm, Friday until 8 pm, Saturday 11 am-8 pm, and Sunday noon-5 pm. Call 404-378-1214.

Museums

Old Courthouse on the Square

Visiting the Old Courthouse on the Square, circa 1898, you catch a glimpse into DeKalb County, which was established in 1822. The Old Courthouse boasts hand-wound clocks installed in 1916, as well as textiles, artifacts and photographs that show you the beginnings of the County through the Civil War to the present. Enjoy the beautiful architecture of the Courthouse built with Stone Mountain granite and Alabama marble. Open Monday-Friday 9 am-4 pm. Contact the DeKalb Historical Society at www.dekalbhistory.org or 404-373-1088.

DEKALB HISTORY CENTER

Pampered Pets

Dog's sure have it good in Decatur thanks to Christine Hawes and her four-legged friend, Sam. Sam is a golden retriever and the inspiration for The Posh Pup. You will find all natural, organic baked goods from biscotti to after-dinner mints—sure to make your pooch drool—and The Posh Pup carries a full line of luxury products that you must see to believe. You'll find all natural bath and spa products, collars, toys, jewelry, and even edible greeting cards. Visit www.poshpupinc.com for more information.

Salons, Spas & Indulgence

salonred✳

One is an award-winning upscale salon—the other an eclectic, child-centered "hair cuttery." Put them both together on the same block and you have Salon Red and Salon Red Kids. Located at 119 and 123 E. Ponce de Leon Ave., just one block off the Historic Decatur Square, these shops cater to the unique beauty needs of the individuals and families in this "small-town" community. Salon Red exclusively carries Bumble and bumble hair care products, alongside trendy handbags and jewelry. At Salon Red Kids, you'll love the great line Wee Ones—high-end hair accessories for girls and babies, including classic hair bows. Don't miss the other Salon Red & Spa in Atlanta at 378 Clifton Rd. Stop by in Decatur, Tuesday-Thursday 10 am-8 pm and Friday-Sunday 9 am-6 pm. Call 404-373-2003 or visit www.salonred.com. The friendly and talented staff at Salon Red treats everyone like family, making it such a fun place to be!

salonredkids

Discover
Helen / Cleveland /
Sautee Nacoochee

White County has been called "The Gateway to the Mountains." It is nestled in the foothills of the Blue Ridge Mountains just 12 miles south of Georgia's tallest mountain peak. It is a county filled with more adventure than you can imagine, from trout streams that run right through towns, a baby hospital filled with cabbage patch kids, a charming alpine Bavarian village, pumpkin farms, gold mines, mountain music and excellent shopping—all within an hour's drive. There are three White County towns that exude the warm, Southern hospitality of the area in very unique ways. Helen, Cleveland and Sautee Nacoochee offer visitors wonderful opportunities for fun and adventure in the Blue Ridge Mountains.

HELEN

Complete with cobblestone alleys and brightly colored buildings, Helen resembles a true alpine village, and is an incredible treat for visitors. In 1969, a group of local businessmen decided to give their sleepy little town a new face. A German face! Gingerbread trim and colors to the buildings gave the town an entirely different look, and soon other businesses followed suit. Many of the townspeople add to the alpine charm of Helen by wearing lederhosen and dirndls. The Bavarian scenes painted on the buildings commemorate the migration of early settlers into North Georgia.

Helen is tucked into the Blue Ridge Mountains on the Chattahoochee River, and has a rich history that is linked to the Cherokee Indians and gold miners. Prior to 1800, there were many Cherokee villages and ceremonial burial grounds scattered throughout what are now known as Helen and Nacoochee valleys. The Indians left the valleys during the 1830s when they were forced to walk the "Trail of Tears" to Oklahoma. Gold was discovered in Nacoochee Valley, inviting thousands of miners into the area to lay their claim. They mined in the area for more than a century. Most of the mining operations ended by the end of the century, and the settlers moved to other areas.

The Gainesville and Northwestern Railroad made its way up the Chattahoochee River to Helen right at the turn of the century, and in 1913 the town was named after the daughter of the railroad surveyor. Although lumber was a great industry for Helen, by the 1960s the town was almost non-existent, with very little tourism. The great "Bavarian" renovation in 1968 ushered in a tremendous flood of tourists, making it one of Georgia's most unique and festive places to visit. Today, the small remote mountain village hosts millions of visitors each year. Its European charm and authentic Bavarian food and drink will make you feel as though you are visiting some small mountain village in Germany.

With the Chattahoochee River flowing from the north edge of town, under Main Street, to the southern side of town, water activities are one of the city's main attractions. During the warm seasons, you can tube or fish to your heart's content. There are also more than 21 waterfalls and hiking trails to explore in the area; however, the main attraction continues to be "food and shopping."

There are some of the most beautiful bed and breakfasts and lodging resorts in this alpine village. From cozy cottages to rustic lodges, you will feel wrapped in the picturesque peace of the mountains wherever you stay. Many have wedding chapels and romantic honeymoon packages available, but they are also perfect for families or group travelers.

CLEVELAND

As the county seat of beautiful White County, thousands of tourists visit Cleveland from around the world each year. Some come to tour the Old Jail, which was built in 1901 (the White County Chamber of Commerce and Welcome Center), others come to hang glide, rappel or climb Mount Yonah, but most come to visit the place that put the town on the map. Cleveland is home to the birthplace of the original "Cabbage Patch Kids." Remember the Cabbage Patch craze that swept the United States during the 1980s? If you've ever stood in line for hours to get one of the adorable, cuddly babies (like we did!), you will love touring BabyLand General Hospital. BabyLand is located in the former Neal Clinic, just two blocks south of the Historic White County Courthouse on Cleveland Square. Mr. Xavier Roberts developed the idea of a custom-made kid "born" in a cabbage patch. His funny faced little kids soon became a national frenzy, with more than 80 million Cabbage Patch Kids being adopted by children since 1978.

SAUTEE NACOOCHEE

This historic, artistic village is a treasure trove of incredible art galleries, unique shops, music, theatre and restaurants, with some of the most remarkable scenery in the country. You'll find antiques, homemade soaps, handmade blankets and fabulous gifts. You can visit a historic grist mill, find the perfect antique or piece of garden art, shop for fly-fishing accessories, paint your own piece of pottery, spend a luxurious day in a beautiful spa, or enjoy a luscious glass of wine. One of Georgia's oldest and largest wineries is located just south of Helen in Nacoochee Village. Habersham Vineyards & Winery has been producing award-winning wines since 1983 and bottles more than 12,000 cases annually.

The valleys of Sautee and Nacoochee offer incredible recreation and adventure for everyone. From horseback riding and rafting to wine tasting and phenomenal shopping, you will love visiting this charming section of North Georgia.

For more information about Helen, Cleveland and Sautee Nacoochee, contact the White County Chamber of Commerce at 706-865-5356 or visit www.whitecountychamber.org. Or contact the Helen Welcome Center at 800-858-8027 or visit www.helenga.org online.

Helen / Cleveland / Sautee Nacoochee Fairs Festivals & Fun

February
Fireside Craft/Art Show

March
Trout Tournament

April
BabyLand General's Easter
Eggstravaganza
Spring Volksmarch

May
Helen Fat Tire Festival
Mayfest
Memorial Day Blast
Sautee-Nacoochee Tour of Homes
Wine Fest

June
Bavarian Nights of Summer (June-
August)
Hot Air Balloon Race
Shrinefest

July
1950s Festival
4th of July Mountain Style &
Fireworks at Dusk

September
BabyLand General Fall Fest
Oktoberfest

October
Oktoberfest

November
BabyLand General's
Appalachian Christmas
Festival of Trees
Lighting of the Village

December
Bi-annual Tour of Homes
Festival of Trees
Lighted Christmas Parade

MAGICAL EASTER EGGSTRAVAGANZA

Babyland General along with the White County Chamber of Commerce play host to the Magical Easter Eggstravaganza that began in Cleveland in 1988. Festival goers enjoy a full day of activities, beginning with a breakfast with the Easter bunny and Cabbage Patch Kids. Then, an Easter egg hunt, where children 10 years and under are invited to participate in finding 18,000 eggs. At noon, a parade is held on the Downtown Square with the famous "Giant Easter Basket Float." Children's rides, arts and crafts, food, dancing, and other activities also take place on the grounds of Babyland from 9 am-5 pm. This annual event takes place on Saturday the weekend before Easter. Call 706-865-5356 or visit www.whitecountychamber.org.

A VICTORIAN COWGIRL

At the entry, you'll be greeted by "A Victorian Cowgirl" sitting on a horse. This fun introduction is just a glimmer of the Southern delights you'll experience at this wonderful shop. Owner Elsie Hogan-Maloy, along with help from local craftsmen, converted a 150-foot chicken house into a beautiful shop filled with true one-of-a-kind treasures. With its 19 beautiful stained glass windows, French doors, stone entry and hardwood floors, Elsie says, "It's the fanciest chicken house in Lumpkin County."

Both inside and out you'll be delighted by this enchanting place. A Victorian Cowgirl is located at 1768 John Crow Rd. between Cleveland and Dahlonega on Elsie's peaceful 26-acre farm. You're invited to wander through lovely rooms filled with amazing cottage and cabin antiques, as well as vintage architectural elements. Unusual items, like hand-painted pottery, luxurious bedding and trendy jewelry—rare treasures you won't find just anywhere. There's even a charming room you can reserve for those special occasions.

Once outside you can explore the streams, ponds and even a waterfall, or the gardens that surround the shop—creating a welcome that dazzles your senses. You will also find a charming "potting shed" out back filled with yard art and gardening supplies. The "Tin Gallery" is filled with art by Tennessee artisans. Clever tin animals line a fence near the shop, and real animals roam freely throughout the property. Elsie says she owns five cats, and each cat owns a dog! A Victorian Cowgirl is open Thursday-Saturday 11 am-5 pm and Sunday 1-5 pm. Visit www.avictoriancowgirl.com or call 706-219-2444. Round up your girlfriends for a delightful day at this charming and eclectic "chicken house." It's well worth the drive!

Artists, Art Galleries, Framing & Photography

SHAPIRO'S Located in the historic and artistic Nacoochee Valley in the Blue Ridge Mountains, you'll find Shapiro's—an extraordinary, contemporary gallery. This log cabin gallery, 2269 Hwy. 17 in Sautee, is a kaleidoscope of handmade works of art from more than 150 artists and craftspeople from across the United States. Susan Shapiro spent more than 20 years as a clay artist, exhibiting in art shows around the country, before she and husband Mike opened one of their galleries in the beautiful Sautee-Nacoochee Valley, just minutes from Helen. Visitors to the gallery will be fascinated by the remarkable pieces of art including: jewelry, pottery, blown glass, wood, mobiles and sculpture. You'll find prints of the Story People by Brian Andreas, clay work by New England potter Tom White, and the latest art watches from WatchCraft's Eduardo Milieres. Stop by Monday-Thursday 10 am-5 pm, Friday-Saturday until 5:30 pm and Sunday noon-5 pm. Call 706-878-1221 or visit www.shapirogallery.com.

Emory and Judy Jones, Freda McAvoy, and Kelvin Morgan invite you to explore Yonah Treasures, which has the feel of a museum, art gallery and country store all rolled into one great shop. It features art from more than 100 area artists, and you'll find Emory's photography, wooden creations, Meader's pottery, jewelry, and much more. Stop by 2047 Helen Hwy. in Cleveland Monday-Saturday 10 am-6 pm and Sunday 1-5 pm. Visit www.yonahtreasures.com or call 706-348-8236.

The Willows Pottery

Located in the foothills of the Blue Ridge Mountains in Nacoochee Village, you'll find The Willows Pottery, a working studio featuring decorative and functional stoneware pottery. You will actually have the chance to see resident potters Emily DeFoor and Betsy Ledbetter work at their wheels. You'll also have the opportunity to create your own masterpiece in the "Paint Your Own Pottery" studio. Stop by The Willows Pottery, 7275 S. Main St. Monday-Saturday 10 am-6 pm and Sunday noon-6 pm. For more information, call 706-878-1344 or visit www.thewillowspottery.com. (See page 163 & 165)

Authentic German architecture, flowing wassergartens (water gardens), Koi-filled lily ponds, breathtaking mountain views and fine Bavarian cuisine is what you will find in this little piece of Alpine heaven. The Edelweiss German Inn & Restaurant has the feel of an Alpine German Inn and is perfect for romantic getaways and special events. Owners John and Ginevra Boyes, and Ed and Laquetta Brummett have created an atmosphere of Bavarian country elegance complete with superb food and world-class service. The Inn has five standard rooms, two luxury rooms with Jacuzzi tubs and outdoor decks, and King Ludwig's Chamber for that special occasion. Each cabin has a fireplace, Jacuzzi tub and a front porch for relaxing. Nestled in the beautiful Blue Ridge Mountains in Sautee, 747 Duncan Bridge Rd. just south of Helen, this inn is the perfect place to celebrate life with good friends and great food. Visit www.edelweissgermaninn.com or call 706-865-7371.

It is described as "peaceful, private and picturesque," and those are understatements. Helen Black Bear Resort is located at 210 Dawn Way in Sautee—just minutes from Helen, at the foot of beautiful Mount Yonah. The lobby is spacious and rustic and features a cozy fireplace, a large antique bar, viewing screen and an outside covered deck. Each cabin includes a hot tub, deck, rock fireplace, fully equipped kitchen and washer/dryer. The 11-room lodge is perfect for special events, reunions and corporate meetings. Adjacent to the lodge is a sweet wedding chapel and gazebo, with a covered pavilion for receptions. In the evening, take a walk down the hill to the Black Bear Dinner Theatre for top-notch live entertainment. Call 877-734-2467, 706-865-0093, or visit www.helenblackbearresort.com, for more information.

A-1 VACATION RENTALS

With everything from rustic hideaways, luxury condos and hillside European chalets, you will find the very best and widest variety in rentals at A-1 Vacation Rentals, 8287 S. Main St., in Helen. Owner Diane Overmier, with her daughter Lauren, her father and stepmother, have more than 25 years experience in the resort management business. They love helping customers find the perfect place for that special vacation to remember. Choose from in-town or out-of-town cabins or chalets with beautiful mountain or river views. A-1 Vacation Rentals is the exclusive property manager for Innsbruck Golf Resort, as well as The Castle Inn, which overlooks the Chattahoochee River and beautiful town of Helen. Whether you are visiting for two nights or even a week's stay, you'll find the perfect place for your family or group. Diane will also help you put together an activity, golf, or a romantic honeymoon package. Call 706-878-0022, 800-395-3644 or visit www.a-1vacationrental.com.

Hotels & Inns

After opening her charming gift shop and dog barkery—Claws and Paws—Deborah Spitzer realized there was not a true "pet friendly" motel in the area. So, she opened the Biscuit Inn, with adorable dog-themed rooms. The four rooms—Duke, Lady, Cookie and Rocky— have cathedral ceilings, hardwood floors, a fireplace and creature comforts, like a pet bed, bowls, a robe and "gourmutt" treats. For reservations, call 706-892-9837. Located on Hwy. 356 just outside Helen, across from the Unicoi State Park—perfect for stretching!

Pampered Pets

Her love of four-legged creatures inspired Deborah Spitzer to open Claws & Paws, Helen's original pet barkery and gift shop at 23 Chattahoochee St. She has three dogs (Freckles, Sam and Spot) and three cats (Rascal, Kallee and Sonny) who are models and taste testers for her unique inventory of "Gourmutt" treats, sweaters, doggy baseball caps, bandanas and toys. She also has unique people gifts! Open daily 10 am-6 pm. Call 706-878-1243. And, if traveling with your pet, call the Biscuit Inn—her pet friendly motel, 706-892-9837.

Restaurants

The Edelweiss Restaurant offers the perfect place to celebrate life with good friends and great food. Guests enjoy an atmosphere of country elegance complete with superb food and world-class service. The Edelweiss German Inn & Restaurant is nestled on a cozy four-acre wooded mountainside in the shadow of Mount Yonah, just three miles south of Helen. From the legendary food to the perfect accommodations, Edelweiss is a unique blend of Bavarian and Alpine Heritage. You'll love visiting the gift shop deli—pack a picnic basket of wonderful sausages, cheese, bread and chocolates—and find a special place to relax. The sausages are made onsite using authentic German recipes handed down for generations.

The Restaurant is known throughout the county as one of the best places to enjoy truly authentic German food. The atmosphere is Old World European, and the owners John and Ginevra Boyes, and Ed and Laquetta Brummett add a family element to the wonderful restaurant.

The menu features appetizers of Marinated Herring, Pommes Frites and German Sausages but is known for its Sauerbraten, Goulash and assorted Schnitzels, including Jager Schnitzel, Rahm Schnitzel and, of course Wiener Schnitzel. The menu also includes traditional American favorites such as hand-cut steaks, chicken and seafood. And, last but not least, dessert—what else but Apple Strudel made by the Executive Chef! Edelweiss is a must on your visit to this beautiful part of North Georgia. Open daily (except Christmas Day) at 747 Duncan Bridge Rd. Visit www.edelweissgermaninn.com or call 706-865-7371.

NACOOCHEE GRILL

Whether your tastes lean toward gourmet and unusual dishes like Duck Breast Salad or to classic comfort foods like crispy fried chicken, the Nacoochee Grill is sure to satisfy! It is located at 7277 S. Main St. in the Nacoochee Village, just one-half mile south of Helen, and is open daily for lunch and dinner. The menu is one of the most extensive and exciting in Northeast Georgia, featuring fresh seafood and hand-cut, fire-grilled steaks. Don't miss the award-winning wines from Habersham Vineyards & Winery. And, for your special events be sure to ask about their catering services. Visit www.nacoocheegrill.com or call 706-878-8020. (See pages 158 & 165)

Spas & Indulgence

Tucked away on a wooded hillside in the peaceful Nacoochee Valley, just south of Helen, the mountaintop house that Mandala occupies provides an ideal spa setting, with comfortable rooms and calm décor. In addition to complete spa services like massage therapy, facials, wraps and soaks, you can treat yourself to relaxation sessions, yoga and t'ai chi classes, hypnotherapy, and weight-loss programs, or visit the gift shop for natural bath and body products. Stop by 47 Wingo Dr. in Sautee Monday-Saturday 9 am-6 pm. Visit www.mandalaretreat.com or call 706-878-0036.

 The bright-blue door and muraled walls of this sweet little gift shop hint at the European atmosphere inside. No trip to Helen's charming Alpine Village would be complete without a visit to Classics. It is an enchanting place, filled with international gifts from well-known artist. You'll find beautiful pieces from Lladro, carved collectibles from Hummel and a beautiful selection of Steinbach Nutcrackers. The shelves are filled with everything from blown glassware and decorative pottery to wall clocks and wind chimes. Be sure to ask owner Judy Holloway and her knowledgeable staff for information about the fun collectors' festivals. Classics, at 8641 N. Main St., is open Monday-Friday 10 am-6 pm and Saturday-Sunday until 7 pm. Call 706-878-1411.

 Kate and Bruce Rodgers began their natural soap business in 1996 with their simple philosophy: "Have faith. Do what you love. Don't make a bigger mess than you can clean up. Use tools rather than machines. Laugh often." Greenstone Soap Company is located at 2276 Hwy. 17, in Sautee—just minutes from Helen. You'll love the wonderful aroma of the natural handmade herbal soaps and bath care products. Try the lavender and oatmeal soap and don't miss the fine gifts like bee's wax candles and organic teas. Open Monday-Saturday 10 am-5:30 pm and Sunday noon-5 pm. Visit www.greenstonesoap.com or call 706-878-5901.

Wines & Wineries

HABERSHAM
Vineyards & Winery

In addition to the wonderful, complimentary wine tasting, fine selection of wines, specialty gifts, and delightful gourmet foods, a visit to Habersham Vineyards & Winery offers visitors a chance to see the barrel rooms and bottling line first hand. Located one-half mile south of Helen in Nacoochee Village—a unique collection of shops and attractions—at 7025 S. Main St., Habersham Vineyards & Winery is one of the largest and oldest in Georgia and has won more than 150 medals in national and international competitions. Most of the grapes used in their wine production are grown in nearby Stonepile and Mossy Creek Vineyards. Native Muscadine grapes are also grown in South Georgia and transported to the mountains for production of their Southern Harvest Wines. Hours are 10 am-6 pm Monday-Saturday and Sunday 12:30-6 pm. Call 706-878-9463 or visit www.habershamwinery.com. (See pages 158 & 163)

Discover Madison

In an 1845 guidebook, Madison was called, "The Most Cultured and Aristocratic Town on the Stage Route from Charleston to New Orleans." Not much has changed in the last 160 years. Madison is still one of the most cultured and sophisticated cities you will visit in the South. Yet, it is still a place where you will see locals entertaining friends on front porches and farmers selling their produce in town on the weekends. Madison has been likened to a "Norman Rockwell Painting," where life moves at a gentle pace.

In the Beginning

The very first inhabitants of this area were the Creek Indians. In 1785, land grants were offered to Revolutionary War soldiers to attract settlers to the area, and several families in the county are still in possession of the original grants. It was at this time that the county was named for the revolutionary war hero General Daniel Morgan, and Madison was incorporated and named for President James Madison. By 1833, the railroad was chartered to go through Madison, but the town's officials would not permit it to run through the town proper.

In 1864, when the Civil War burned through the South, battles destroyed railways, factories, bridges and homes. Entire towns were burned, but Madison holds the honor of being called, "The Town Sherman Refused to Burn," or "The Town Too Pretty To Burn!" Senator Joshua Hill, an anticessionist, was credited with saving Madison by convincing General Slocum to post guards at all of the homes throughout the town instead of burning them. Unfortunately, his own plantation was burned to the ground by Union troops. It wasn't until 1908 that the present Confederate Monument was erected in the Town Square.

The town was once populated by wealthy cotton planters and merchants who built many of the extraordinary antebellum homes you see today in the Historic District. These fine examples of Federal and Greek Revival architecture encompass almost the entire town, making Madison's Historic District one of the largest in Georgia. The Morgan County Courthouse, which was built in 1905, has been recently refurbished, and has been used as a filming site for television and cinema.

Visiting History

A tour through Madison's Historic District will include several exciting and important historical buildings. The Madison-Morgan Cultural Center, which is located in the restored 1895 School Building, features exhibits depicting local life during the 19th to early 20th century. Heritage Hall, a magnificent 1811 Greek Revival home, is an integral part of Madison's Historic District. It is noted for its unique "window etchings," which appear in seven of the eight rooms. (These were done by daughters and granddaughters of the second owner, Dr. Elijah Evans Jones.) The beautiful architecture, period furnishings and original oil paintings create an elegant setting for both private and public functions. The home, called Heritage Hall, was donated to the Morgan County Historical Society in 1977 by Sue Reid Law in honor of her grandmother and the home's final resident, Mrs. Fletcher Manley. Another remarkable, historic home you will see is the Rose Cottage. It was built by Adeline Rose, a woman who was born into slavery, and later earned her living by taking in washing and ironing for 50 cents a load. (She did most of her early work for the boarders of the Hardy House, which was owned by the family of the famous comedian Oliver Hardy.)

The Reason You're Here!

Today, thousands of visitors make their way to this wonderful small town. Whether Madison is your only destination, or you are following Georgia's Antebellum Trail, be sure to tour the magnificent Historic District, the gardens, the churches and the galleries. Here you will also find excellent shopping that dazzles your imagination, mouth-watering dining and great lodging accommodations for you to enjoy a charming Southern experience. We've found some of the most delightful cafés, top-rated restaurants, wonderful specialty shops, and unusual antique shops, selling everything from "Granny's Peach Jam" to hand thrown pottery. Along the way, we've discovered that the people of Madison are its greatest attribute. They are friendly, helpful, and will welcome you with big smiles to their historic city. It certainly is easy to see why *Travel Holiday* magazine voted Madison the "#1 Small Town in America," and we're sure you'll agree!

For more information about Madison, contact the Madison Morgan County Welcome Center at 800-709-7406, 706-342-4454 or visit www.madisonga.org online.

Madison
Fairs Festivals & Fun

February
Casino Night

March
Antiques Show and Sale
Taste of Madison

April
Madison Fest/Bluegrass Festival

May
Spring Tour of Homes

June
Chamber Music Festival

July
Independence Day Concert and
  Picnic
Sunflower Festival

September
Corvette Show on the Square

October
Jacks Creek Farm Festival
Lake Oconee Jazz and Blues
  Fest

November
Cotton Gin Festival
Merchants Holiday Open House

December
Christmas Rush Road Race
Holiday Tour of Homes

SALLY'S

Business owners Sally Overfelt and Barbara Voyles have been friends for more than 25 years, and love being able to share their interests and love for people in this charming specialty store. From top-of-the-line cookware and whimsical tabletop décor to unique gadgets, you will find a remarkable array of extraordinary kitchenware and accessories at Sally's. They offer the finest in kitchenware with a touch of style, including items by All-Clad, Chantal, Oxo, Doughmakers and Sabatier. You'll also find linens by Heritage Lace and Park, and products by Caldrea, which provide a top-notch cleaning experience. Tucked away in Madison's Historic Downtown Square, Sally's—where style and function come together—is a favorite of both locals and tourists alike. Stop by 125 W. Jefferson St. Monday-Friday 10 am-5:30 pm, Saturday until 5 pm, and Sunday 1-5 pm. Visit www.sallysofmadisonga.com or call 706-342-8222.

Simply Southern

This beautiful and fascinating store started "simply" when Lesley Taylor discovered monogramming as a way for identical twin daughters Caroline and Sarah Beth to have their own identities. She and her mother, Gwen Turner, started with a small space, offering the folks of Madison "Simply Southern" personalized keepsakes. They soon grew into the 1830s antebellum home at 270 S. Main St. in the Historic District, which they renovated and love. Simply Southern features custom monogramming and engraving, unique gifts and accessories for you and your home, as well as Crabtree & Evelyn, and so much more. You'll be enchanted by the delightful and charming mother/daughter owners that make shopping this store such fun. Open Monday-Saturday 10 am-5:30 pm and Sunday 1-4 pm seasonally. Don't miss the other location in Eatonton, just south of Madison. Call 706-343-1001 or visit online www.simplysouthernonmain.com.

MADISON INTERIORS MARKET

Local designers have credited Madison Interiors Market in *Southern Living* as being a haven for decorators and designers. The Market is located in a renovated cotton warehouse at 144 Academy St. in Madison's Downtown Historic District. It is an upscale shopping experience with a fine selection of furniture, Oriental rugs, accessories, and art by regional artists, with much more in the 20,000 square feet. With more than 75-handpicked dealers, Madison Interiors Market is the largest upscale dealers market in the state of Georgia. Stop by Monday through Saturday 10 am-6 pm and Sunday noon-5 pm. For more information, call 706-342-8795 or visit www.madisonmarkets.com.

Art Galleries

STONEBRIDGE
WESTERN TREASURES
and Fine Art

Nestled in the Madison storefronts of Jefferson Square Parkside at 191 W. Jefferson St., Stonebridge Western Treasures and Fine Art continues to fill a unique niche for both beginning and seasoned art collectors in the area. Owners John and Joyce Stevens hope to see others become as enthusiastic as they are about fine art, which is why they have created a beautiful gallery filled with treasures from across the West.

As John and Joyce traveled throughout the years, they were inexplicably drawn to the history and beauty of the American West, and began acquiring carefully selected works of art. Their gallery showcases a variety of artwork portraying the artistry and spirit of the West—the hopes and dreams of cowboys, the life of settlers and pioneers, and the breathtaking scenery of our vast country. Connoisseurs of all things Western will find an exciting collection of original oils, watercolors, pastels, sculptures, prints and posters by some of the leading artists in America.

Additionally, the gallery specializes in handcrafted jewelry by Western and Native American artists, along with carefully chosen pieces from local artisans. You will find a wide selection of home accessories, gift items and rugs reflecting the feel of the American West. For a literal "taste of the West," try some of the delicious Southwestern dips, soups and dressings.

"We want to share our love of the American West with people who might also come to appreciate all that's unique about that part of our country," share John and Joyce. They have indeed done a wonderful job of bringing "the heart of the West to the heart of the South" in this outstanding gallery. Designers and interior decorators are encouraged to contact the gallery for special assistance. Stop by Tuesday-Saturday 11 am-6 pm. Visit www.stonebridgetreasures.com. or call 706-342-2841.

CULTURAL CENTER

Since 1976 visitors have been entertained, thrilled and inspired by the exhibits, special events and performances of the Madison-Morgan Cultural Center at 434 S. Main St. in Madison. Permanent museum exhibits depict life in the region during the 19th and early 20th century, including "A History of the Piedmont," "The Schoolroom," "Boxwood Parlour," and "Arts & Crafts Room." For more information and hours, call 706-342-4743 or visit www.madisonmorgancultural.org online.

Morgan County African-American Museum

Located in the circa 1895 Horace Moore House at 156 Academy St. in Madison, the Morgan County African-American Museum was founded in 1991 by Deacon Martin L. Barr and Rev. Fred Perriman. Don't miss the "Shona Sculpture Collection" from Zimbabwe. Learn the plight of a people and it's culture, and celebrate African-American history. Open Tuesday-Friday 10 am-4 pm and Saturday noon-4 pm. Call 706-342-9191.

THE ROGERS HOUSE

Into architecture? You'll find a fine example of the Piedmont Plain style architecture when you visit the Rogers House at 179 E. Jefferson St. in Madison. It was typical of the houses built throughout the rural South during the early 1800s. The Rogers House has been carefully restored through photographs and historical archives. Open Monday-Saturday 10 am-4:30 pm and Sunday 1:30-4:30 pm. Contact the Morgan County Historical Society at 706-343-0190.

Heritage Hall

An integral part of Madison's historic district, Heritage Hall was built in 1811 by Dr. William Johnston and occupied from 1830-1876 by Dr. Elijah Evans Jones—a prominent physician and major shareholder in the Georgia Railroad. The home, located at 277 S. Main St., is maintained by the Morgan County Historical Society, and has been restored because of its architectural and historical significance. Its authentic period furnishings provide an elegant setting for unforgettable special events. Open Monday-Saturday 11 am-4 pm and Sunday 1:30-4:30 pm. Visit www.friendsofheritagehall.com online or call 706-342-9627.

ROSE COTTAGE

Adeline Rose purchased her home—land in 1891, lumber in 1893, and then began building Rose Cottage. She lived in the house for more than 66 years before her death in 1959. In 1996, the City of Madison moved Rose Cottage to its present location at 179 E. Jefferson St. Today, the Morgan County Historical Society manages this historic home in tribute to the labor of love of a woman who was born into slavery and released at two years of age. Rose Cottage is open for tours Monday-Saturday 10 am-4:30 pm and Sunday 1:30-4:30 pm. Call 706-343-0190.

STEFFEN THOMAS MUSEUM & ARCHIVES

The Steffen Thomas Museum and Archives is an organization dedicated to the life and work of the late artist (1906-1990) who immigrated to the United States from Germany in 1928. Located in a beautiful pastoral setting at 4200 Bethany Rd. in Buckhead (just eight miles southeast of Madison). Exhibitions of Thomas' sculpture, paintings, watercolors, mosaics, graphics, charcoal drawings and ceramics are on display Tuesday-Saturday 1-4 pm. Call 706-342-7557 for tour information or visit www.steffenthomas.org online.

Georgia Trend magazine touts this enchanting museum as, "Madison's newest cultural jewel, and in some ways its most impressive." Located on the Historic Town Square at 290 Hancock St., the Madison Museum of Fine Art features a sculpture garden with pebble paths, and a "Mary Garden" with plants and legends from Medieval times. You'll also love the museum store! Visit Monday-Saturday 1-5 pm and Sunday until 4 pm. Call 706-342-2007 or visit www.madisonmuseum.org online.

Books

Grab a favorite book and curl up on the comfy green sofa with the store cat, Eve! Family-owned-and-operated by Susan Kurtz and Elizabeth Meyer, Dog Ear Books has become a Madison favorite for young and old alike. The children's section is filled with the newest, most beautiful titles, as well as classics. The shelves also hold all the latest adult favorites—fiction, nonfiction, mystery, religion, health, music and architecture. Call 706-342-3460; visit www.dogearbooks.com; or stop by 142 Academy St.

Cabins, Cottages, Bed & Breakfasts

When you are ready to leave the world behind for a little while, Southern Cross Guest Ranch is waiting for you. It stretches across 200 acres of gently rolling hills in Georgia's Historic Heartland, offering guests blissful seclusion, wonderful horseback opportunities and, of course, true Southern hospitality. This incredibly beautiful Bed and Breakfast is located just outside of Madison at 1670 Bethany Church Rd, (between Atlanta and Augusta). Southern Cross is an all-inclusive working guest ranch with more than 150 horses, so visitors can horseback ride for hours through lush wooded trails and beautiful green meadows. If you are a beginner, riding lessons are available on horses matched to your experience, but guests may also trot off on their own to explore the beautiful countryside.

Owner Inge Wendling has always had a passion for horses, and with the development of Southern Cross, has found a way to share it with others. She and her two sons are wonderful hosts who will make your stay as exciting and action packed or as peaceful and relaxing as you desire. The all-inclusive package includes up to four hours of horseback riding, three delicious meals a day, pool and hot tub, and a choice of beautifully decorated rooms. The inn itself is a 12,000 square foot Southern, antebellum mansion with gleaming hardwood floors, oriental rugs and exquisite antiques. You can choose a room with a rustic, western theme or one decorated in beautiful, Victorian style. All rooms feature king size beds, a TV, a VCR and a private bath. Premium rooms also offer fireplaces and whirlpool tubs. A private chef is responsible for a delicious mix of international cuisine, as well as local favorites

For information or reservations, call 706-342-8027 or visit www.southcross.com online.

HALLIE JANE'S

Market *Catering*

Whether your gathering is large or small, black-tie or tie-dye, Hallie Jane's Market and Catering will ensure it is very special. It is one of Madison's premier catering companies, specializing in off-site catering services for private and corporate events of all sizes. Owned by David and Hallie Duan, Hallie had the fortunate opportunity to travel extensively throughout the United States and abroad, and is able to draw upon those experiences to create her exciting and impressive menus. You will find it all—delicious traditional, ethnic and fusion cuisine. Hallie has a signature "Baked Cajun Crawfish Dip" that customers buy by the pound! You'll also love the self-serve lunch buffet of soups, salads and desserts that change daily. Be sure to try the decadent pecan bars! Hallie Jane's Market and Catering is located at 140 Academy St., and is open Monday-Saturday 11 am-3 pm. Visit www.halliejanes.com online or call 706-342-2837.

Be sure and check out Amici Italian Café while in Madison. See page 119 for full details.

Gifts, Jewelry, Clothing and Home Accessories

Two great shops under one roof! Located in an 1800s building in Historic Downtown Madison at 172 S. Main St., Amelia's offers a wonderful selection of women's apparel and accessories from Gotcha Covered, French Dressing, Tribal and Glima to Brighton, Hobo and Emily Ray. For shoes choose from Yellow Box, Born, Tsonga and much more! When your wardrobe is complete, wander into The Ruffled Rooster where you'll find distinctively different doo-dads and décor such as Yankee Candle, Arthur Court, Lampe Berger, Hillhouse Naturals and, of course, a selection of roosters to crow about! For a glimpse into this wonderful store, visit www.ameliasonmain.com online or stop by Monday-Saturday 10 am-5:30 pm and Sunday 1-5 pm. For more information, call 706-342-2986.

The Ruffled Rooster

Gourmet, Specialty Foods & Wines

Simply put, it's old-fashioned goodness on Madison's historic downtown square. Just follow the incredible aroma to Antique Sweets, 132 E. Washington St., which has captured the attention of every sweet tooth and chocoholic in town. This enchanting candy store is the long-time dream of mother and son, Patty and Patrick Alligood, and with help from Patty's sister—Debby Owens, who owns The Fudge Factory in Dahlonega—that dream has been fulfilled. Glass cases feature rich chocolates, golden pralines and soft heavenly divinity, and an antique breakfront holds gift-boxed candies ready to give. Patrick is "the confectioner" and customers love watching as he prepares small batches of confections in the store's kitchen, and, of course, he needs testers! Everything is delicious! There is even a sweet "Kid's Corner" for candy by the piece. Open Monday-Thursday 10 am-6 pm, Friday-Saturday until 8 pm, and Sunday (seasonally) 1-5 pm. Call 706-342-0034.

The Squished Grape

From the moment Ginger Doshier-Simmons tasted her first wine—at the age of 26—she was mesmerized by the different qualities and complexities that the art of wine involved, and she was hooked for life! She and husband Curt opened The Squished Grape, in Madison, to feature unusual, value-priced wines from around the world, as well as high-end collector's wines like Silver Oak and Opus One. The Squished Grape is open Tuesday-Thursday 11 am-5 pm and Friday-Saturday until 6 pm. Call 706-752-0052.

Hotels & Inns

MADISON

Travelers have come to expect the best from Hampton Inns through the years, and this Madison inn certainly lives up to those expectations. Conveniently located at 2012 Eatonton Rd., Hampton Inn has all of the amenities to accommodate a corporate or leisure guest. The 62 rooms open to indoor corridors, and all feature irons and ironing boards, two telephone lines and data ports, high-speed wireless Internet, 25-inch televisions—which include HBO, CNN, ESPN, Fox News, as well as a complimentary newspaper. Before you venture into this remarkable historic town to sightsee or to shop, enjoy a complimentary, extended breakfast buffet. The Inn also offers a fitness area and an outdoor pool. The friendly staff members want your stay here to be the most pleasant part of your trip, and they are extremely helpful with information about all of the galleries, museums, parks, restaurants and tours. For more information or reservations, call 800-HAMPTON, 706-342-9003 or visit www.hamptoninn.com online. It is the very best in "historic hospitality!"

Salons, Spas & Indulgence

GiGi's Salon and Day Spa— In 1986, GiGi Gerhardt studied under two very famous British stylists and credits this difficult training for the success she enjoys today as one of Madison's favorite hairdressers. Gigi's Salon and Day Spa is located at 223 S. Main St., in a beautiful antebellum home built in the 1830s. The Salon offers beautiful hairstyles, as well as manicures, pedicures, facials, massage and a variety of professional products. Be sure to browse the boutique, filled with antiques, handbags, gifts and jewelry. The Salon is open Tuesday-Saturday 10 am-6 pm, Thursday until 8 pm. Call 706-342-0965.

Discover
Marietta /Woodstock /
Canton

MARIETTA

Marietta welcomes visitors to her city with all the grace and charm of a true Southern belle. Just 25 miles north of Atlanta, this beautiful Southern city is drenched in Civil War history and filled with exciting adventure and recreational opportunities. The first thing you will notice about Marietta is that it is such a pretty city. The tree-lined streets and beautiful parks surround magnificent Victorian homes and historic sites. The Historic Downtown Square is filled with wonderful antique stores, unique boutiques and fabulous cafés and restaurants.

Historic Marietta

This vibrant hub of north Georgia was originally organized as one of 20 counties from the original Cherokee County, and became the Cobb County seat in 1834. Just 30 years later Civil War broke out in America and Marietta was the site of an important battle. In 1864, General Sherman marched his 100,000 troops from Chattanooga to Marietta and forced the city's surrender. The Marietta History Museum documents the city's history from the early Native American inhabitants and the Gold Rush through the Civil War, World War II and its recent history.

The Marietta Square

This is the perfect place to start your visit. The Downtown Square includes the vintage 1898 train depot, which is home to the Marietta Welcome Center and the Kennesaw House, which houses the Marietta History Museum. The famous "Gone With the Wind Museum: Scarlett on the Square" is located within a vintage 1880 warehouse. Just a few miles away from the Square, you'll find the Marietta National Cemetery, the Confederate Cemetery and the Kennesaw Mountain National Battlefield Park. On the north end of the square, there is a bandstand, which is the center for numerous city festivals and the site of the decorated Christmas tree during the holidays. Shopping Marietta's Square will include an eclectic mix of fabulous finds, including Victorian and American antiques, primitives, collectibles, pottery, gourmet foods, architectural elements and gifts for the garden.

Scarlett on the Square!

Margaret Mitchell's best selling novel *"Gone With the Wind"* premiered as a movie in 1939, receiving eight Oscars, including Best Actress for Vivien Leigh as "Miss Scarlett." In 1989 the movie won the People's Choice Award for the "Best Picture Ever Made." The Gone With the Wind Museum affords die-hard romantics to relive moments with Scarlett and Rhett, Melanie and Ashley, and the folks of a genteel pre-war South. The museum features original costumes, props, books, posters and interesting exhibits that tell the incredible story of the people of Tara.

The Big Chicken

What is red and white, 56-feet tall and one of Marietta's most interesting landmarks? It's hard to miss the famous "Big Chicken" that was erected at the corner of Highway 20 and U.S. 41 to draw attention to an old Marietta restaurant called Chick, Chuck and Shake. Today, the Big Chicken stands in front of a local restaurant where you will find a gift shop that includes lots of Big Chicken memorabilia. You might hear locals use the landmark chicken in their directions to "turn at the first light past the Big Chicken," or "just down the street from the Big Chicken." Marietta is "A Lot to Cluck About."

WOODSTOCK

Located in the southernmost part of Cherokee County, just 30 miles north of Atlanta, you'll find the charming little town of Woodstock, one of the county's oldest towns. The first train depot was built here in 1879, and the first gristmills in the county were located here. The Woodstock Visitors Center is located downtown at Dean's Store, where you can stock up on brochures of all that the town has to offer. Be sure to visit the beautiful gazebo and water fountain in Woodstock City Park. It's a great place to relax and count your shopping bags!

CANTON

Established in 1833 as the Cherokee County seat, Canton was originally known as Etowah. Its name changed to Canton in 1834. It evolved through the years from an unsettled Indian territory to a prosperous mill town made famous by "Canton Denim," a high-quality denim produced by Canton Cotton Mills. The mills operated from 1899 to 1981, helping Canton to become a commercial and social center of Cherokee County. Another reason for Canton's viable growth is its location at the foothills of the Blue Ridge Mountains along the banks of the Etowah River. It is an incredibly beautiful place to visit and play, and a wonderful place to shop!

For more information about Marietta, contact the Marietta Welcome Center and Visitors Bureau at 770-429-1115, 800-835-0445 or visit www.mariettasquare.com online.

For more information about Canton and Woodstock, contact the Cherokee County Chamber of Commerce at 770-345-0400 or visit www.cherokeechamber.com online.

Marietta / Woodstock / Canton Fairs Festivals & Fun

April
Canton's Bluegrass Concert Series (Apr-July)
Taste of Marietta
Woodstock Rocks! Summer Concert Series (Apr-Aug)

May
Arts & Crafts Festival (Woodstock)
Cherokee Indian Festival and PowWow
Festival of the Arts (Canton)
May-retta Daze Arts & Crafts Festival (Marietta)
Memorial Day Celebration (Woodstock)

June
Woodstock Brown Bag Concert Series (Jun-Sep)

July
Fireworks Extravaganza (Woodstock)
Fourth in the Park (Marietta)
Fourth of July Celebration (Canton)

September
Antique Festival (Marietta)
Art in the Park (Marietta)
Bike Rodeo (Woodstock)
Glover Park Brown Bag Concert Series (Marietta)
Riverfest (Canton)

October
Big Chicken Chorus Concert (Marietta)
Fall Festival (Woodstock)
Halloween Happenings (Marietta)
Harvest Square Arts & Crafts Festival (Marietta)
Kidfest (Woodstock)
Taste of Canton

November
Holiday Festival of the Trees (Canton)
Holiday Festival of the Wreaths (Woodstock)
Holiday Open House (Marietta)

December
Holiday Jubilee (Woodstock)
Holiday Tree Lighting (Marietta)
Hometown Christmas (Canton)
Marietta Pilgrimage Christmas Home Tour
Santa on the Square (Marietta)

Antiques, Gifts & Home Décor

 The Ivy Garden

This quaint shop is a must-see! The Ivy Garden is a two-story "Old House" filled with delightful antiques and gifts. It is also one of the few shops in the area to offer handcrafted items from local artists. In addition to painted furniture, home and garden décor and one-of-a-kind handmade jewelry, there is a large selection of "Red Hat Society" items. (Owner, Lisha Carrier began a chapter of Red Hatters in the area.) With reservations, any group can enjoy a "Picnic on the Porch"—a delicious lunch of sandwiches, salads and desserts. Stop by to sample a cup of gourmet coffee and a piece of biscotti. Located off Canton Hwy. at 126 Barrett Rd. in Holly Springs (5 miles south of Canton), this delightful shop is open Monday-Saturday 10:30 am-5 pm. For more information, call 770-479-2647.

The Wild Honeysuckle
for the home

As you walk through the doors of The Wild Honeysuckle, you'll know you have found something different. You are transcended to a shop reminiscent of those found on a trendy city street, yet as welcoming as one found on Main Street in Anytown, USA. The store's clever vignettes showcase a unique mix of home accents, fine furniture and gorgeous gifts, while giving the customer endless design ideas and reasons to linger.

The Wild Honeysuckle offers a gift registry for weddings, births, anniversaries or graduations. Customers can also take advantage of the extensive design services by owner Janel Ideker—she enjoys working with a client's existing collection, adding pieces and accents to create a new ambiance.

The Wild Honeysuckle, 2295 Towne Lake Pkwy. #140 in Woodstock, is open Monday-Saturday 10 am-6 pm or call 770-516-1427.

DuPRE'S
ANTIQUES & INTERIORS

Harry DuPre continues a 127-year-old family tradition in operating DuPre's Antiques & Interiors, 17 Whitlock Ave. S.W. in Marietta. Harry's great, great grandfather opened a retail business at this very location in 1877. It is located at the Historic Marietta Square, where Andrews and his Union soldiers met, preparing for their famous train raid during the Civil War. Today, the store features quality antiques and wonderful collectibles. You'll find books, clocks, furniture, glass, lamps, china and unique architectural elements. It's no wonder DuPre's has been voted one of the top five antique shops in the Atlanta Metro area in an *Atlanta Journal-Constitution* poll.

Open Monday through Saturday 10 am-5:30 pm and Sunday 1-5:30 pm. Call 770-428-2667 or visit www.dupresai.com.

BRENDA'S
HOUSE OF FLOWERS

Skip Shipman gave his wife Lyn an incredible Christmas present in 1996. Lyn was looking for something to do after moving to Atlanta from Phoenix where she had managed several departments at the Arizona Biltmore, a five-star resort. When he asked her what she had liked the most at the Biltmore, she said managing the floral department. So, Skip purchased Brenda's House of Flowers in Woodstock for his wife.

After Lyn was at Brenda's for several months, Skip took a 90-day leave of absence from his position as CEO of a small Atlanta-based company to install new technology, initiate marketing and sales programs, and develop a business plan for the shop. To make a long story short, he never went back. Skip and Lyn are now living the "American Dream." Skip says, "I go to work every morning with my best friend and wife, Lyn."

Teleflora, the floral industry's largest wire service, bestowed Brenda's with its most prestigious award, as one of their "Top 50 Retail Florist" in America. Brenda's has won this honor for the last six years! Brenda's was selected as Cherokee County's "Small Business of the Year" by the Chamber of Commerce, voted "The Best of the Best" florist by *The TowneLaker* magazine and the *Atlanta Journal-Constitution*

Brenda's has become the first choice for birthday, anniversary and wedding arrangements, with designs ranging from traditional and formal to fun and contemporary. You will also find a large selection of wonderful gift baskets. To view Lyn's exciting floral creations, visit www.brendashouseofflowers.com or stop by 9010 Main St. Monday thru Friday 9 am-5:30 pm and Saturday 9 am-2 pm. For more information, call 770-926-3306 or 800-562-4297.

Ladyslipper
RARE PLANT NURSERY, INC.

Located in a beautiful verdant part of Georgia, there is a magnificent nursery of flowers and rare plants called Ladyslipper Rare Plant Nursery. This nursery has become a favorite place for locals and visitors throughout the state. In fact, customers drive from great distances to browse the beautiful gardens at 7418 Hickory Flat Hwy. in Woodstock.

Owner Lula Norris was born and raised on a farm in Tennessee and moved to Georgia during the 1980s. She brought with her a real love for flowers. In fact, she says she has never wanted to do anything more in life than work with plants, flowers and nature. Lula has been in the nursery business for more than 15 years. Ladyslipper Rare Plant Nursery is family-owned-and-operated, and the staff is friendly and extremely knowledgeable about the unique rare plants. Lula and her team are available to help you create and maintain a garden that will delight from season to season.

At Ladyslipper you'll find popular "Southern" beauties—a gorgeous collection of rare plants that will impress even the most avid gardener. If you enjoy container gardening, this is definitely the place to shop for unusual pots and beautiful plants. Choose from a wide variety of plants, such as lacy ferns, dripping ivies, awesome annuals, gorgeous grasses and tasty herbs. The charming gift shop on the property is filled with home and garden delights such as hand-made wind chimes and yard art. Whimsical little fairies seem to peek from almost every corner of the store, including a special line from a local artisan.

Ladyslipper Rare Plant Nursery is open Monday-Friday 8 am-5 pm and Saturday until 4 pm. Call 770-345-2998.

Pampered Pets

Kreature Komforts OF MARIETTA, INC.

When John Soper left the hustle and bustle of the "corporate world," his business went "to the dogs!" Literally! Kreature Komforts, 31 Mill St., #300, is devoted entirely to the canines and felines of Marietta and the people who love them. You'll find hundreds of lines of essentials for "debonair dogs and sophisticated cats," like designer collars, leads, beds, clothing and toys. At the gourmet bakery, choose from natural preservative-free goodies, or as a special treat, order a bone-shaped Birthday Cake! There is a display of luxury pet furniture at the front door and clever pet paraphernalia in every corner of the store. If you need help with your selection, simply confer with the "administrative assistant"—John's adorable Sheltie—"Callie." Kreature Komforts is located on the Historic Marietta Square and is open Tuesday-Saturday 8 am-5 pm. Call 770-428-8616 or visit www.kreaturekomforts.net online.

THE AVENUE®

The Avenue concept, introduced in 1998, offers an outdoor, pedestrian-friendly setting featuring shopping, dining and pampering. In contrast to an ordinary mall, this "Main Street" pedestrian center is smaller in scale and appeals to the discriminating, and often time-constrained shopper. If you are looking for high-quality merchandise in a convenient setting, this is the place for you! All three Georgia area Avenues combine premier national retailers, select local merchants and specialty restaurants in an attractive, open-air setting. The Avenue is a shopper's paradise—Ann Taylor, Talbots, Williams-Sonoma, Chico's, Coldwater Creek

and many more fine retailers and restaurants.

You'll find first-rate shopping at all three venues. For more information visit online www.theavenuealist.com.

Marietta – East Cobb – 4475 Roswell Rd. – 770-971-9945

Marietta – West Cobb – 3625 Dallas Hwy. – 678-594-6738

Peachtree City – 239 City Cir. – 770-486-6587

(Color photo featured in front section of book.)

Discover
Milledgeville

Like a true "Southern belle" the city of Milledgeville charms visitors with her magnolia scented beauty, fascinating history and gracious hospitality. Called Georgia's Antebellum Capital, Milledgeville was Georgia's fourth state capital from 1807-1868. The city was named for John Milledge, former Governor of Georgia, whose family dates back to the original colonists of Georgia. Just like Washington D.C., Milledgeville was specifically built to be a state capital, and was laid out in checkerboard fashion with four public squares. The State House Square was the highest point of the city, overlooking the river and was chosen as the site for the state's Capitol Building.

While Milledgeville served as the political center of Georgia, many notable Georgians and famous visitors were attracted to the city. Secession was declared here in 1861, catapulting Georgia into the War Between the States. General Sherman marched through Milledgeville in 1864, seizing the town for two days. Fortunately, he spared many of the fine Federal style, Greek Revival, Victorian and Classic Revival homes there.

Capitals

The Old Capitol Building, 201 E. Greene St., was built in 1807 and is considered the finest example of Gothic Greek Revival architecture in a public building in the United States. It served as Georgia's seat of government until 1868. Today, the ground floor of the Old Capitol is Georgia's Old Capital Museum, where you will see exhibits and interpretations of the historical and cultural heritage of Milledgeville. Since 1879, Georgia Military College, a two-year junior college, now utilizes the gothic style capitol.

While Milledgeville served as Georgia's capital city, eight governors lived in The Old Governor's Mansion, from 1839 until 1868. The remarkable historic building was built in high-style Greek Revival architecture, and was designated a National Historic Landmark in 1973. One of the most outstanding and influential governors to serve Georgia and live in the Mansion was Governor Joseph E. Brown. He was governor during three important periods of Georgia's history: the Antebellum period, the Civil War, and the Reconstruction. During General William Sherman's "March to the Sea" the Governor's Mansion was confiscated to be used as Union headquarters, and thousands of Union soldiers marched through Milledgeville. Just four years later the government seat was moved to Atlanta and the Mansion was used as a barracks for the Georgia Military College cadets, and has been a part of the Georgia College & State University. Recently the Mansion underwent an outstanding renovation and restoration. The building was restored as accurately as possible to its original state in lighting, layout, paint and woodwork. Even the original picket fence around the building was reproduced. The Old Governor's Mansion is located in Historic Downtown Milledgeville on the corner of Clarke St. and U.S. 49 and is open to the public for tours Tuesday-Saturday.

Columns

The best way to discover all that this Antebellum Capital City has to offer is to take a Walking Tour of "Milledgeville's Capitols, Columns & Culture." The Milledgeville CVB will help plan tours and guided trolley tours by appointment. You will be able to tour the historic churches; St. Stephen's Episcopal Church, c. 1841 and the Sacred Heart Catholic Church, c. 1874; the Flannery O'Connor Room in the Georgia College & State University library; the historic Masonic Hall, with its 87-foot unsupported, circular, three-story stairway; and the Old Governor's Mansion, which was occupied by General Sherman.

Surrounding one of the antebellum homes called Lockerly Hall, you'll find the Lockerly Arboretum, one of Milledgeville's beautiful treasures. It is a private, non-profit educational support facility located on 50 acres of the former plantation. Here you will see a fascinating variety of cataloged plants and trees from all over the world. Visitors, students and garden clubs are welcome at no charge.

Another notable point of interest in Milledgeville is the picturesque farm of Andalusia. It was here that the legendary American author Flannery O'Connor lived from 1951 until her death in 1964. She often described the operation of the dairy farm on which she lived, and drew from it many of her characters, settings and situations. The farm is open for public touring Monday, Tuesday and Saturday 10 am-4 pm or for group tours by appointment.

Culture

There are exciting and fun celebrations and festivals held throughout the year in Milledgeville. On the second weekend in April is the annual Spring Tour of Homes, showcasing some of Milledgeville's most beautiful homes. During the week of Halloween is the CVB's annual Haunted Trolley Tour. Take a guided ride through Milledgeville's Historic District and hear the fascinating tales of ghosts and goblins. For fall fun try the Sweetwater Festival held every year on the first Saturday of November. This festival is fun for the whole family. During the Holiday Season a must-see is the Old Governor's Mansion all decked out in authentic 19th century décor. Witness the Mansion transform itself into a true Victorian Christmas delight.

The culture of Milledgeville is also greatly impacted by Lake Sinclair. This lake community provides a beautiful, laid-back venue for living in Milledgeville that draws visitors and new citizens from across the nation. Lake Sinclair was recently declared the "Cleanest Lake in the State." With more than 500 miles of shoreline, it encompasses 15,300 acres for swimming, boating, fishing and camping. Boats dot the horizon of the lake year round and the picnic areas and campsites are always full. Full-service marinas, restaurants and charter services make the lake accessible and fun for visitors, and the "lake people" are extremely friendly and helpful. Lake Sinclair is known to be one of the best fishing holes in the entire country, and a seasonal retreat for Atlantans and snowbirds. Linda Kerce, one of Milledgeville's most successful business people has a beautiful home on the lake and is known as one of the city's most celebrated entertainers. During the holidays you will see her entire estate outlined in lights across the lake.

There are so many wonderful places to see and people to meet in Milledgeville. You will love the easy-going gait of the people and enjoy being part of their beautiful community; even if it is just for a short visit. There are wonderful shops to discover, fantastic cafés to try, historic museums to explore and a beautiful lake that will afford hours of pleasure on the water. Enjoy your stay in Historic Milledgeville, a welcoming city of "Capitals, Columns & Culture." You won't be disappointed!

For more information, contact the Milledgeville-Baldwin County Convention and Visitors Bureau at 800-653-1804, 478-452-4687 or visit www.milledgevillecvb.com online. Or, contact the Milledgeville Baldwin County Chamber of Commerce at 478-453-9311 or visit www.milledgevillega.com online.

Milledgeville Fairs Festivals & Fun

April
Spring Tour of Homes

August
Hamp Brown Bottom Festival

October
Haunted Trolley Tour

November
Sweetwater Festival

December
Antebellum Christmas at Old
Governor's Mansion
Christmas Parade

The best way to take in the charming town of Milledgeville is to first stop by the Milledgeville-Baldwin County Convention & Visitors Bureau. The Welcome Center is located at 200 W. Hancock St. in an early 1900s building that once served the city as Post Office and then the Library. A two-hour guided trolley tour is available Monday-Friday at 10 am and Saturday 2 pm. Driving through the landmark Historic District includes visits to St. Stephen's Episcopal Church, circa 1841; the Old State Capitol, circa 1807; and Lockerly Hall, circa 1839. Georgia's Old Capital Museum and gift shop is located on the ground floor of the Old State Capitol (Milledgeville was the fourth capital of Georgia) and Lockerly Arboretum showcases a wide variety of flora native to the area. This site encompasses almost 50 acres of gardens surrounding Lockerly Hall, a Greek Revival plantation. Be sure to visit the gift shop at the Milledgeville-Baldwin County CVB for interesting memorabilia and souvenirs. Hours are Monday-Friday 8:30 am-5 pm and Saturday 10 am-4 pm. For more information, call 478-452-4687, 800-653-1804 or visit www.milledgevillecvb.com online.

This charming antique store is located in an 1890s building at 126 S. Wayne St. in Historic Downtown Milledgeville. The shop at its former location in Macon was featured in *Cotton & Quail Antique Gazette* and *Southern Living* magazine. For more than 30 years, owners Dave Sanford and Brenda Morrison have gained knowledge of antiques through furniture refinishing and use this expertise to offer reasonably priced, high-end antiques. Stop by Monday-Saturday 10 am-6 pm to receive a warm Southern welcome and shop in a comfortable atmosphere. Call 478-452-3100 or visit www.camelliacottageantiques.com.

BLACK SHEEP ANTIQUES

When Diana and Ken Brittingham retired, they found a brand new life and career. Diana got the "antique bug" and soon Ken had to buy an entire building to house all of her finds. Black Sheep Antiques, 125 S. Wayne St., is an interesting collection of antiques and home décor with something for every room and everyone. You'll find primitive furniture, antique stained glass and iron pieces, as well as collectible Depression glass and McCoy pottery. Whether you are looking for a massive antique armoire or a small piece of art, Diana and Ken probably have it. Milledgeville old-timers will recognize the building as the old local drug store and soda fountain that was built in 1867. The store's name, by the way, came from Ken, who laughingly says that he was the "black sheep of six children." The store is open Tuesday-Friday 10 am-6 pm and Saturday until 5 pm. For more information, call 478-453-7148.

Grapevine Antiques & More

With two stories filled with more than 50 booths in 30,000 square feet, you are sure to find the perfect treasure at Grapevine Antiques & More. This amazing antique mall is located along the Antebellum Trail in the heart of Historic Milledgeville at 117 W. Hancock St. You will meet the four great owners (long-time friends) and have so much fun shopping this extraordinary collection of fine antiques. Open Monday-Saturday 10 am-6 pm and Sunday 1-5 pm. Call 478-451-0556

Artists & Art Galleries

Villane's

Art Glass Studio

Growing up in a family of artists, Villane Waldhauer remembers aromas of cloves, lavender and turpentine that her mother used to mix her paints. After a 25-year nursing career, Villane finally yielded to her passion of becoming a full-time artist. She began to work with "hot glass" in 2000, perfected the art of glass design, and opened Villane's Art Glass Studio, 103 W. Hancock St. in Milledgeville, "where jewelry is art!" Villane's specialties include paperweights and lampwork beads. Open Monday-Saturday 10 am-6 pm. Call 478-414-8770.

Bed & Breakfasts, Cabins & Cottages

Antebellum Inn
BED & BREAKFAST

Downtown Milledgeville boasts a wealth of beautiful Greek Revival, Classic Revival and Victorian homes and buildings. Among these sparkling gems, along the historic Antebellum Trail is the breathtaking Antebellum Inn, 200 N. Columbia St. Stately columns and wide wrap-around porches create a timeless beauty and grandeur for this premier guest inn. It is the perfect place for weddings, receptions, bridal and baby showers, or family reunions. The Inn features two parlors and five bedrooms with private baths, each dressed in the most luxurious of linens. Every room is equipped with cable television, a VCR, private telephone lines and computer modem hook-ups. Each morning you will enjoy a gourmet breakfast in the elegantly decorated dining room. Antebellum Inn is true Southern comfort at its best. Visit www.antebelluminn.com online or call 478-453-3993.

THE GUEST HOUSE

The Guest House is a charming bed & breakfast, tucked behind an 1840s Victorian-style cottage at 520 W. Hancock St. It is located in Milledgeville's Old Capital Historic District, just one block from The Old Governor's Mansion. The Guest House caters to adults and can be rented either as a one-bedroom or a two-bedroom suite. The suites have private baths, a parlor area, an eating area and private entrance. A deluxe continental breakfast and snacks await you in the kitchen. A washer and dryer may tempt you to an extended stay. Proprietor Betty Snyder has been involved with the arts and local Milledgeville history for the past 30 years and she invites her guests to make themselves at home amid her art and early attic antiques. For more information, call 478-452-3098.

Camping & RV Parks

LITTLE RIVER PARK CAMPGROUND & MARINA

Fishermen have long been attracted to Lake Sinclair, and as soon as they cross into Baldwin County they head for Little River Park Campground & Marina, 3069 N. Columbia St. in Milledgeville. This premier campground and marina is a long-time tradition on the lake, servicing thousands of customers with gas, food and friendly Southern hospitality each year.

Owner Linda Kerce acquired the 16-acre camping/fishing hub from the Gheesling family, who has owned this and the well-known restaurant Choby's since the early 1980s. She has moved the restaurant from its original location just across the street to the park, giving water customers a wonderful place to relax and enjoy some of the best Southern cooking in the state. She has created a pristine community for the extended-stay campers. "This is an absolutely, beautiful area." Linda says, "We have a long stretch of natural area that's never been touched." There are towering pine trees on the water's edge, a perfect place for RVers. There is also a store and covered patio for guests.

Little River Park offers perfect accommodations for tournament contestants with a fully stocked bait and tackle shop, ice, snacks, coffee, hot dogs, and cold drinks. Full-service camping facilities are available year round for RV travelers who want to park and stay awhile. Now with the famous restaurant Choby's on-site, Little River Park is truly full service. You'll love this little Southern slice of heaven. For information or reservations, call park manager David Johnston at 478-452-1605.

Fashion & Accessories

Tré Bella

While Rayna Jones studied at Georgia College and State University, she realized that there was not a unique boutique in Milledgeville that tailored to young college students. Tré Bella, 106 W. Hancock St., definitely fills that gap. It is a slightly Bohemian store filled with scarves, belts, purses, jewelry and clothing from wonderful lines. Rayna carries the styles she loves—unique lines of designer jeans from 7 For All Mankind, and clothes from Free People. You'll see these fun styles in magazines like *Lucky, Marie Claire* and *InStyle.* Her unique hand-made jewelry, navel rings, brooches, toe rings, hair accessories and even cell phone charms are trendy and fun. Tré Bella is open Monday-Friday 10 am-8 pm and Saturday until 6 pm. Call 478-452-3110.

J.C. GRANT COMPANY
JEWELERS

Any stop in Milledgeville should include a visit to J.C. Grant Company Jewelers at 116 S. Wayne St. This is not your ordinary jewelry store. You won't find bright lights and fast talking salespeople here. It is the oldest retail business in town, family-owned-and-operated, and steeped in local history. This jewelry store is a landmark. J.C. Grant Company opened in 1886, and is the area's premier jewelry store with an accredited gem lab, graduate gemologist, as well as on-site repairs for watches and jewelry. But J.C. Grant Company is more than just jewelry! Stop by and take a look at the wonderful gifts and decorative accessories—perhaps you'll find a Milledgeville souvenir or even that special piece you've been looking for. Whatever your interest, J.C. Grant Company is one-of-a-kind and should be a definite stop. Open Monday-Friday 9 am-6 pm and Saturday until 2 pm. Call 478-452-2222.

The Old Governor's Mansion

Milledgeville, Georgia

Completed in 1839, The Old Governor's Mansion is one of the finest examples of High Greek Revival architecture in the nation. Designed by noted architect Charles Clusky, an Irish immigrant, and built by Timothy Porter of Farmington, Conn., The Mansion looms over Milledgeville, with its stately columns and imposing facade. Serving as the residence of Georgia's chief executives for more than 30 years, The Mansion's history encompasses the Antebellum period, the Civil War and the early Reconstruction phases of the state's history. During the Civil War, The Mansion was claimed as a "prize" in the "March to the Sea," when General William T. Sherman headquartered in the building in 1864. Following the Civil War, Georgia's seat of government was relocated to Atlanta in 1868. The Mansion was given to Georgia Normal & Industrial College (currently known as Georgia College & State University) in 1889.

Beginning in the late 1990s, an initiative was begun to return The Mansion to its antebellum splendor. Following five years of intensive historical, structural and material research, The Mansion began its restoration process in November of 2001. Funded through the Georgia General Assembly and a generous grant from the Woodruff Foundation, The Mansion's original layout, colorations, lighting and appearance have been restored with love and care. Of special note are the restored facade and the intricate gilding on the interior dome. Also, a Visitors' Center, which contains a gift store, accentuates the main building.

Stop by 120 S. Clarke St. Tuesday-Saturday 10 am-4 pm and Sunday 2-4 pm, with tours available on the hour. For more information, visit www.gcsu.edu/mansion or call 478-445-4545.

(Color photo featured in front section of book.)

GEORGIA'S OLD CAPITAL MUSEUM

Be an eyewitness to prehistoric Indian cultures that thrived in the Milledgeville area. Learn about Georgia's traumatic secession from the Union in 1861 and the tragic War Between the States that followed. A visit to Georgia's Old Capital Museum gives visitors a glimpse into Baldwin County's rich history, from the founding of Georgia in 1773 through the 61 years Milledgeville served as the State Capital and beyond. Located in the restored 1807 Gothic Revival Statehouse at 201 E. Greene St. on Old Statehouse Square, the museum is only a stone's throw from an ancient Indian mound site. The capitol itself is the earliest public building documented in a Gothic Revival style in the United States. Don't miss exhibits such as the "Long Road to Recovery," which covers the Reconstruction era and the latter days of the 19th century. In "The 20th Century and Beyond Gallery" changing exhibits rotate every few months. The Museum is open Tuesday-Friday 10 am-noon and 1-3 pm, and Saturday 10 am-noon. For more information, call 478-453-1803 or visit http://museum.gmc.cc.ga.us online.

Start with an Awesome Onion, Oysters on the Half Shell, or Buffalo Shrimp. Then get serious with some of the best fried catfish or shrimp you will ever taste. Pile on sides like crispy fries, homemade cole slaw or buttery grits, and you'll have yourself a true Southern meal. Linda Kerce moved the Milledgeville trademark restaurant Choby's across the street to Little River Park. It still retains the same delicious menu items as when the respected Gheesling family started it during the early 1980s. Choby's at Little River has been completely refurbished including a large-covered deck that overlooks Little River Park and Lake Sinclair. Guests can enjoy the outstanding service and wonderful ambience as they dine in the main dining area, the "porch," the deck, or the piano bar. Linda also encourages customers to arrive by boat. You will have help tying up, enjoy a tram ride to the restaurant, and feel comfortable knowing that your boat is in good hands—because Linda owns the Marina too!

Linda Kerce is an amazing hands-on owner. She must never sleep, because she is also the owner of Serenity Wellness Spa & Salon, and Truss Specialties, a long-time respected truss building company. She cheerfully admits to being a workaholic. She says, "My life is centered around work and family. I wake up happy, and go to bed happy." This dynamite Georgia native loves life on the lake and everyone she meets—she never meets a stranger.

Choby's at Little River is located at 3065 N. Columbia St. It is open Thursday-Sunday 4:30-9 pm and Friday-Saturday until 10 pm.

Oh yes, be sure you save room for one of the delicious desserts like Gourmet Turtle Cheesecake, Key Lime Pie or the Chocolate Lovers' Dream —which actually weighs a pound! For more information, call manager Debbie Bailey at 478-453-9744.

This unique, very happening restaurant and bar at 119 S. Wayne St. in Milledgeville is in the large basement of the 1830s Goldstein Building. Dim lighting and soft jazz music set the stage for an impressive menu. From in-house, hand-cut steaks grilled to perfection to crab cakes, lamb chops, seared duck breast and sashimi tuna, there is something for everyone. Be sure to save room for the simply delicious made-from-scratch desserts. Open for dinner Tuesday-Saturday 5-10 pm and cocktails 5 pm-2 am. For reservations, call 478-452-8119.

Salons, Spas & Indulgence

Imagine that you are surrounded by soothing music and exotic fragrances while you sip on a refreshing beverage and revel in a luxurious massage or refreshing facial. As your worries and stress melt away, you are swept into complete serenity. Sound like heaven on earth? It almost is. Actually, you will experience all of this and so much more at the enchanting Serenity Wellness Spa & Salon, 107 Sportsman Club Rd. in Milledgeville. This award-winning European-style salon and spa is a place where a simple cut and curl or body massage becomes a soothing experience for the mind and body.

Owner Linda Kerce admits that pampering and spas are two of her passions. So much so that she usually chooses her vacation destinations based on the spas. After years of visiting spas in the United States and Mexico, Linda decided to bring the special experience home. She is an energetic and savvy businesswoman who spent many years in the construction business. Linda combined her construction know-how with her spa experience to transform a vacant factory into a glorious center for pampering. She considers it her gift to the community. Linda designed Serenity Wellness with all of the special qualities she loved in the favorite spas she had visited in Atlanta, Las Vegas and Cancún. Whether it was the special services, unusual equipment, elegant décor or simply the tranquil feel, Linda worked to bring what she loved most to the Spa. No detail is missed—different rooms, like the Rainforest Room, are decorated with natural, rich textures, luscious plants and fine art.

The staff at Serenity is warm and generous, and more than anything, they want to pamper you so that you look and feel beautiful. Serenity offers a variety of services. If you want a massage, you can choose from Swedish, Sports, Neuromuscular, Deep Tissue and even the heavenly Heated Stone Massage. Or, maybe you'd like to indulge your skin with Serenity's Signature Facial, a special European Seaweed Treatment. If you want to lose inches, try one of

Serenity's ultimate slimming solutions, like the Cellulite Treatment or the European Body Wrap. Other services include manicures, pedicures, hydrotherapy, bronzing, waxing, makeup, hair and more. There really is so much to choose from! From beginning to end, Serenity offers you a premiere spa experience. It even uses the well-known Repêchage products, which offer "Beauty from the Sea," ensuring that you receive only the best. Serenity's unique gift boutique is an absolute must.

You may also want to spend time refreshing your body with physical activity. At Studio at Serenity, you'll be able to slim down, shape up and feel great by attending a group Stott Pilates class or even scheduling a one-on-one training session in the fully equipped Pilates Studio. Linda's latest addition, a complete physical therapy clinic with more than 25 years combined therapist experience, accepts Medicare, Medicaid and most insurance.

"Making people the best they can be," is Serenity's motto, and we're sure that you'll discover that to be true. No matter what you're looking for in a day spa experience, Serenity is sure to have it. Open Tuesday, Wednesday-Friday 10 am-6 pm, Thursday until 8 pm, and Saturday 9 am-4 pm. Visit www.serenitywellnessspa.com or call 478-453-8158.

Discover Newnan / Old Town Sharpsburg

Newnan and Sharpsburg are part of Coweta County, which was part of the Creek Nation, named for the tribe headed by half-Scott, half-Creek William McIntosh, Jr. He surrendered lands to the Federal government in the 1825 Treaty of Indian Springs. The beautiful scenery of Coweta County has drawn film crews from across the world to shoot a number of movies and television shows. It is also home to numerous "famous folk," including the late columnist and author Lewis Grizzard; Ellis Gibbs Arnall, former Attorney General and Governor of Georgia; novelist Erskine Caldwell; football great Drew Hill, and superstars Alan Jackson and Doug Stone. It was also the home of author Margaret Ann Barnes, who penned *"Murder in Coweta County."*

NEWNAN

Historical Newnan was settled around 1828, and became the county seat of Coweta County. It was named for General Daniel Newnan, who was a soldier in both the Indian Wars and the War of 1812. He was also a member of the Georgia General Assembly and later Georgia Secretary of State and a United States Congressman. The founding fathers of Newnan laid out the town in a grid pattern with the impressive courthouse as the center of the town. They named the streets for famous politicians and presidents Washington, Madison, Jackson and Jefferson. You will hear quaint chimes announcing the hour from the bell tower of the courthouse. It has even been the site of many movies and television shows, including the murder trial immortalized in the book, *"Murder in Coweta County."*

The railroad helped to bring economic prosperity to Newnan during the 1800s. In fact, the town was listed as one of the wealthiest towns per capital in the United States. It was during this time that most of its beautiful antebellum homes were built. Fortunately, they were spared by the Civil War. The war came close to Newnan during the Battle of Brown's Mill in 1864, just three miles south of town. This battle resulted in the defeat of Federal troops by Confederate General Joseph Wheeler. General Wheeler's headquarters was one of the mansions in the "City of Homes," Newman's Historic District.

It is called the "City of Homes" because of its remarkable examples of unique architecture. You will find homes in Victorian and Craftsman, Georgian, Greek Revival, Plantation, Colonial and Federal styles in the Historic District. The Historical Society sponsors an annual Tour of Homes, which includes The Male Academy Museum, Newman's first private boys' school.

OLD TOWN SHARPSBURG

This historic village has seen enormous growth and notice of late. The town has become a quaint, charming tourist attraction. Restored buildings have been turned into antique and collectible shops and cafés, and the people are excited about the growth of their beautiful town.

Perhaps one of the best ways to learn about the history of Sharpsburg is to visit one of the town's—and indeed the state's—historic treasures, the old Bridges and Cole Store. For many decades the store was a town center—a place where everyone gathered to buy just about anything they needed, and to share news with neighbors. The building was built more than a century ago, with a brick in the building bearing the date 1861. Many of the Sharpsburg residents remember playing in the store as children, maybe even getting a prized piece of candy from the glass display. The original owners closed the store during the early 1980s, but Sharon Hazel opened it again in 1984 as Old Town Antiques. It is now an emporium for antiques and gifts and retains many of its original features —wonderful remembrances of the town's past.

For more information about Newnan and Old Town Sharpsburg, contact the Coweta County Convention and Visitors Bureau at 800-8-COWETA, 770-254-2629 or visit www.villagesofcoweta.org online.

Newnan / Old Town Sharpsburg Fairs Festivals & Fun

April
Old Town Sharpsburg Spring Festival

July
Fourth of July Parade and Fireworks
Watermelon Festival

September
Coweta County Fair
Newnan Festival Days & Ice Cream Social
Old Town Sharpsburg Fall Festival

October
Downtown Trick or Treat
Taste of Newnan

November
Newnan Holiday Open House
Old Town Sharpsburg Christmas Open House

December
Christmas Parade (Newnan)
Dickens of a Christmas (Newnan)
Newnan's Candlelight Tour of Homes

A visit to Old Town Antiques & Gifts, 132 Terrentine Rd., is truly a walk back in time. Folks from all over the country come to Sharpsburg just to see this historic building and enjoy a glimpse into the past. Locals still know the building as the Bridges and Cole Store, a general and dry goods store that was part of Sharpsburg's history for more than 100 years.

Today, it has been kept historically intact, with original floors, counters, rolling ladders, shelving and a coal bin. Old Town Antiques & Gifts is a remarkable collection of fine antiques and treasures, including owner Sharon Hazel's enchanting Old World Santas. Year-round you'll find Sharon's Santas throughout the store—amazing creations with hand-sculpted faces and boots from clay, and made with antique quilts and fabrics, sheep's wool, fur trim and vintage toys. Each one is hand-made, signed and dated. All are extremely collectible! Open Wednesday-Saturday 10 am-5 pm. Call 770-252-9400. *(Color photo featured in front section of book.)*

Collectors' Corner

Ladies, we have a wonderful day planned for you! It just might take the entire day to see, experience and taste all of the wonderful treats that await you at Collectors' Corner in Sharpsburg. This rambling yellow house, located at 8861 Hwy. 54, is a 22,000-square-foot collection of new and old with a charming tearoom and a friendly staff.

The first floor is a meandering layout of wonderful rooms filled with gifts, home accessories, furniture, collectibles, holiday décor, and so much more. The Thomas Kinkade Gallery showcases the "light illuminating" canvases of the famous artist, with a varied selection of collectibles representing his works. A sunny garden room is filled with whimsical birdbaths, wind chimes, garden gifts and accessories. You'll also love the ladies boutique, which offers a great selection of Brighton products, fashionable clothing, accessories, and an array of exciting jewelry and handbags. For younger customers, another area is brimming with gifts, educational toys, clothing and keepsakes for ages birth to teen. Each room is filled with treasures at every price from lamps, custom florals and tabletop accessories to sumptuous bath/body products and delicious Georgia jams, jellies and can-dies. The second floor is occupied by more than 30 antique dealers who offer a variety of antique furniture, glassware, vintage collectibles, and more.

There is truly something for everyone in this collection of treasures. Open Monday-Saturday 10 am-6 pm and Sunday 1-5 pm. visit www.collectors-corner.net or call 770-251-6835.

Shop till you drop, then relax for lunch or dessert in the charming Jasmine Tea Room, which offers a varied menu of soups, sandwiches, salads and special entrees. The Tea Room is open for lunch Monday-Saturday 11 am-4 pm and Sunday noon-4 pm. Call 770-254-8564. *(Color photo featured in front section of book.)*

Hotels & Inns

Newnan is a historic treasure and picturesque town nestled in the countryside, just 38 miles south of Atlanta. Surviving the Civil War intact, it is known as the "City of Homes" for its wealth of antebellum structures. Newnan's unique location and size create an atmosphere of metropolitan culture and small town ambiance.

The friendly faces at the Comfort Inn invite you to enjoy the atmosphere, culture, history and hospitality that are uniquely Newnan. Located at 590 Bullsboro Dr., it is the perfect place for a relaxing break and to "take in the sights." The hotel features spacious rooms with hi-speed Internet, cable TV, micro/fridge, iron, hair dryer and coffee maker. Stay one day, stay two, stay awhile, or simply stay—you just might like what you find! Visit www.choicehotels.com/ires/hotel/ga294 or call 770-502-8688.

Photography

RICHARDS STUDIO OF PHOTOGRAPHY

Even the most camera-shy person will love having their picture taken at Richards Studio of Photography. Owners Eric and Dawn Richards are devoted to making you feel at ease in front of the camera. Eric is a Certified Professional Photographer and achieves a timeless quality in his work. With Richards Studio, 149 Main St. in Sharpsburg, your photos will be more than another picture—they will be a work of art. Call 770-252-4250 or visit www.richardsstudio.us.

Quilts, Needlework & Stitchery

Mitchell's Last Chance Gift Shop

Jean Mitchell is known far and wide as "The Quilt Lady," and this suits her just fine. "I've been quilting all my life," says the soft-spoken artist, "since I was about eight years old." Jean's mother taught her and her sister the art of quilting using flour sacks for fabric, and it has been her passion ever since. Residents of Old Town Sharpsburg are used to seeing Jean at her quilting frame in the front yard of her store, Mitchell's Last Chance Gift Shop, where she displays her beautiful creations for sale. She quilts eight hours a day. "The more I quilt," she says, "the more I want to quilt." Jean's quilts have been showcased at the Modern Primitive Gallery in Atlanta, and grace the homes and businesses of collectors throughout the country. Visit her gift shop at 176 Terrentine Rd. in Old Town Sharpsburg Tuesday-Saturday 10 am-5 pm. You'll have the chance to visit with Jean and maybe even get the chance to see her at work on one of her masterpieces. For information, call 770-927-6204.

Discover Perry

City leaders invite visitors to "Stop, Shop, Stay and Play in Perry," a quaint, charming town with the population of 10,000 in the heart of Georgia. Perry was founded in 1821 through a treaty with the Creek Indians, incorporated in 1824, and remains as the county seat of Houston County. It was named in honor of Commodore Oliver Hazard Perry for his triumph at Lake Erie in the War of 1812. The town is located on Big Indian Creek, which attracted early settlers to take advantage of the fertile soil and favorable climate for cotton, peaches, pecans, grains and peanuts. The earliest industries in the town were cotton gins, gristmills and sawmills.

Because of its location at the intersection of four highways, Perry is called the "Crossroads of Georgia." Its location has had a tremendous impact on tourism throughout Perry's history, making it the town's number one industry today. Perry is also located in the Historic Heartland Region and is an important part of the Georgia Antiques Trail, the Golden Isles Parkway, the Peach Blossom Trail and the Andersonville Trail. Another important contributor to the growth of tourism in Perry is the New Perry Hotel. The historic hotel, then known as the Cox Inn, was a vital part of the town's heritage and served travelers dating back to the 1800s. Today, there are more than 23 hotels in Perry.

Celebrations and Festivals

Perry is a city of many festivals, including the Mossy Creek Barnyard Festival held in April and October each year. Whiffs of award-winning barbecue cooking over open pits, sounds of fiddles and children with painted faces welcome visitors to this favorite celebration. It's held among the old homestead buildings that are scattered throughout the terraced woods. You will enjoy bluegrass bands and dance teams. You can even take a lesson in playing mountain dulcimers. Old-timers are at work making soap, building wooden canoes, carving decoys, building fishing rods, making pottery and cracking bullwhips. Kids will love piling into a hay wagon for an old-fashioned hayride and petting the friendly farm animals. It's fun for the entire family!

The Georgia National Fair is held annually in October; a 10-day event that celebrates Georgia's youth, agriculture and heritage. There are food booths, midway rides, street entertainers, exhibits and nightly fireworks. Concerts at the Reaves Arena feature top-billed entertainers, and you might even see a circus performance. The Fair is held at the Georgia National Fairgrounds & Agricenter, which is a state-of-the-art facility on 1,100 acres. This multi-purpose facility is also the center for annual trade shows, livestock events, horse shows, fairs and sporting events.

Shop, Stay and Play in Perry

The renovated downtown area of town is called "Old Perry." It is a charming village with specialty shops and a friendly "down South" atmosphere. Beautiful tree-lined streets, year-round flowers and comfortable benches create an inviting welcome for visitors. Poke through antique shops and bookstores, then have lunch or grab a cup of coffee and piece of pie from one of the sweet cafés or restaurants.

The self-guided walking/driving tour of Perry starts and ends at the New Perry Hotel on Main Street. This historic hotel was the original stop for the stagecoach, built in the 1850s. From there you'll see historic homes and churches, the oldest bank in Houston County, the Sam Nunn Museum, the Masonic Lodge, the Houston County Courthouse, and the Perry Players Community Theatre.

Finding a great place to stay in Perry is definitely no problem. Besides the beautiful landmark New Perry Hotel, there are many hotels, inns and RV parks to choose from. Whether you plan to stay for a day or a week, we know you'll have a wonderful "Southern experience" in Perry, Georgia.

For more information about Perry, contact the Perry Area Convention and Visitors Bureau at 478-988-8000 or visit www.perryga.com online.

Perry
Fairs Festivals & Fun

February
Georgia National Rodeo

March
Peaches to the Beaches Antiques
and Yard Sale

April
Beltista Home and Garden Show
Mossy Creek Barnyard Festival
Perry Dogwood Festival

July
Big Bang Boom – July 4th
Celebration

October
Fall Challenge/Taste of Perry
Georgia National Fair
Mossy Creek Barnyard Festival

November
Best of Downtown Perry

December
Christmas at the Crossroads

Known as "The Crossroads of Georgia," the quaint, but thriving, city of Perry will remind you of a time when gentility and hospitality were the norm. Its beautiful Dogwood tree-lined streets and colorful azaleas and camellias will take your breath away. You'll enjoy joining in the many celebrations that occur here throughout the year—fairs, festivals, craft shows and concerts. This cherished town is part of Georgia's famous Antique Trail and home to the Georgia National Fairgrounds & Agricenter. The Fairgrounds has grown to 1,100 acres and is dedicated to giving Georgia's youth a place to show, learn and compete in the annual Georgia National Junior Livestock Show and Rodeo. A visit to the Perry Area Convention & Visitors Bureau at 101 General Courtney Hodges Blvd. is the best way to discover all Perry has to offer. The CVB is open Monday-Friday 8:30 am-5 pm and Saturday 10 am-4 pm. Call 478-988-8000 or visit www.perryga.com.

Antiques

CARRIE LYNN'S ANTIQUES

Carrie Lynn's Antiques may be the best-kept secret in Middle Georgia. Located in a charming 1920s bungalow at 901 Northside Dr., it is filled with an amazing selection of quality antiques and home décor. Owner Jillinda Falen has been dealing in antiques for more than 20 years and writes a weekly "Antiques" column in Perry's local newspaper. She is also an estate liquidator, so her inventory is constantly changing. Open Monday-Saturday 11 am-5:30 pm. Call 478-218-7754 or visit www.antiquesingeorgia.com online.

Joe and Connette Gayle began buying wonderful antiques years ago, and stored many in an old backyard shed. People began to call and come by to ask, "What do you have in 'the shed'?" So, they opened Antiques From The Shed in 1975, with an emphasis on Early Americana and country furniture. Their specialty niche is "pre-machine" antiques, and any piece with a history. The Shed is located at 1139 Macon St. in Perry and is open Monday-Saturday 10 am-5 pm. Call 478-987-2469.

Easy Living Garden Center
Antiques & Collectibles

Easy Living Garden Center is a unique store with lots of charm and Southern hospitality. This family-owned business in Perry carries a variety of reasonably priced antiques, collectibles, garden accessories and much more. Don't miss the historical landmarks located within the Center and say hello to Petie and Angel—the resident Jack Russell terriers that love to greet customers. Stop by Easy Living Garden Center at 400 N. Perry Pkwy. Monday-Saturday 9 am-5 pm or call 478-987-8910.

GEORGIA NATIONAL FAIRGROUNDS & AGRICENTER

The Georgia National Fairgrounds & Agricenter is a state-owned, multipurpose 1,100 acre complex. It is the site for conventions, meetings, livestock and horse shows, concerts, rodeos, RV rallies, trade shows, and sporting events; a center for diverse activities in Perry. Since its opening in June 1990, the Agricenter has attracted more than 11 million people. The state-sponsored Georgia National Fair runs for 10 days starting on the fifth Friday after Labor Day. The "Top 50 North American" Fair has won 56 International Association of Fairs and Expositions (IAFE) awards for its agricultural, competitive exhibits, and communications programs. The  Georgia National Fair has been designated a Southeast Tourism Society "Top 20 Event for October" nine times. The Georgia National Junior Livestock Show & Rodeo takes place in late February. The Georgia National Fairgrounds & Agricenter is your family's center for year-round events! Visit www.gnfa.com online or call 478-987-3247.

Children's

Established in 1979 in Historic Downtown Perry, the Sugarplum Tree, 917 Carroll St., has continued to garner raves through the years for its beautiful clothing and old-fashioned customer service. Nancy Jackson strives to provide a selection of children's clothing and gifts that cannot be found in malls or department stores. And, she keeps customers returning by constantly changing the lines offered and only using manufacturers who will stand behind the quality of their merchandise. You'll love the fact that Nancy still provides many services like layaway, free gift-wrapping, baby registry and monogramming. Sugarplum Tree is open Monday-Friday 10 am-6 pm and Saturday until 5 pm. For more information, call 478-987-0970.

Fashion & Accessories

MeMe's
On Carroll

The window display at Meme's On Carroll, 913 Carroll St. in Perry, gives you just a hint at the captivating personality of the owner Diann Hutcheson. Her personality and flair for fashion and jewelry make it a fun, trendy place to shop. Diann worked in the corporate world and then as a stay-at-home mom until fulfilling a childhood dream of owning her own boutique. Meme's features fashions with lines such as James Jeans and Bentley A. Stop by Tuesday-Saturday 10 am-5 pm or call 478-987-0642.

Long-time friends Francie Hargrove and Marti Tolleson combined their talent and flair to create this beautiful store. Two Friends, 909 Carroll St., is filled top-to-bottom with a little of everything—Vietri dinnerware, monogrammed bags and purses, fabulous jewelry, and so much more. It is a "must see, must visit" store in Perry that will become one of your favorite places to shop. Open Tuesday-Friday 10 am-5:30 pm and Saturday until 5 pm. Call 478-987-0751 or visit www.twofriends2.com.

This warm and friendly gift shop is filled with lovely accessories, furniture and custom-made floral arrangements. Carlton Interiors, 903 Carroll St. in Perry, features beautiful lamps and accessories by Chelsea House, custom-made jewelry by Anthony Alexander, and jackets by Anage. Owner Joyce Carlton can also help you with your home interior design. Visit Carlton's Monday-Saturday 10 am-5 pm. For more information, call 478-987-4511.

Hotels & Inns

The original Perry Hotel was built in 1870 to accommodate the stagecoach line and the railroad extension into town. Later the New Perry Hotel was rebuilt on the same site, 800 Main St., and still maintains the historic ambiance of its glorious past. The hotel stands in a magnificent flower garden that blooms year-round. The 25 hotel rooms and 17 poolside rooms are beautifully dressed with fine furniture and luxurious bedding. Please visit www.newperryhotel.com or call 478-987-1000.

As one of the nation's leading chains of quality, value-priced hotels, the Hampton Inn in Perry, at 102 Hampton Ct., lives up to its reputation for excellent service and outstanding amenities. Coffeemaker, wireless high-speed Internet and movie channels are standard in all of the comfortable rooms. Guests are also treated daily to a complimentary hot breakfast bar and a newspaper. For more information, call 478-987-7681, 800-426-7866 or visit www.hampton.com.

JONES JEWELERS, INC.

This "old-fashioned, small-town" jewelry store has been a Perry landmark and treasure for more than 55 years. Barbara Jones continues the tradition her parents began long ago in Jones Jewelers, Inc., 904 Carroll St. Jones Jewelers specializes in fine jewelry, china, crystal, Georgia Historical plates and first-rate costume jewelry. The store is now serving a second generation of brides in Middle Georgia. Open Monday-Friday 10 am-5:30 pm and Saturday until 4 pm. Call 478-987-1531.

THE RESTAURANT
at the NEW PERRY HOTEL

Beautiful gardens along with Southern charm create a warm atmosphere for two or 200 at The Restaurant at the New Perry Hotel. Breakfast, lunch and dinner are served in the same timeless tradition known for generations, with great menu selections. The Tavery, a full-service tavern, is located on the property and offers outdoor seating, where locals and tourist gather to relax. Whether sharing a meal, a cocktail or planning a wedding, you will find quality and service are always their goals. Stop by 800 Main St., visit www.newperryhotel.com or call 478-987-1073.

Sweet Southern hospitality is always on the menu at The Front Porch Tearoom, 922 Carroll St. Betty Hotchkiss and Sandra Morgan have created a beautiful place with an inviting charm—the perfect setting for a delightfully elegant lunch or tea. A light lunch or tea is served Tuesday-Saturday 11 am-5 pm, and a full-afternoon tea is offered by reservation. Enjoy lunch on the main floor or reserve The Attic, a banquet room that overlooks Historic Downtown Perry for a special event for adults or children. Call 478-987-1866 or visit www.frontporchtea.com.

 **Card Carousel**

This is the perfect place to sit for a while, listen to good music, enjoy a refreshing Blue Bell ice cream cone, or a cup of freshly ground coffee, and then shop. Card Carousel, 807 Carroll St., is a unique combination of collectibles, ice cream, coffee, and of course, wonderful Hallmark cards. After retiring from the Perry Hospital, Nadine Weems worked at the Card Carousel part-time for six months before purchasing it in 1998. She still loves every minute of her day—meeting new people, scooping ice cream, and telling them about Historic Perry. Don't miss the magnificent dolls by Madame Alexander. Card Carousel is open Monday through Friday 9:30 am-5:30 pm and Saturday until 5 pm. For more information, call 478-987-5211.

Discover
Rome / Cave Spring

You won't be hearing "Buon Giorno" here in Rome, unless it's followed of course by "Y'all!" Rome, Georgia, like its big sister in Italy, has become known as the "City of Seven Hills," but it is Southern through and through. The rebirth that began in downtown became the finest Victorian city center in Georgia, with a thriving downtown area now referred to as the, "Between the Rivers Historic District." The spires, turrets and grotesques that adorn the downtown area are links to a past filled with legend and adventure.

Historic Rome

Rome wasn't built in a day! Historians tell us that Hernando DeSoto may have passed through the area as early as 1540, and was later inhabited by the Cherokee and Creek Indians. The city is surrounded by the Etowah, the Oostanaula and the Coosa Rivers, and was originally known as "Head of Coosa." During this time, it was a thriving little community where some of the Indians owned businesses. Major Ridge and John Ross, prominent Cherokees in Rome, owned ferryboats, farms and a trading post. The abundance of water and timber and the seven hills made it a perfect place for a trading center and town.

During the late 1830s, the interaction of the white settlers and Cherokees was important to the history and shaping of what is now known as Rome. One of the last Cherokee's in Rome was John Ross who was forcibly evicted from his home before Rome could be founded. The town's name was changed to "Rome" by men who discovered the area and knew it had the appropriate resources to be a prosperous city. The name was suggested because the area's seven hills were similar to the "Seven Hills" in Rome, Italy. Eventually, the name was one drawn out of a hat! Rome received its charter in 1834 and soon became a main river port between Alabama and Georgia.

Unfortunately, Rome suffered terrible damage and loss during the Civil War. Many of the churches and buildings on Broad Street were used as hospitals for both Union and Confederate soldiers and headquarters for the Union troops. When General Sherman and his troops left Rome, they burned most of the city.

Rome was literally rebuilt from the ashes. The three rivers, which had attracted the city's earliest founders, once again provided water and a source for manufacturing and new life. Today Rome is a diversified hub of Northwest Georgia–a world-class destination.

Rome's Seven Hills

The seven hills of Rome include Myrtle Hill, Blossom Hill, Jackson Hill, Lumpkin Hill, Old Shorter Hill, Clocktower Hill and Mount Aventine.

Myrtle Hill is named after the Vinca minor, commonly called myrtle or the flower of death, that grew wild on the hill. Myrtle Hill Cemetery replaced the original Oak Hill Cemetery, and is listed on the National Register of Historic Places. One thing that makes Myrtle Hill Cemetery so unique is that it is the only location in the State of Georgia where a First Lady of the United States is laid to rest. During the Civil War, this hill's elevation made it a chosen "look out" spot by the Union army. Today, it is a beautiful landscape of terraced slopes, beautiful oaks and magnolias. **Blossom Hill** is the location of the Bruce Hamler Water Treatment Plant, which pumps more than 10 million gallons of water each day from the Oostanaula and Etowah rivers. **Jackson Hill** is located on the south end of Blossom Hill, and is the location of the Rome Convention and Visitors Bureau, Rome Visitors Center and Coosa Valley Regional Development Center. The hill was the original site of Fort Norton from 1863-1864. **Lumpkin Hill** is one of the original Rome cemeteries, known as Oak Hill Cemetery, where many of the original townspeople were buried. **Old Shorter Hill** began as the Cherokee Baptist Female College in 1834, which was later renamed Shorter Female College. Several other educational facilities utilized the site before demolition in the late 1970s. The stone walls that line Third Avenue today were once the walls from the college. **Clock Tower Hill** is perhaps Rome's most recognized and most visible landmark. Listed on the National Register of Historic Places, the Clocktower stands in the center of town. Mr. James Noble, Sr. formerly of Cornwall, England led the movement to upgrade the city's water supply with the proposed construction of the water tower. The clock was added in 1872. The structure is 104 feet tall with a nine-foot face. The clocktower has commemorated the history of Rome for 134 years and welcomes visitors by announcing each hour with a beautiful chime. The last of the seven hills is **Mount Aventine**, a four-acre enclave between S. Broad Street and the Etowah River, which was developed in 1875 and is named after ancient Rome's Mount Aventine. During the middle 1800s, workers at the Noble Foundry would test fire cannons across the Etowah River into Aventine's northern ridge. It is also the location of a Jewish cemetery dating back to the 1875.

The Chieftains' Major Ridge

One of Rome's fascinating attractions is the Chieftains Museum/ Major Ridge Home. It is a site on the Trail of Tears National Historic Trail, and was the house and property of the prominent early 19th century Cherokee leader Major Ridge.

Who was this famous Cherokee warrior who paid with his life in an effort to save his people? Major Ridge was a full-blood Cherokee warrior who was known as "Ca-Nung-Da-Cla-Geh," which meant "he who walks on mountains." The whites simply called him "Ridge." He was a fierce warrior in the last series of border wars against the white settlers in Georgia, and was reported to have taken many scalps during his youth. He married a Cherokee woman named Susanna (Sehoya) Wickett, and built a homestead in the area around 1800. When Andrew Jackson, during the war of 1812, bestowed the rank of Major upon Ridge, he took it as his first name. When the U.S. decided to move all of the Indians to Oklahoma during the early 1830s, Major Ridge tried to convince others that the only way to save their people was to move west. He was shot during an ambush after he settled in the Cherokee's new home. He was considered to be a traitor by his people due to his act of signing the treaty for the removal of the Cherokees to modern day Oklahoma. His original log framed cabin home is called "Chieftains." It served as a trading post for the Indians. Today, it is the location of Chieftains Museum/Major Ridge Home. It tells the Ridge story with permanent exhibitions, a diorama of a 16th century Indian Village and Cherokee pottery recovered during excavations on the site.

Oak Hill – The Martha Berry Museum

The beautifully preserved 170-acre estate and home of Martha Berry is located just outside downtown Rome at Oak Hill. Martha Berry is considered one of the most outstanding women in Georgia history. With a desire to educate the poor rural Appalachian youth, Berry founded a log-cabin school that eventually became Berry College, one of the premier small colleges in America. The Martha Berry Museum is located on the grounds of Oak Hill and houses a collection of Berry memorabilia.

CAVE SPRING

Just 15 miles southwest of Rome, you'll find the historic, Southern community of Cave Spring. The town is named for the natural limestone cave and spring just off the square in Rolater Park. The cave is filled with incredible stalagmites and a legendary "Devil's Stool" formation. It is believed to be the site where the early Cherokee Indians held their tribal meetings. The spring water has won awards for its purity. You can bring your own jug and fill up!

A day in Cave Spring means a day of wonderful shopping and history. It has more than 90 historic buildings and sites listed on the National Register of Historic Places. The town boasts a lovely square with a variety of shops and diners. If you love antiquing, Cave Spring is definitely the place to shop. It is filled with charming antique stores.

For more information about Rome, contact the Greater Rome Convention and Visitors Bureau at 800-444-1834, 706-295-5576 or visit www.romegeorgia.org online. Guided tours of Myrtle Hill Cemetery and Historic Downtown Rome available.

Rome / Cave Spring Fairs Festivals & Fun

January
Martin Luther King Celebration

April
Steeplechase Kingston Down
Single A Affiliate Rome Braves
Season Opener

May
British Car Show at Berry College

June
Cave Spring Arts Festival

July
Georgia Cup Pro-Am Cycling

September
Rome International Film Festival
Armuchee Blue Grass Festival
Berry Ford Festival
Running Water Pow Wow and
Ripe Corn Festival

October
32nd Peach State March
Festival
Chiaha Harvest Festival
Trick or Treat on Broad Street
Trout Unlimited Chili Cook-Off

November
Christmas Parade
Fine Wine Festival

December
Candles and Carols of
Christmas Past
Holiday Art Space Tour

GREATER ROME CONVENTION AND VISITORS BUREAU

The historic and natural beauty, along with the sweet welcoming smiles of her people, draw visitors from across the country to the small Southern city of Rome. The quaint Victorian charm and architecture of the "Between the Rivers Historic District" makes this beautiful Main Street City a favorite place to visit. The Greater Rome Convention and Visitors Bureau's Visitor Center is located at 402 Civic Center Dr. in the 1901 Historic Train Depot, with an attached caboose serving as the Last Stop Gift Shop featuring Rome gifts. This is the best place to start your day of discovery. Stop by Monday-Friday 9 am-5 pm and Saturday until 3 pm. For more information, call 706-295-5576, 800-444-1834 or visit www.romegeorgia.org.

ANTIQUES ON BROAD

When driving through the Historic District of Rome, a stop by Antiques On Broad, 114 Broad St., will not leave you disappointed. Located in a beautiful 19th century building that originally housed a hardware store, you'll find 7,500 square feet of the finest antiques ever assembled. Approximately 50 dealers offer antiques, fine furniture, home décor, vintage jewelry and linens. You'll quickly realize that you've stepped into a decorator's shopping dream.

Fueled by her love of antiques, owner Patsy Lake has created a stunning display of antiques with a welcoming atmosphere. Antiques On Broad is open from 10 am-5:30 pm Monday-Saturday and 1-5 pm on Sunday. For more information, call 706-295-0015.

Fine European and American antiques, estate jewelry, antique Persian rugs, and more than 2,500 volumes of used and rare books are at home here in The Roman Antique Mall & Expo in Rome. This historic building at 233 Broad St. has been renovated with great care to preserve the original heart pine floors, brick walls and high tin ceilings. With 15,000 square feet, the building holds more than 40 booths and consignment items. Take a walk through the past and enjoy their great selection of furnishings, pottery, crystal, china and antique art. Periodically there is a free Appraiser's Corner and book signings by Rome area writers. Owner Julie Armas has honored her late mother, Carolyn Atkins' passion for antiques by creating one of Georgia's most charming antique malls. Open Monday-Saturday 10 am-6 pm and Sunday 1-5 pm. Call 706-290-1900 or visit www.theromanantiquemall.com.

Country Roads Antique Mall

Vintage glassware and antique furniture from 1850-1950 and everything in between is at Country Roads Antique Mall. Since opening in 1987 at 19 Rome Rd. in Cave Spring, it has grown to include 30 dealers who offer quality antiques and collectibles. Open Monday-Saturday 10 am-5 pm and Sunday 1-5 pm. Call 706-777-8397.

Christa Grant has always said she was "born 100 years too late." Her love and passion for preserving history led to her amazing business Christa's Etc., 10 Alabama St. in Cave Spring. Christa's is an extraordinary collection of fine antiques, restored lamps, great collectibles, and much more. Call 706-777-3586.

Art Galleries

Established in 1976 to provide arts programs and services for Rome and Floyd County, the Rome Area Council for the Arts (RACA) produces, presents and sponsors programs in the literary, performing and visual arts. No matter your age, student to senior, you will enjoy RACA's many wonderful exhibits and programs throughout the year. RACA is located in a turn-of-the-century building at 248 Broad St., and is open Monday-Friday 9 am-5 pm. Older Rome generations will remember the building as the McDonald-Brown General Store, and more recently the McBrayer Bros. Furniture store. The RACA gallery includes painting, pottery, sculpture, photography, printmaking, textiles, woodworking and glass work by local and regional artists. The gift shop also offers books by local authors and artists, as well as tapes and CDs by local musicians and storytellers. You'll love getting this glimpse into Rome Area's artistic past and present. The gallery exhibits change monthly—so visit often! For more information, call 706-295-2787 or visit www.romearts.org.

Children's

Imagine the look of joy on your little girl's face as she gazes through the "nursery window" to select her newborn baby doll. She will apply to adopt, select her very own baby, and then have a picture taken as the nurse gently places the baby in her arms. This unforgettable moment at Ginger's Dollings, 247 Broad St. in Rome, is the only adoption center within "Specialty Shops" in Georgia and is brought to you by Lee Middleton Original Dolls. Owner Suzanne Gay purchased this charming store from her dear cousin, Ginger who opened it more than 20 years ago. They carry a wonderful selection of Rome souvenirs, children's gifts, collegiate items, and locally made Carol Marie's Fudge. You will also find Corolle Dolls, All God's Children, Madame Alexander, Breyer Horses, Ty, Barbie, and more. Ginger's also has a great facility for children's parties. Open Monday-Saturday 10 am-5:30 pm. Call 706-232-1260.

Smartypants

This upscale resale boutique for tots to teens is Rome's exclusive children's consignment shop. Julie Roberts is the young, energetic owner of Smartypants, 514 Broad St. As a teen, Julie learned to make her clothing allowance stretch by being an avid resale shopper. She studied fashion merchandising and design in college and had several years in retail management and international staffing before opening her cool store. The apple green walls with pink accents provide a fun atmosphere for the children's boutique, which offers a wide selection of gently loved apparel. The shop also features a selection of maternity wear, a collection of new accessories and jewelry, a variety of mirrors, and painted furniture. Visit Smartypants Monday-Friday 10 am-5 pm and Saturday 10 am-3 pm. Call 706-234-8528.

Cosmetics, Health & Beauty Products

Drop by Dragonfly Dreams, 100 W. Second Ave. in Rome, and get what you need for a dreamy home-spa experience. Amy Gossett, a former Respiratory Therapist, carries on a family tradition of soap making and continuously adds new products to her existing line. Amy is also the creator and manufacturer of the internationally known "Mud-n-Scrub" clay foot scrubber sold in fine spas, salons and boutiques. Visit www.clayandsoapstudio.com or call 706-291-9144.

Fashion & Accessories

Two best friends—one fabulous store! Melanie Morris and Mimi Weed grew up together in Rome, and both are from retail families. Mel & Mimi, 203 E. 8th St. is located in a historic 100-year-old Victorian house they have decorated with lots of fun color and attractive displays. They carry a variety of looks and styles in order to appeal to teenagers, single girls, fun moms and even hip grandmothers. It's a great "girlfriend" store! You will find clothes from great lines like Lilly Pulitzer, Karen Kane, Trina Turk, Seven Jeans, and many more. The entire home is filled with Southern hospitality and "bling," and each room holds a mix of fashion clothing and one-of-a-kind gifts. Mel & Mimi's is open Monday-Saturday 10 am-5:30 pm. For more information, call 706-295-4203.

Paula's Silver and Gold

"Life's too short to wear ugly accessories!" At least that's what Paula Conaway says, and she should know. As the owner of Paula's Silver and Gold, she is dedicated to helping her customers find just the right accessories they're looking for. Paula's Silver and Gold, 236 Broad St. in Rome, is a wonderful family owned accessory boutique that houses more than 250 different kinds of shoes, stunning silver and gold fashion jewelry, and fun clothing for sizes juniors to 3X, including petites. You'll find just the goody you're looking for to put the finishing touch on any outfit. It's the perfect combination of style and affordability, with a strong dose of "country" customer service. You may even be waited on by Paula's husband or her nine-year-old son Dallas—a seasoned salesperson-in-training. You truly will receive service with a smile here. Paula's Silver and Gold is open Tuesday-Friday 10 am-6 pm and Saturday until 4 pm. Call 706-232-0033.

Whether you're a Southern belle or a fashion diva, there is always something new and fresh at Country Cousins, 8 Rome Rd. in Cave Spring. Owner Donna Staples first established this wonderful boutique in 1991 as a country gift shop. Through the years it has evolved to specialize in ladies accessories and boutique gifts, including Vera Bradley handbags and luggage, Swarovski crystal jewelry, and Brighton accessories. In fact, Country Cousins is among a select few stores who've been designated as a Brighton "Heart Store" nationwide. You'll definitely want to attend at least one of more than 12 annual events hosted by Country Cousins, featuring new products, sales or just "girlfriend shopping." Stop by Monday-Saturday 10 am-6 pm and Sunday 1-5 pm. Call 706-777-0523.

Furniture, Gifts, Home Décor & Interior Design

When venturing through Rome, don't miss out on the beautiful display of products at The Forrest Interior Design & Gifts, 440 Broad St. After years of working in the industry, owner Nadine Headrick along with her daughter and designer Paula W. Conaway, and friend and designer Crandel Allmon finally decided to "do it on their own—together." With more than 20 years of retail and design experience, this family affair is poised to provide you with whatever the occasion requires. The designers have studied internationally, gaining an extensive knowledge of product and design. Let the design staff change your dreams into reality. Having a hard time dreaming something up? Well, you're in luck. If you see it in a magazine or a book, then they can go out and find it for you, too. From floral arrangements to draperies to just about anything you can think of, they can design it. And, their prices are unbelievable!

People travel from all over the South just to shop at The Forrest. The selections are one-of-a-kind. Visiting anytime would be wonderful, but if you happen to be around during the Christmas season, you're in for a real treat. The whole store is turned into a winter wonderland. By the way, they also do Christmas decorating that will take your breath away. No cookie cutter looks here! They serve both residential and commercial customers and they have decorated for caterers and even the prestigious annual Steeple Chase in Rome. They will travel anywhere, from Florida to California, so if you're looking for that old-fashioned kind of service—the kind you used to get—then the ladies of The Forrest are the right ones for the job. Give them a call, they're waiting for you! Call 706-802-1400 or visit Tuesday thru Saturday 10:30 am-5:30 pm.

the Country CRAFTSMAN

If you've been looking for American country reproductions that accurately interpret the simple hand-built furniture of our forefathers, your search is over. Mike Wofford, owner of The Country Craftsman, 53 Rome Rd. in Cave Spring, has been handcrafting furniture since he was a young boy. He specializes in creating what you want with uncompromising precision and dedication. In his 3,000-square-foot workshop Mike creates one piece at a time using timeless techniques that have been proven over the centuries and still remain the best today. There really is nothing that can top the beauty or strength of a quality handmade piece of furniture. For more information, be sure and give Mike a call at 706-777-8343 or stop by Monday thru Friday 9 am-5 pm and Saturday 9 am-1 pm.

A trip through Rome's Historic Downtown would not be complete without a visit to this wonderful shop. Dasha Style & Color is located between the rivers at 412 Broad St. The shop's aromas of Alexandria's fragrance lamps and coffee from the Appalachian Coffee Company—blended, roasted and bagged in the Blue Ridge Mountains—accentuate an eclectic mixture of children's clothing, gifts, home décor and jewelry. Owners Bruce and Sherri Wallace strive to have a variety of items that are different and unique, like distinctive handiwork of local artisans, craftsmen and manufacturers. Sherri and her son are also artists and you will find their artwork throughout the store. At Dasha Style & Color, you'll find a gift for any reason and any season! Open Tuesday, Thursday-Saturday 11 am-5 pm, and Wednesday until 4 pm. For more information or to schedule an appointment, visit www.dashastyleandcolor.com or call 706-235-5002.

Gourmet & Specialty Foods

Martha Jane's Home Style Fudge

Martha Jane Montgomery was the famous "fudge lady" in Cave Spring for more than 28 years, supplying the town with delicious fudge from her secret recipe. She passed the apron strings down to her daughter Lynn Petty, who has taken her mother's place at the stove in producing mountains of absolutely delicious fudge. Folks follow their noses to Martha Jane's Fudge, 22 Alabama St., where Lynn is busy cooking up batch after batch of fudge in the conventional flavors but also like Tiger Butter, Chocolate Coconut, Rocky Road, Maple Nut and more. It is also a great place to grab a cup of Neighbor's gourmet coffee in flavors like Snickerdoodle or Southern Pecan and browse through the selection of great gifts. Martha Jane's Fudge is open Monday-Saturday 10 am-5 pm and Sunday 1-5 pm. For more information, visit www.marthajanesfudge.com or call 706-777-8544.

Hotels & Inns

Widely recognized in the Southeast by its familiar Southern colonial design, the folks at Jameson Inn strive to provide excellent customer service by making you feel right at home—Southern style. It's the perfect place to have the "perfect stay" every time. From the deluxe-continental breakfast to the great rooms and the wireless high-speed Internet, your needs are being taken care of. So, whether you're spending that special weekend in Rome with friends or you're visiting on business, Jameson Inn is there for you. Because the owners are so proud of their company, a guest loyalty program called Jameson Stock Awards has been added—allowing you as its customer, to share in its growth. So, when planning your trip, remember Jameson Inn is your home away from home. Located at 40 Grace Dr. SE. For more information, call 706-291-7797, 800-526-3766 or visit www.jamesoninns.com.

When the Hawthorn Suites in Rome broke ground in March 2004, an excitement permeated this small Georgia town. The historic early 20th-century building at 100-110 W. 2nd Ave., was getting a new chance at life, once again finding a place in the future of Rome. Less than a year later, construction was finished and the building was dedicated in December 2004. It opened its doors to a new day and time and has become a vital role in Rome's ongoing downtown revitalization. The building was restored to the grandeur of its early days—a link between its history and the present community. Southern hospitality is served up in generous helpings throughout the hotel—from the hot buffet breakfast bar and Waterfront Bar & Grill to the charming gift shops and salons, you'll be pampered and cared for in true Southern style. The hotel features spacious suites, full or efficiency kitchens, exercise facilities, and onsite laundry service.

In every room, you'll see photographs that tell the history of the building and city. Over the last 105 years the building has had many lives. It was home to Champion Garment Co., Riddle Office Supply, and even a roller rink on the 3rd story—the floor is still banked and, for several years the building was home to Battey Machine Company, so many people still call it "The Battey Building." During the early 1980s, the building housed apartments and businesses, but it was closed in the late 1980s and remained empty for more than 15 years. In 2004 a group of visionaries teamed with Hawthorn Suites to create a wonderful new hotel that will provide a beautiful home to future travelers. For more information or reservations, call 706-378-4837, 800-527-1133 or visit www.hawthorn.com.

OAK HILL
& The Martha Berry Museum

You will at once recognize this magnificent antebellum home as the Carmichael Mansion in the film "Sweet Home Alabama." Oak Hill & The Martha Berry Museum stand as a testament to a long-ago genteel time and pay tribute to one of the country's most amazing and outstanding women—Martha Berry.

Martha Berry grew up in a life of luxury in this beautiful mansion, but as a young woman, was always deeply moved by the plight of the poor Appalachian youth. She left the comforts of her privileged childhood home to found a log-cabin school that has grown into one of the premier small colleges in America. Berry College is now located on 28,000 acres and is recognized for its strong academic program and the opportunities it provides for religion-in-life experiences. The Oak Hill Mansion remained in the Berry family until Martha's death in 1942 when it became the property of Berry Schools. Today, the estate is known as Oak Hill and The Martha Berry Museum.

The home has been preserved as it was when she lived there, and serves as a welcome center for visitors. You may tour the entire grandeur of Oak Hill including Aunt Martha's Cottage, the home of Miss Berry's beloved cook and house servant Martha Freeman; the Carriage House, which houses Martha's vintage vehicles; formal gardens and trails; and the Original Cabin, which is known as "The Birthplace of Berry College."

The Martha Berry Museum, the Garden Room and the Oak Hill Meadow are available for special events. Call 706-291-1883, 800-220-5504 or visit www.berry.edu/oakhill, for more information or reservations. Located at 24 Veterans Memorial Hwy. in Mount Berry just outside of Rome.

Restaurants, Special Events & Tearooms

A stroll along Rome's Historic Broad Street is not complete without a stop at Harvest Moon Café—unwind on the patio or the sunny rear deck, or soak up the unique atmosphere inside. Built in 1895 as the Faye department store, it has been converted into a casual, yet urban environment with folk art from around the world.

As featured in *Southern Living*, the eclectic menu "tempts even the stodgiest diner." The Moon is famous for its sweet-potato chips with blue-cheese dip, spicy pimento cheese and huge burgers. If craving something more sophisticated, the crab cakes have received rave reviews. Everything is made from scratch, including all the delicious cakes, desserts and breads. Located at 234 Broad St. and open Monday-Tuesday 11 am-2 pm, Wednesday-Saturday 11 am-10 pm and Sunday 10:30 am-2 pm. Call 706-292-0099 to reserve the mezzanine or for catering services.

To walk into the Victorian Rose Tearoom and Café, 510 Broad St. in Rome, is like walking back in time. You'll love the time you spend here! Owner George Kastanias and his two daughters Dawn and Holly offer afternoon teas along with soups, salads and sandwiches to satisfy your hunger and longing for peaceful relaxation. The quality of service and Victorian era feel will make your experience an excellent one, time after time. Within this original Fire House—the old ones with the horse-drawn fire truck—you can also visit the Red Hat

Boutique. George's mother-in-law runs the boutique! Yes, this is a family venture. Family is important to George, as seen in his community work at the local soup kitchen and family resource center. Don't miss this one! Open 11 am-4 pm Monday-Friday. Call 706-232-3911.

Linen tablecloths, beautiful glassware and fresh-cut flowers create a sophisticated elegance for your special occasion at Magretta Hall. Owner Audrey Polczynski has created an enchanting ambience of a bygone era in the historic building at 201 Broad St. in Rome. Magretta Hall is a full-service restaurant that is perfect for special events, like weddings and wedding receptions, rehearsal dinners, business meetings, or even a simple gathering of special friends. Audrey is

a wonderful chef and caterer, and she brings a wealth of experience and flavor to each event. The Hall is available for parties with 20-250 guests, but Audrey can cater events for as many as 1,000 at the facility of your choice. Don't miss the Southern cuisine lunch buffet on Tuesday and Sunday 11:30 am-2 pm. For more information, call 706-234-6636 or visit www.magrettahall.com.

T. Martooni's
Great Food and Spirits

Who says you've got to be in New York City to experience an upscale Martini Bar? Forget all the chaos that goes with New York City. T. Martooni's Great Food & Spirits—named after Dean Martin's famous flub after one too many martinis—is the place to go and experience the elegant yet casual atmosphere of a fine dining restaurant. Located in Historic Downtown Rome, at 239 Broad St., it is the area's only martini bar. T. Martooni's offers a wide selection of wines and mixed drinks, as well as superb food in a unique 1920s décor. All food and desserts are prepared in house, from the 'Ing-Bing' Spinach and Artichoke Dip to the 'Ritzy' Baked Stuffed Shrimp. Your experience awaits, go uptown, go T. Martooni's. Visit Tuesday-Thursday 5:30-9 pm, and Friday-Saturday 5:30-10 pm. For more information, call 706-295-7070.

Discover Roswell

The Cherokee Indians called it the "Enchanted Land." Located on the northern banks of the Chattahoochee River, Roswell continues to enchant visitors with gentle glimpses of history around every corner. In fact, it is called the town "Where Yesterday Is Not So Long Ago." From the churches, cemeteries and beautiful plantation homes you will discover the history of this town from its Cherokee and Gold Rush beginnings to present day Georgia's 6th largest city. You will also discover that even with so much growth and prosperity, Roswell has been able to retain its small town atmosphere and yesteryear charm. The city's natural beauty is astounding, and it is recognized as a thriving arts community. Outdoor recreational opportunities abound in beautiful parks, nature centers, historical walking tours and fun festivals.

"Golden" Beginnings

The community of Roswell was founded in 1839 by Roswell King, who had been attracted to the area because of the discovery of "gold" in North Georgia. As he traveled the ancient Indian trails along the Chattahoochee River, he discovered the vast forests and waters of Vickery Creek. It was here that he envisioned a mill powered by the rushing water and the beginnings of the community that would soon be known as Roswell. The area had a much earlier history however. It had been a land inhabited by the Cherokee Indians, and white men were forbidden on the land by Georgia law. The lure of gold was stronger than fear of retribution or even danger by the Cherokee, for settlers began to pour into the area and the Indians were forced to adapt to the "white man's ways." In fact, the Cherokee's adaptation to their new life is quite an amazing piece of history. By 1821 one of the leaders named Sequoyah had created an alphabet consisting of 85 letters called the "Talking Leaves." Thousands of Cherokee learned to read and write and even started the first Native American newspaper called "The Cherokee Phoenix." They became shop owners, storekeepers and farmers. Even with this amazing progress, Georgia declared the Cherokee nation illegal and took possession of the land, and President Andrew Jackson approved removal of the native people. They traveled west on the path that would become known as "The Trail of Tears."

Roswell King began work on the community's first cotton mill in 1838, which was later incorporated as the Roswell Manufacturing Company. The success of the mill and the lure of homesites drew families to the area. During the Civil War, the mills played a large part in history. When Brigadier General Kenner Garrard arrived in Roswell in 1864, workers at the cotton mills flew a French flag, hoping that the statement of neutrality would save the mills. When General Sherman later found the claim to be false he ordered the mills destroyed and everyone connected (mostly women and children) arrested and charged with treason. The beautiful homes and churches, however, escaped damage and the city began to rebuild. The mills were rebuilt, and the textile industry once again allowed Roswell to grow and prosper. Visitors can still tour many of the magnificent homes today.

Roswell celebrated its 150th year (Sesquicentennial) in 2004, a city that Mr. Roswell King would be proud of today. Visitors can enjoy tours of Antebellum Barrington Hall, Bulloch Hall and the Archibald Smith Plantation.

Roswell's Civil War Sites

On July 5, 1864 the Union army skirmished with the Confederate soldiers, who were guarding the road to Roswell. Their mission was to capture Roswell's covered bridge entry to the city. In order to avoid the Union army gaining access through the bridge, Confederate Capt. James R. King, grandson of City founder Roswell King, ordered that it be burned. The Covered Bridge Site is 50 feet downstream from the Roswell Road Bridge. The burned bridge was rebuilt in1869 and stayed in use until 1925 when it was replaced by the current bridge. The Woolen Mill Site is the site of the Ivy Woolen Mill, which produced items for the Confederacy, and became Union General Dodge's headquarters during occupation. Shallowford Site was the waist deep river site where the Union Calvary fought their way across, causing the Confederate troops to retreat to defenses around Atlanta. The Entrenchments South of the River are the remains of the entrenchments constructed by the Union forces to secure the army's hold of the south shore of the river. More than 27,000 soldiers camped between these entrenchments and the river. The Roswell Presbyterian Church on Mimosa Blvd. was built in 1840 and served as a Union hospital. Much to the dislike of Rev. Nathaniel Pratt, mass was given to the Union solders here. Great Oaks - Rev. Nathaniel Pratt's House, served as Union Army 15th Army Corps headquarters for General John Logan. The Roswell Cotton Mills, on the banks of Vickery Creek, were constructed in 1853, and burned by Union forces on July 7, 1864. Only the brick foundations and a few walls remain. And last, McAfee's Bridge Site, was a covered toll bridge built in 1834, and was the site of a skirmish in July 1864. The bridge was destroyed by the Union forces.

Shopping and Dining in Roswell

Crispy fried chicken, homemade biscuits and gravy, fried green tomatoes, and of course outstanding barbecue are all on the menu in Roswell—along with a cool glass of sweet tea of course. You will be delighted with the variety of fine restaurants, cafés and tearooms in Roswell, serving down home country to elegant continental cuisine. In period buildings to tiny tucked away downtown corners, you'll find wonderful places to enjoy lunch or dinner.

Antique markets, gift shops, bookstores and art galleries will draw you inside their charming shops with a selection of items that rival the stores of Atlanta (without the traffic!). We know you will enjoy your "Lady's Day Out" in beautiful and charming Historic Roswell.

For more information about Roswell, contact the Historic Roswell Convention and Visitors Bureau at 800-776-7937, 770-640-3253 or visit www.cvb.roswell.ga.us online.

Roswell Fairs Festivals & Fun

February
Roswell Roots

March
Great American Cover-Up Quilt
Show

May
Colors Festival of Arts
Concerts Series (May-October)
Memorial Day Ceremony and
Picnic
Roswell Artwalk

June
Roswell Magnolia Storytelling
Festival

July
Butterfly Festival
Fourth of July Fireworks
Extravaganza

August
Roswell Heritage Music Weekend

September
Labor Day Celebration &
Fireworks
Raiford Gallery Anniversary
Show
Roswell Arts Festival
Roswell Historical Society
Antique Show & Sale

October
A Haunting of the Hall
Halloween Hikes
The Roswell Woman – Health,
Beauty and Fitness Expo
The Taste of Roswell
Youth Day Parade and
Celebration

November
Genesis Annual Art Exhibit

December
Christmas in Roswell

BULLOCH HALL &
ARCHIBALD SMITH PLANTATION HOME

Built in 1840 by Major James Stephens Bulloch, grandson of Governor Archibald Bulloch, Bulloch Hall has been described as one of the most significant homes in Georgia. This magnificent Greek Revival mansion was the childhood home of Martha (Mittie) Bulloch Roosevelt, the mother of our 26th president Theodore Roosevelt. Mittie's other son Elliot was the father of Eleanor Roosevelt, who married Franklin D. Roosevelt, and became our nation's first lady. The home sits on 16 acres with a third-mile trail that meanders through a big leaf magnolia grove into "Mittie's Garden." The house is open for tours on the hour Monday-Saturday 10 am-3 pm and Sunday 1-3 pm, with the last tour at 3 pm. Visit www.bullochhall.org online or call 770-992-1731.

When Archibald and Anne Smith constructed their Roswell home during the mid 1800s, they had no idea that it would be preserved through many generations as an untouched historical treasure. Now owned by the City of Roswell, the Archibald Smith Plantation Home at 935 Alpharetta St. remained in the Smith family for 150 years, and has become one of the best examples of architectural, cultural and historical interpretation in the region. Visitors may tour 12 original outbuildings on the historic landscaped grounds. Hourly tours are available Monday-Friday 11:30 am-2:30 pm, and Saturday 10:30 am-1:30 pm. For information, call 770-641-3978.

Named after Mittie Bulloch, Theodore Roosevelt's mother, this charming tearoom and café is the perfect place to celebrate any special occasion in Historic Downtown Roswell. Mittie's Tea Room Café, a 20-year tradition, is located at 1169 Canton St. and offers both Low and High Tea luncheon menus for groups and individuals alike. The café is enchanting, with indoor and outdoor seating, and the service is outstanding. You'll have a hard time deciding on one dish, because everything looks and tastes delicious. Quiches are baked in a light oatmeal crust, and the popular crepes are fluffy and tender. With choices like Lob-

ster Bisque, Crab Stuffed Portabella Mushrooms and their famous Chicken Salad, you will want to visit Mittie's time and again. Call 770-594-8822 for more information or catering, or visit www.mitties.net. Open daily, 9 am-4 pm.

Famous for its "fried Cajun pickles" and homemade fare, Andy Badgett's Fickle Pickle Café is a Roswell favorite. Located at 1085 Canton St. in a charming Victorian house, everything is homemade and delicious, right down to the mayonnaise and ketchup. Piled high sandwiches on homemade bread, fresh salads and filling sides make a perfect meal. Of course, you won't want to leave without a carrot-cake cookie!!! Open for lunch Monday-Saturday 11 am-4 pm and dinner Tuesday-Saturday 5-9 pm. Visit www.ficklepicklecafe.com or call 770-650-9838.

It has been said of this magnificent antebellum plantation that, "No home in the South has extended more true and simple hospitality than Great Oaks." Built in 1842, it was the manor house of a plantation that produced sorghum, corn and wheat and home to Reverend Nathaniel A. Pratt, first minister of Roswell Presbyterian Church, and his wife Catherine, daughter of founder Roswell King. Today, The Gardens at Great Oaks is a magnificent setting for your special celebrations, weddings, receptions, private dinners, corporate retreats and the pride of Roswell. A beautiful gazebo graces a traditional English flower and herb garden, and the vegetable garden is a masterpiece. (Be sure to ask James about the

"secret" that makes his garden so prolific!) The Gardens at Great Oaks is located at 786 Mimosa Blvd. For more information or reservations, call 770-693-6010 or visit www.historicgreatoaks.com online. *(Color photo featured in front section of book.)*

As part of Roswell's 640-acre Historic District, the Roswell Convention & Visitors Bureau offers a complete picture of this charming city. The Visitors Center is located at 617 Atlanta St., near antebellum homes, historic sites, art galleries, restaurants, shops, lodging and much more. Numerous tours are available in Roswell and the yearlong calendar is filled with special events. The Visitors Center will provide you with all the details while showing you true Southern hospitality. Open Monday-Friday 9 am-5 pm, Saturday 10 am-4 pm and Sunday noon-3 pm. For assistance, contact the Visitors Bureau at 770-640-3253, 800-776-7935 or visit www.cvb.roswell.ga.us online.

Specialty Shops

Scentimentals Awaken your senses as you step through the doors of Scentimentals, 944 Canton St. in Roswell's Historic District, a boutique specializing in luxuries for you and your home. Certified by the International Fragrance Foundation, mother and daughter owners Anne and Tara, along with their fine staff, offer expertise and guidance as you select from the world's finest fragrances and pampering essentials for bath and body.

Linens, candles, home-care products and accessories help fill this shop with wonderful temptations. Fun things to wear such as trendy tops, jackets and jeans, flirty skirts and dresses, and resort wear from Fresh Produce Sportswear, along with "just have to have it" handbags, jewelry and accessories make shopping at Scentimentals a delightful way to spend the day. Shop Monday-Saturday 10:30 am-5 pm. For more information, call 678-795-9222.

The Shoppes of Plum Tree Village

Influenced by the Queen Ann and Gothic Victorian buildings up and down Canton Street, Buddy and Sandra Milton have created a remarkable 21st Century retail village nestled in the 19th Century Historic District of Roswell. Stop by this pedestrian-friendly retail village that combines the historical charm of the 1800 circa buildings with a contemporary feel of galleries, shops and boutiques. Surrounded by flower gardens and fragrant fruit trees, the Gazebo lends a "South of France" dining atmosphere to this charming collection of shoppes.

The light-flooded **SLM Studio & Gallery**, 770-587-0978, showcases the contemporary mixed-media paintings and sculptures by Sandra Milton.

The BILT-House, 770-552-8581, is an up-scale shop, featuring contemporary women's sportswear and home furnishings, as well as great jewelry and designer accessories. Call 404-816-7702 to find out about the Buckhead location.

Browse through **Uniquities**, 770-998-5557, for eclectic old world furnishings, oriental rugs and gifts from around the world. Window fashions and designer services are also available.

A 150-year-old farmhouse transformed into six rooms of color and whimsy is **V-Originals**, 770-645-0199. You will find handmade items created by each of the five on-site artists.

The **Taylor Kinzel Gallery**, 678-352-1986, showcases a wide variety of original oils, sculpture, glass and unique jewelry.

Relax, strengthen your body and breathe in a beautiful, peaceful environment at **Plum Tree Yoga**, 678-585-0500. Classes are offered seven days, all levels.

For more information on The Shoppes of Plum Tree Village, 1035-1065 Canton St., visit www.plumtreevillage.net online or call 770-992-1200. *(Color photo featured in front section of book.)*

Discover Smyrna

Smyrna is a smart, stylish and fascinating city with a bustling social center, community spirit and sweet hometown feeling. It is called "The Jonquil City" because of the abundance of the fragrant yellow flowers blooming in gardens and along the streets throughout the area. Located only ten miles northwest of Atlanta, Smyrna is a very integral element of the Atlanta Metropolitan area.

The revitalized downtown area, called "The Village Green," is a lively mix of residence and retail, charming homes, vibrant restaurants and unique shops in the bustling social center called the "Market Village." *(Color photo featured in front section of book.)*

Smyrna History

Smyrna was first known as Ruffs Siding, and later as Varner's Station. At one time, all of Cobb County was equally divided between the Cherokee Indians and the State of Georgia. When a settlement deeded all the land to the state in 1831, settlers began to find their way to a religious campground here, which was later permanently established. It became the center of social and religious life of the county, and from this, the Methodist Church was organized in 1838. Religion played such an important part in Smyrna's birth that the people chose a name from the book of Revelation in the Bible for their city. Smyrna was one of St. Paul's seven churches in Asia.

Smyrna Treasures

Start your tour of Smyrna with a visit to Aunt Fanny's Cabin. This historical log cabin is the Smyrna Welcome Center, and has an interesting history. It was originally a restaurant founded in 1941 by Isoline Campbell MacKenna Howell. In 1948, Hester and Marjorie Bowman bought the restaurant and elevated its reputation to almost celebrity status. In fact, many celebrities frequented Aunt Fanny's

Cabin, which was known for its authentic Southern food and rustic atmosphere. The restaurant grew and flourished through the decades, but closed in 1992. The City of Smyrna purchased the original log cabin and moved it to its present location as the Smyrna Welcome Center. Here you will find information on all of the city's local treasures, historic cemeteries, city tours and seasonal festivals.

During the 1980s, Smyrna city leaders decided to take steps to revitalize the downtown area. Their desire was to create a sense of family and community, "a village to call home." This concept became The Village Green, a community center that included a state-of-the-art library, city hall, garden and beautiful arboretum. This was all done in a Williamsburg style, with a brick road that circles a central fountain. It is a beautiful landmark and a tribute to the forward thinkers in Smyrna. The Market Village includes more than 40,000 square feet of retail space and top rated restaurants. Enjoy your visit to Smyrna, we sure did.

For more information about Smyrna, contact the City of Smyrna at 770-434-6600 or visit www.ci.smyrna.ga.us online. Or, contact the Cobb County Convention and Visitors Bureau at 800-451-3480, 678-303-2622 or visit www.cobbcvb.com online.

Smyrna Fairs Festivals & Fun

March
Spring Fling - Easter Egg Hunt

April
Spring Jonquil Festival & Market Village Crawfish Boil

May-July
Summer Concert Series

August
Birthday Celebration

September
Spice of Life – Food & Cultural Celebration

October
Fall Festival & Octoberfest in the Market Village

November
Tree Lighting and Holiday Festivities

December
Saturday with Santa

Children's

A Funky Place To Shop & Play!™

Owners Holli Cash and Cheryl Pefianco call their store, "A Funky Place To Shop and Play!" Planet Me, 1290 W. Spring St., in Smyrna Market Village is a combination of trendy merchandise and unconventional services in a very family-friendly environment. Cheryl and Holli drew their inspiration for their unique store from what they knew best—their children. Using them as their "test market," the ladies filled the store with gifts targeting itty-bittys, tweens, teens and those who will always be young at heart. From the latest toys to trendy jewelry, they have gifts for everyone—even the family pet. Services include complimentary gift-wrapping, birthday party events, a comprehensive gift registry, express call-ahead curbside gift services, personalization, embroidery and shipping. Planet Me is more than a gift shop; it is an intensely personal shopping experience. (And so much fun!!) It is a festive venue to shop for merchandise that is trendy, funky and fun without compromising on solid moral character. For information, call 770-436-4FUN (4386) or visit www.theplanetmeshop.com. Hours are Monday-Wednesday 10 am-7 pm, Thursday until 8 pm, Friday-Saturday until 9 pm, and Sunday 12:30-4 pm.

Fashion & Accessories

Ruby Jean's

Stephanie Townsend comes from a long line of shop owners. And while she draws on her mother's and grandmother's retail expertise, her shop, Ruby Jean's is actually named after a special aunt who is as sweet and Southern as this delightful store. Ruby Jean's is located at 2968 Atlanta Rd. in one of Smyrna's oldest homes. The home, which is known as the "Gautschy House," was built in the early 1900s. Stephanie has filled each room with wonderful women's fashions, fabulous jewelry, and one-of-a-kind accessories for the home and garden. You'll find unique fashions for a special night out, as well as great casual wear and you'll especially love the reasonable prices. There really is something for everyone here. Ruby Jean's is open Monday-Saturday 10 am-6 pm and Sunday noon-5 pm. Call 770-431-4660 or visit www.rubyjeans.net.

THE SHOPPE IN THE BACK

You've probably heard the old saying that "Back Door Guests Are Best." Well, everyone is a special "back door guest" at this bright and fun shop in Smyrna. The Shoppe in the Back is located in Smyrna Market Village at 1295 W. Spring St., and it's as bright and colorful as its creative owner Blaire James. Filled with chic separates for every woman, you'll love this store. Blaire has impeccable taste and a talent for finding unique lines that will flatter every age and shape. She carries beautiful designer clothing, jewelry and accessories, as well as cosmetics and bath and body products. You will find career bags by Marka; flirty, sweet dresses by Plenty; Red Engine jeans; and jewel-neck tunics by Forty. The designs are young and fun, yet classically stylish. Whether you need an outfit for a night on the town or new work attire, Blaire has got you covered! The store is open Monday-Wednesday 11 am-5pm, Thursday-Saturday until 7 pm, and Sunday noon-5 pm, (but you'll have to use the back door!) Visit www.theshoppeintheback.com or call 770-436-9972.

It didn't take long for the people of Smyrna to discover Kara Shaw and fall in love with her beautiful Village Green Flowers & Gifts, 1260 W. Spring St. Kara, with her amazing staff and their artistic talents, as well as the careful selection of high-quality, unique flowers have made this shop a favorite for upscale arrangements and floral design. You might not find the ordinary and overused mums and daisies, because Village Green carries unique flowers like Leptos, Calla Lilies, Bells of Ireland and Hyacinths. The creations are extraordinary and unusual! Many customers love the work so much they have Village Green on retainer for holidays and special occasions!

Whether you need a simple arrangement for your dining room table or your entire house decorated top to bottom for that special occasion, Kara and her staff will work their magic with the fabulous blooms and gorgeous greenery. One of Kara's favorite tips, "Place arrangements next to your bedside so they are the first thing you see in the morning and the last thing you see at night." Village Green Flowers & Gifts is open Monday-Saturday 10 am-6 pm. Visit www.villagegreenflowersandgifts.com online or call 770-435-9393, 866-435-9393.

Gifts & Home Décor

Carole Scott's customers tell her that they come to her beautiful Smyrna shop just to escape their stressful day. Love Street Gifts & Gardens, 1295 Concord Rd. is located in a charming 1920s craftsman's bungalow surrounded by a beautiful garden of year round color. In the garden area, you'll find an amazing selection of yard art, seasonal plants and containers, so you can buy it planted or do it yourself. The shop received *Atlanta Magazine*'s "Best of Atlanta 2004" award for "Best Garden Whimsey." Inside the cottage, delightful rooms burst with wonderful unique gifts and accessories from the whimsical to the sublime. Choose from well-known lines such as Vera Bradley, The Thymes, and many more.

We loved the great jewelry and handbags, as well as the selection of funny cards, napkins, magnets and wall plaques. Open Monday-Saturday 10 am-6 pm and Sunday noon-5 pm. Visit www.lovestreetonline.com or call 770-434-8578.

home accessories

unique gifts

interior design

RED DOOR INTERIORS

There's a question circulating in the quaint town of Smyrna—so, what's behind the pretty "red doors"? Owners Kimberly and John Gangemi have created two very special shops to meet their clients' interior design and home decorating needs. Red Door Interiors—the original store— at 1260 W. Spring St. is located in the heart of downtown at Smyrna Market Village. You'll discover lovely home décor treasures and gift items from candles, artwork and stationery, to unique seasonal gifts. You are sure to find just that special something. Open Monday 10 am-6 pm, Tuesday-Wednesday until 7 pm, Thursday until 8 pm, Friday-Saturday until 9 pm, and Sunday noon-6 pm. Visit www.reddoorinteriors.com or call 770-444-9664.

The newest store, RDI Home is located at 3310 Atlanta Rd., just a short drive from Red Door Interiors. Stop by this location if you are starting a new decorating project, or just looking for that one special item. This unique shop offers a full-line of home furnishings with complete interior design services. RDI Home is open Monday-Saturday 10 am-6 pm.

Karen's Gifts Karen Wilson started her gift shop as a hobby by displaying a few specialty items placed in a small corner of her husband's pharmacy. That "corner" expanded twice, until she finally had to move to its present location at 3988 Atlanta Rd. The joke in Smyrna had been, "Oh your gift shop has a pharmacy!" As a full-time owner, Karen insists that she has the best job in the world—shopping for a living. Gifts from Karen's include all types of local art, woodwork, furniture, baby and collegiate items, special occasion flags and wonderful collectibles from Byers Choice and Gail Pittman. Karen strives to find as many goodies as possible from small companies so that the selection is unique and special. She offers monogramming and engraved jewelry, and her signature gift wrap is always free. Customers love knowing that they can come in, select a gift, and leave with a beautiful present ready to give. You will find something you didn't know you always wanted here, and you will love the friendly attention from this charming Southern lady. No matter the occasion, Karen's Gifts has the "perfect" gift. The store is open Monday-Friday 9 am-6 pm and Saturday until 5 pm. For more information, call 770-435-9800 or visit www.karensgiftsofatlanta.com.

 It's a Smyrna favorite for finding affordable antique or new furniture and is as pretty as its name. Love Street Home, 1125 Concord Rd., is situated a few blocks down the street from its sister store Love Street Gifts & Gardens and is a one-stop shop for your interior design needs including treasured home accessories and quality furniture. Owners Carole and George Scott offer everything from Shabby and Urban Chic to traditional, as well as original oil paintings and frames that are very reasonably priced. You'll find a large selection of iron wall décor, lamps, linens for beds, bath and kitchen, and silk and dried flowers. Love Street Home is also a distributor for the well-known Tyler Candles from Tyler, Texas. Browse the charming vignettes of Love Street Home Monday-Saturday 10 am-6 pm and Sunday noon-5 pm. For more information, call 678-556-3878 or visit www.lovestreetonline.com.

Atkins Park Restaurant enjoys a colorful history as the oldest continuously licensed tavern in the Highlands area of Atlanta, and shares its name with the original community developed in 1910. In fact, one of the first homes erected is now the second story of Atkins Park in Atlanta. With that history and success Atkins Park Tavern was born in Smyrna, and has also become a "favorite neighborhood tavern and eatery"—perfect for a family dinner, a relaxing weekend brunch or a late night drink with friends. Owners Kevin Drawe and Stuart Corriher are proud to have a wide-ranging list of wines and beers. Executive Chef Richard Hamlin adds spice and flair from his native Louisiana to create an eclectic menu with an influence of Cajun and Creole. Including such wonderful items as Fried Green Tomato Benedict and Drunken Pork Tenderloin. Be sure to ask about the annual Spring Crawfish Boil, Octoberfest, and the Smyrna Hops and Barley Beer Tasting events. Atkins Park Tavern is located at 2840 S. Atlanta Rd. in Smyrna and Atkins Park Restaurant is located at 794 N. Highland Ave. in Atlanta. Atkins Park Tavern is open Monday-Friday 11-4 am, Saturday 11-3 am and Sunday 11 am-midnight. For more information, call 770-435-1887 or visit www.atkinspark.com online.

Owners Tim Langell, Joe Romano and John Gibney met their freshman year of high school in New York, and have been friends for more than 25 years. Armed with a secret recipe from a family friend, they opened Zucca Bar and Pizzeria, and were instantly successful. Even better, executive chef Danny Arturo, who specializes in authentic, home-cooked, Italian menu favorites, joined the dream team. A few of Zucca's thin-crust, New York style specialty pizzas are White Pie, Chicken Parmesan and Pizza Margherita. The menu also includes wonderful calzones, salads, appetizers and pasta dishes, as well as fresh chicken, veal and seafood entrées that will keep you coming back until you've tried them all. Whether you are planning a large gathering of family and friends or just an intimate night out, Zucca is the place to be. The owners invite you because . . . "NYC is so far away, and life's too short to eat bad pizza!" Stop by 2860 Atlanta Rd. in Smyrna Market Village Sunday-Wednesday 11 am-midnight, Thursday until 2 am, Friday until 4 am, and Saturday until 3 am. For more information or reservations, call 770-803-9990 or visit www.zuccany.com.

Discover Social Circle

Almost 50 miles east of Atlanta, in the Historic Heartlands of Georgia, you'll find the sweet, friendly town of Social Circle. During the 1800s, the community was located at the junction of two old Creek Indian paths (known today as Cherokee Rd. or Highway 11 and Hightower Trail). The Creek Indians used these two trails for fur trading.

For Namesake

How did this town get such a charming name? A legend has been passed down through many generations about its origin. The legend says that a group of men who were meeting at the crossroads were sitting around the well having their "usual" drink. A stranger approached and was greeted with such warm hospitality that he said, "This is surely a social circle!" A replica of that original well was erected in the center of Social Circle as a symbol of the city's beginnings, characterizing the spirit of friendship that permeates the entire city.

Rich in History

The Georgia Railroad brought prosperity to Social Circle, which lasted until 1864 when Civil War broke out in the South. Until that time Social Circle had become quite the "shopping hub," with people coming from as far away as Decatur to trade. When Sherman marched through Social Circle with his torch, he had with him young Lieutenant Vallance of Genesco, New York. Although Vallance helped General Sherman burn most of the town, he pledged that he would come back one day to help restore what he had destroyed. History tells us that he did, indeed return, with a half-house style of architecture from New York and the first "Jersey cow." As you tour the historic homes in town, you will see an example of Vallance's half-house style in the Annie Gresham House on W. Hightower Tr.

After the war until the 1920s, growth continued in Social Circle because of its cotton production. It was during this time that many of the city's beautiful antebellum homes were built. One of these incredible homes in the heart of the Historic District is known as The Blue Willow Inn. The magnificent Greek Revival mansion was a place that inspired Margaret Mitchell to write *"Gone With the Wind."* Today, it is a remarkable restaurant that has gained fame and recognition by *Southern Living, A Taste of Home, USA Today, Gourmet, Food and Wine*, and *Guideposts* magazines. The tables are always set with Blue Willow china and fresh cut flowers, and the food is a sampling of the down-home Southern comfort food you will find throughout the area. There are many lovely historic homes to tour in Social Circle. You'll find beautiful examples of Colonial Revival, Federal, Gothic Revival, Neo-Classical, Plantation Plain, Second Empire, Queen Anne, Victorian and Italianate. The Josiah Clark Townhouse, c. 1838 is believed to be the oldest standing home in Social Circle.

Legendary "Friendship"

The town's hospitality and charm is displayed throughout the year, but the one festival that really sums up the atmosphere of Social Circle is the Friendship Festival held each October. It includes a 5K race, arts and crafts, food booths, music, and of course a parade.

The locals of Social Circle have a lot to live up to in their unusual name, and they do it with ease. The entire town is ready to welcome you into their "Circle," anxious to tell you the stories and legends of their beginnings. As participants of Georgia's Treasures Along I-20, they open the doors to their wonderful restaurants, antique and collectibles shops, fine art galleries, and even a 1920s General Store with broad smiles and warm handshakes. You will find some of the best the South has to offer in Social Circle. Be sure to make a wish at the famous well!

For more information about Social Circle, contact the City of Social Circle Better Hometown at 770-464-1866 or visit www.socialcirclega.com online.

Social Circle
Fairs Festivals & Fun

January
Classic Car Cruise In (Jan-December)

March
Easter Egg Hunt

May
Better Hometown City-Wide Yard Sale

July
Christmas in July
Social Circle Freedom Celebration

September
Social Circle Fair
Social Circle Tour of Homes

October
Annual Friendship Festival

December
Christmas Toys for Tots
Circle of Lights Christmas Celebration

Antiques, Gifts & Home Décor

BALDWIN ANTIQUES Nancy Baldwin carries on a tradition and business that she and her late husband Ed began back in 1984. They lovingly restored the historic building at 128 S. Cherokee Rd. in Social Circle and Baldwin Antiques has continued to grow and prosper ever since. Customers appreciate a wide variety of wonderful antiques along with fair prices. The store is open Monday-Wednesday and Friday 10 am-4:30 pm, Saturday until 5 pm, and Sunday noon-4 pm. Call 770-464-2139.

The endearing mother/ daughter owners Sara Thomas and Jeri Headrick have a very faithful following in Social Circle. In fact, it is their faith in God that inspired them to open their beautiful one-of-a-kind store. Gabriel's, 132 S. Cherokee Rd., is a favorite place to shop for quality antiques, unique home décor and special gifts. Look for special items from Vera Bradley and Lampe Berger. Gabriel's is open Monday 11 am-5 pm and Tuesday-Saturday 10 am-5:30 pm. Call 770-464-0670.

Artists & Art Galleries

VISUAL PRAISE
FINE ART STUDIO & GALLERY

Leslie Young Marks is a Holy Spirit-inspired artist who uses the visual arts to reveal her insight into God's Word. A lifetime of training and instruction in classical realism has aided Leslie in being able to capture the personality of her subjects on canvas. She and her husband Bill own and operate Visual Praise Fine Art Studio and Gallery, 119 S. Cherokee Rd. in Social Circle. Here you will enjoy samples of Leslie's incredible pieces of art, from original oil paintings to limited edition signed and numbered prints. Leslie's portraits and paintings are displayed internationally in many private collections, and her oil and pastel works have won numerous awards. To meet with Leslie about commissioning a portrait, stop by Monday-Saturday 10 am-5 pm. For more information, or to ask about art classes for beginners, intermediate or advanced artists, visit www.visualpraisefineart.com online or call 770-464-2300.

Cottages

THE HOLLY HOUSE

Decorated in wonderful period antiques and furnishings, The Holly House, 128 Holly St., is a quiet retreat for weekends, getaways or special events. Steve and Kathy Trantham have renovated and decorated this Registered Historic Home with care—preserving its historic significance. A fully equipped kitchen is available, so you'll feel right at home. This cozy cottage is within walking distance of everything Social Circle has to offer. For reservations, call 770-464-3811.

Realtors

Simpler Times Realty

Diane Johnson is a Social Circle native who knows and loves her town and its history. As owner of Simpler Times Realty, 188 Thurman Baccus Rd., Diane helps you find the perfect place to fit your needs. She works in all aspects of real estate, including historical homes, single family, first-time homebuyers, commercial and investment properties. She treats customers like family, and you will love having her as your realtor. Call 770-464-1800 or visit www.simplertimesrealty.com.

Blue Willow Inn ®
Restaurant and Gift Shop

"True grit" meets "Southern grits" in this *Gone with the Wind* inspiration. That's right; the home that houses the Blue Willow Inn Restaurant is said to have been the model for Margaret Mitchell's very own Tara. In fact, Mrs. Mitchell was a frequent visitor to the home while she was married to Red Upshaw (her inspiration for Rhett Butler), whose cousin built the magnificent Greek revival in 1917. Customers say they almost expect to see Miss Scarlet sweep down the stairs to join them for dinner, and we're sure you'll be swept away too. Not only will you love the Blue Willow's atmosphere with its elegant rooms and glorious gardens, but its food will leave you speechless.

Billie and Louis Van Dyke purchased the home in 1991, after much soul searching and prayer. Soon after opening, the late columnist Lewis Grizzard stopped in Social Circle on his search across the South for the best fried green tomatoes. He not only touted Billie's

tomatoes, but he let his readers know that the Blue Willow Inn was one of the best restaurants in the South. It has been featured in *Southern Living, Guideposts* and *Gourmet* magazines, as well as *USA Today,* and the Food Network named it one of America's "Top Five Bodacious Buffets." Bodacious is indeed the word to describe its incredible Southern-style buffet. You'll pile your plate high with all your favorites—chicken and dumplings, turnip greens, sweet potatoes, fried chicken, homemade rolls, desserts and much more. Billie says some customers eat their main course, retire to the front porch for a rest and then return for dessert and coffee. The Van Dykes keep the charm of the Old South alive in this remarkable restaurant at 294 N. Cherokee Rd. (Hwy. 11—four miles north of I-20, exit 98). Open for lunch or dinner Tuesday-Sunday. Call 800-552-8813, 770-464-2131 or visit www.bluewillowinn.com.

Specialty Shops

Dolls & Stuff Faye Kitchens and Debra Hales are mother/daughter owners of one of the largest display stores in the state of Georgia. Dolls & Stuff, 124 S. Cherokee Rd. in Social Circle, is filled with collectible dolls and doll accessories. Faye has been a passionate doll collector for many years and has more than 500 dolls! They carry the popular and collectible Lee Middleton dolls, and many other famous lines. The store is open Monday-Saturday 10 am-5:30 pm. Visit www.dollsandstuff.com or call 770-464-0203.

Discover
Stone Mountain

Stunning emerald forests, a cobalt-blue lake, fragrant magnolias and amethyst mountain laurels are just a few of the magnificent treasures of nature you will discover in beautiful Stone Mountain. You will also be surrounded by specialty shops and restaurants that offer distinguished items for everyone in the quaint Stone Mountain Village. The Village was established in 1839, and was listed in the National Register of Historic Places in 2001. There are more than 275 properties in the Historic District that date from the 1830s to the 1940s. Saturday walking tours highlight the development of the Village, from Main Street to the historic neighborhoods.

First named New Gibraltar, Historic Stone Mountain Village was once a railroad community and the center for Georgia's granite industry. In fact, Stone Mountain itself is purportedly the largest mass of exposed granite in the world. The mountain is believed to have originated more than 300 million years ago from intense heat and pressure forcing molten material upward. The gradual cooling through the centuries resulted in the compact, uniform granite crystals you'll see today. Granite taken from Stone Mountain has been used in the construction of the U.S. Capitol, the Panama Canal and many other structures in the world. Take a cable car to the top of the mountain to see the famous spot where parts of *"Apollo 13"* were filmed. At night, the north side of Stone Mountain becomes a screen for the popular Lasershow Spectacular.

Shop Till You Drop

The Village is now a thriving artist community, offering numerous specialty stores, antique shops, galleries and restaurants. If you are interested in historic architecture, you will love the tree-lined streets surrounding the Village, which are filled with stately antebellum homes, quaint Victorian cottages and bungalows. The city cemetery is within walking distance of Main Street, and is a great way to discover Stone Mountain's historic past. Shopping the artistic Stone Mountain Village will be such a treat. You will find exquisite handcrafted jewelry, Civil War memorabilia, fine art, and Georgia-made pottery. Indoor and outdoor restaurants offer everything from German, Italian, Mexican, Irish, Southern and American cuisine, and you'll find that the bed and breakfasts and hotels all seem to combine the atmosphere of the past with modern amenities.

A Little Culture Anyone?

Art plays such an important role in Stone Mountain. The citizens celebrate art by making it part of their daily lives. It is in the handcrafted pieces of jewelry, pottery or birdhouses you'll find in the many stores. It is in the music and literary works of local artists. But nowhere in Stone Mountain is it more celebrated than in the historic trolley station that has been transformed into the incredible "ART Station." ART Station galleries and theatre showcase the works of well-known Southern artists, actors, authors and playwrights. It is an arena for new plays and new pieces of art from contemporary artists. Three visual arts galleries feature the creativity of painters, sculptors, photographers and craftsmen. The ART Station theatrical season includes new dramas, comedies and musicals, many with a slight "Southern accent."

For more information about Stone Mountain Village, contact the Stone Mountain Village Visitors Center at 770-879-4971 or visit online at www.stonemountainvillage.com. Or, contact DeKalb County Convention and Visitors Bureau at 800-999-6055, 770-492-5000 or visit online at www.atlantasdekalb.org.

Stone Mountain Fairs Festivals & Fun

April
    Stone Mountain Village Walking Tours (April-October)

June
    Stone Mountain Village Arts & Crafts Show

December
    Holidays in Stone Mountain Village

To cultivate a garden is to walk with God.
–C. Bovee–

Southern Artistry

Virginia Mason's late husband was a well-known Georgia artist whose pottery is shown in the Smithsonian, and he even made a piece that was presented as a gift to Queen Elizabeth. After working at his side for more than 30 years, Virginia decided to open a gallery showcasing the work of Southern artists. Her beautiful gallery Southern Artistry is located at 965 Main St. in Stone Mountain's Historic Downtown.

Southern Artistry features wonderful woodcraft, fused glass, beautiful jewelry and one of the widest selections of functional pottery. All pieces are handmade by Southern artists—50 of them are from Georgia. Southern Artistry has been nominated by *Niche* magazine as one of the "Top 100 Retailers of American Crafts." Virginia is extremely knowledgeable and willing to help you choose that perfect piece. Open Monday-Saturday 10 am-5 pm and Sunday 1-5 pm. Call 770-469-9456.

The Village Inn
Bed and Breakfast

Built in 1820 as a roadside inn, this stately historic B & B was one of the few buildings to be spared during the Civil War, because of its use as a hospital. The Village Inn Bed & Breakfast in Stone Mountain was renovated in 1995 and restored as a luxury bed & breakfast with a romantic "Gone With the Wind" theme. Owner Ashley Anderson welcomes guests to indulge themselves in a "reverie of yesteryear" with comfortable modern amenities. Themed rooms, like The Angel, The Rhett Butler, and The Scarlett, are furnished with elegant linens, furniture and art. The third floor has a magnificent two-room suite called The Ballroom Suite, which is perfect for honeymoons, anniversaries, or special nights out. Beautiful rooms, flawless details, and personal attention from Ashley make each visit to The Village Inn, 992 Ridge Ave., a memorable event. For more information, visit www.villageinnbb.com online or call 770-469-3459.

Gifts & Home Décor

After collecting everything imaginable for more than 40 years, Clif and Jeanette White found a way to share their interests with others when they opened Swan Galleries in 1988. This wonderful collectibles shop is located at 933 Main St. in the original Stone Mountain Inn Hotel, which was built in 1905. You will love browsing through the exclusive collection of Wee Forest Folk, and the sparkling cases of Swarovski crystal. No matter what you love to collect, the Whites will help you find it. Open Monday-Saturday 10 am-5 pm. Call 770-498-9696.

Stone Mountain General Store

Need a bag of birdseed? How about a handsome rooster plate to hang? Maybe a piece of Lodge Cast Iron Cookware, a jar of delicious Georgia peach preserves, or an American flag? Even owner Jane Phillips has a hard time describing Stone Mountain General Store at 935 Main St. With more than 5,000 unique items filling this historic building, the store draws visitors from around the world. Jane and son Mike run the place, and rely on husband/father Ottis—an expert hardware man. As a family business, everyone lends a hand, even Jane's 90-year-old mother Agnes Birts (Gran as she's known to all). From an extensive selection of kitchen gadgets to a variety of outdoor accessories, you'll find a little of everything. Youngsters can even ride the antique toy horse, Big Bronco! Open Monday-Saturday 10 am-6 pm and Sunday noon-5 pm. For more information, call 770-469-9331 or visit www.stonemountaingeneralstore.com.

Jewelry

Not only is Stones a must-see destination shop in Stone Mountain Village, it is the most unusual jewelry store that you will ever visit. Their unique hands-on approach to jewelry making has earned them the title "The Un-Jewelry Store." Their philosophy is simple...find the most unusual as well as some of the better-known beads and gemstones, then make one-of-a-kind jewelry items. Necklaces, bracelets, rings, and earrings are made on-site, and custom designs are their specialty. With one of the largest selections of loose beads, temporary strands, instruction books and tools in the Southeast, Stones is a favorite for those who want to make their own jewelry, or like to design a piece and have it assembled by the knowledgeable staff. Stones also offers repair and redesign services, and classes for basic beading, knotting and more. In addition, the shop has an area devoted to crafters and artists. Stop by 951 Main St., call 770-469-5536 or visit www.stones-jewelry.com.

Restaurants

The Village Corner This outstanding German restaurant and bakery has become a destination point for locals, as well as tourists to Stone Mountain. Established in 1974, The Village Corner, 6655 James B. Rivers Dr. is owned-and-operated by Hilde and Claus Friese, who are originally from Germany. Feast on delicious baked goods and German specialties like Sauerbraten, Spaetzle and Schnitzels. The Village Corner is open Tuesday-Saturday 8 am-midnight and Sunday 10 am-10 pm. Visit online www. germanrestaurant.com or call 770-498-0329.

Discover Warm Springs / Pine Mountain

There is nothing like a quaint Southern town to refresh your spirit, and that's exactly what the sweet Georgia towns of Pine Mountain and Warm Springs do. Living up to their names, these beautiful towns entice visitors far and wide by offering a little something for everyone—great shopping, rich history and lovely wilderness. We know as you meander through their streets, you'll fall in love with them as much as we did. You never know, your simple vacation may just turn into a lifelong love affair with this part of Georgia. Enjoy!

WARM SPRINGS

Within just an hour of Atlanta you'll find the historic and very beautiful little town of Warm Springs. It was a little town that almost died, but since 1982 has grown in size and reputation to be a tourist favorite. During the very early years the beautiful rolling hardwood forests were inhabited by the Creek and Iroquois Indians, who used the eternally warm waters of the mountain springs. History tells us that they would bring their sick and wounded to be "healed" in the warm mineral waters. The tradition continued through the years, drawing settlers to the area they named "Warm Springs." In 1832 David Rose built a beautiful "resort area" near the springs, and in 1893 the 300-room Meriwether Inn was built. It had a dance pavilion, a tennis court and even a bowling alley. This resort soon became the "in" place for a summer retreat.

History comes alive in Warm Springs, and the experience is truly Southern. Off Main Street and through the courtyards of Bullochville and Magnolia, you'll find unique shopping opportunities and delightful restaurants. Located at the southern end of Warm Springs is the famous Little White House, where President Franklin Roosevelt is said to have spent his happiest times. There are two museums that chronicle FDR's life in Georgia and outline the interesting history of this Victorian town.

The Warm Springs

President Franklin Delano Roosevelt first brought national attention to Warm Springs in 1924, when he visited the heated mineral waters as treatment for his polio. The water's buoyancy seemed to restore feeling to his legs and relax his muscles. The springs maintain an 88-degree temperature and flow at 914 gallons per minute. Visitors are still welcome to feel the actual spring and hear its history. Roosevelt fell in love with the rolling hills and natural beauty of Warm Springs and built a home here; a small six room cottage called "The Little White House." It was here that he lived during his visits to the rejuvenating mineral springs, and it was here that he is believed to have developed his New Deal policies that changed our nation. Roosevelt is also responsible for starting the first institute for polio rehabilitation, where patients would come to exercise in the warm springs. In April 1945, President Roosevelt suffered a massive stroke and died while sitting for a portrait by Russian artist Elizabeth Shoumatoff in the living room of the cottage. The unfinished portrait still hangs in the den of the house. His 1938 convertible Ford and 1940 Willys Roadster are also on display at the Little White House, as well as the wheelchair that he designed.

A New Life for Warm Springs

Although Warm Springs is today a successful vibrant town, just 20 years ago it was on the brink of extinction. After the death of Franklin Roosevelt, the town began a decline that threatened its existence, with businesses closing and citizens moving to bigger cities. A spark of revitalization was ignited in 1969 when Paul and Grace Bolstein from Florida began to purchase property in Warm Springs attempting a "face lift." They added front porches, boardwalks, gingerbread trim and stained glass to many of the buildings. As hard as they tried, the Bolsteins were unable to see their dream become reality when illness struck in 1983.

It was at this time that a woman by the name of Jean Kidd accidentally stumbled into Warm Springs on the way to Callaway Gardens in Pine Mountain. "We couldn't even get a cup of coffee," Jean says, "And grass was knee-high in the sidewalks." As she and her friends sat there on the curb admiring the quaint buildings, a man happened by who offered to sell her the town and she bought it. Imagine having to explain that purchase to your husband! Jean's ability to see through the weeds and need of the near ghost town was its salvation. It was a "village reclaimed from the dusty history books." She immediately began to seek out investors and merchants—most of whom were her girlfriends—to relocate in Warm Springs, and slowly the town began to take on a new life. Business owners opened bed & breakfasts, tearooms, antique shops, and boutiques. Jean was also instrumental in reviving the Little White House.

There is an extraordinary and charming area of downtown in a quiet, peaceful courtyard called Bullochville. Brightly painted cottages and lofts, house wonderful items such as antiques, collectibles, handcrafted woodwork, pottery, and even homemade fudge! On any given day you might see an artist making wind chimes or carving something from a piece of wood.

Each shop takes on a flavor of its own, and each does its part in blending past with present and future. Today, Warm Springs is a town filled with excitement again, and the people are as friendly and warm hearted as the "warm springs" themselves.

PINE MOUNTAIN

Brimming with beauty, adventure, history, azaleas, and graceful Southern charm, Pine Mountain is called a vacationer's dream. It is located just one hour southwest of Atlanta at the foothills of the Appalachian Mountains, and is known for its abundance of quaint shops and distinctive historical charm. It is also known as "Gateway to Callaway Gardens," a magnificent garden resort with a host of activities during the year.

From antiques and handcrafted treasures to fine art, you'll find it all in the picturesque streets of Pine Mountain, which has been called "an antique lover's paradise." There is even an old-fashioned general store in its fourth generation of family service.

The Glory of Callaway Gardens

Pine Mountain's and one of Georgia's number one tourist attractions is Callaway Gardens. It is one of the main reasons tourists travel to this small Georgia town. Callaway Gardens was created in 1952 by Cason and Virginia Callaway, whose dream was to create a place "where man and nature worked together to the benefit of both." They built the amazing preserve around the discovery of the rare "Plumleaf Azalea," which grew naturally in the woodlands. The Callaways worked tirelessly in creating a 14,000-acre residential community with the beautiful gardens as a centerpiece. Virginia Callaway once said, "All who come will be heirs to the richness of this natural area." The magnificent retreat remains a place of solace, inspiration and discovery for everyone. The pristine lakes, natural woodlands, stunning flora and fauna, hiking and biking trails, 63 holes of championship golf and educational centers offer visitors outstanding opportunities for recreation in one of the most beautiful places on earth. You may also visit the lodge and spa at Callaway Gardens beginning Fall, 2006.

FDR State Park

You can combine your love of history with exciting outdoor activities here in Pine Mountain. The beautiful 9,047-acre FDR State Park offers fishing, boating, hiking, camping and rustic cabins just minutes from town. The largest state park in Georgia offers more than 40 miles of hiking trails with spectacular waterfalls and breathtaking views.

A Fantasy in Lights

If you are lucky enough to be visiting Pine Mountain during the holidays you are in for a magical adventure. Eight million colored lights sparkle their welcome to visitors during the annual "Fantasy in Lights." Since its opening in 1991, this holiday extravaganza has delighted all ages with dozens of lighted scenes, music, and of course Santa Claus. You can drive through the light show in your own car, or ride in the open air "Jolly Trolley," and be entertained by costumed characters, live entertainment and special music.

Shop In Style

As you stroll along the revitalized downtown shopping district, you are sure to find something for that special someone. Shop in many of the upscale, high-quality gift shops and boutiques—many of which are located in restored turn-of-the-century buildings. Of course, all that shopping will make you hungry. Why not dine in the delightful tearoom, or choose from one of the many, delicious restaurants.

Whether you are here in Pine Mountain for a day, a weekend or an extended stay, you will love every minute of your visit. There is so much to see and experience, and it is such a beautiful place, from the flowers on the doorsteps of the quaint downtown shops to the acres of stunning blooms at Callaway Gardens.

Lions and Tigers and Bears!

If wild adventure is what you want, you can get "up close and personal" to hundreds of exotic animals at the 500-acre "Wild Animal Safari." Grab a bag of their special food and feed and touch the animals as they come up to examine your car. You will see lions and tigers and bears of course, as well as giraffes, zebras, camels and even alligators. Buffalo, llama, rhino, monkeys, and tropical birds call the park home, as well as some animals you've probably never heard of before like zedonks, yakatusi and gaur. Kids will also love "Old McDonald's Farm," the Petting Zoo, Baby Land USA and (yikes) the Snake Pit!

For more information about Warm Springs, contact the FDR/Warm Springs Welcome Center at 800-337-1927, 706-655-3322 or visit www.warmspringsga.ws or www.visitmeriwether.com.

For more information about Pine Mountain, contact the Pine Mountain Tourism Association at 800-441-3502, 706-663-4000 or visit online at www.pinemountain.org.

Warm Springs / Pine Mountain Fairs Festivals & Fun

January
Callaway School of Needlearts
– Callaway Gardens
FDR's Birthday Celebration
– Warm Springs

February
Taste of Pine Mountain

March
Azalea Festival – Warm Springs
Spring Celebration, Plant Fair
and Sale – Callaway Gardens

April
Annual Commemoration
Ceremony
Azalea Festival
Pine Mountain Days Festival
Warm Springs Spring Fling
Festival/Roosevelt Days

May
Master Water Ski & Wake Board
Tournament – Callaway
Gardens
Memorial Day Weekend
Celebration

June
Annual Fishing Rodeo
FSU "Flying High" Circus
– Callaway Gardens

July
July 4th Celebration in Warm
Springs
Pine Mountain's Old Fashioned
4th of July
Surf and Sand Spectacular
– Callaway Gardens

September
Harris County Cattlemen's
Association Rodeo
Sky High Hot Air Balloon Festival
– Callaway Gardens

October
Annual Harvest Hoe Down
Art at Oak Grove's Fall Fringe
Fling
Chrysanthemum Festival
– Callaway Gardens
Ole Chipley Town Fair

November
Annual Candlelight Tour Festival
in Warm Springs
Chrysanthemum Festival
Fantasy in Lights at Callaway
Gardens
The Steeplechase at Callaway
Gardens

December
Fantasy in Lights at Callaway
Gardens
Warm Springs Holiday Activities

Pine Mountain.
Georgia

Gateway To Callaway Gardens

Located just an hour southwest of Atlanta, Pine Mountain's picturesque streets and downtown charm is a must see. This charming town is full of locally owned shops, filled with delightful treasures—far away from the chaos. Dining is also a pleasure with a variety of casual and gourmet eateries. Each serves delicious food—served with down-home hospitality.

Pine Mountain is also known as "The Gateway to Callaway Gardens"—a destination that attracts thousands of tourists to its lovely gardens, world-class golf courses and special events.

For more information, stop by Pine Mountain Tourism Association at 101 E. Broad St., call 706-663-4000, 800-441-3502 or visit www.pinemountain.org online.

FDR/Warm Springs Welcome Center

Warm Springs' history dates back to when Indians used its springs as a source of healing. More recent history includes President Franklin Delano Roosevelt using these same springs with hopes of improving his polio stricken legs. FDR eventually built a home in Warm Springs and enjoyed traveling throughout the county along the Meriwether-Pike Scenic Byway, which is a 55-mile loop retracing some of his favorite routes.

To learn more about the Byway and Warm Springs history, visit the FDR Warm Springs Welcome Center, 1 Broad St., Monday-Saturday 10 am-5 pm and Sunday 1-4 pm. Call 706-655-3322, 800-337-1927 or visit www.visitmeriwether.com.

Sweet Home Antiques

As one of four businesses created by the talented team of retired attorney Bruce Thompson and Dr. Phillip Rogers, Sweet Home Antiques has served as a catalyst for the renaissance of downtown Pine Mountain. The shop is located in the midst of two turn-of-the-century blocks of buildings at 149 Main St. and is the perfect setting for the remarkable antiques and furnishings from around the world. The owners travel to England and France several times a year in search of unique furniture, accessories and artwork; however, they also carry an extensive selection of American antiques and Southern primitives. The store is open daily 10 am-6 pm. Call 706-663-7776.

Chanticleer, 141 Main St., has established itself as a destination shop for those seeking the unique in continental antiques, unusual decorative accents and gifts, and gourmet foods. Located in one of a row of turn-of-the-century buildings in the heart of Pine Mountain, Chanticleer is one of four incredible shops created by Phillip Rogers and Bruce Thompson. But, the talent doesn't stop there. Manager Meg Russell, who has a knack for exquisite floral design, is responsible for the creative design and displays throughout the store. She will arrange any of the extraordinary silk flowers in the container of your choice. Stop by daily 10 am-6 pm. For more information, call 706-663-7878.

Antiques & Crafts
UNLIMITED MALL

You will want "unlimited" time to browse the incredible Antiques & Crafts Unlimited Mall in Warm Springs. It is located just two miles north of Warm Springs 7679 Roosevelt Hwy. There are 114 shops under one roof—each with beautiful displays of fine antiques, collectibles, arts and crafts. Dovie Geter and her husband built the 5,000 square foot mall in 1977 and success soon followed. In fact, business was so good she built a 10,000 square foot addition in 1992. Each vignette is creatively decorated, giving shoppers wonderful ideas as to how the items will look in their homes. The mall features exquisite antique furniture, crystal and china, vintage linens and clothing, toys, books, and estate jewelry. Be sure to visit the Visions Art Gallery featuring regional artist Arthur Riggs, who brings to life his "visions" through unique colors and technique. Shop daily 10 am-6 pm. Visit www.acum.org online or call 706-655-2468.

MAIN STREET EMPORIUM

Antiques, collectibles, vintage linens, unique decorator and gift items, and old books—just a few of the wonderful items you will find inside Main Street Emporium in Pine Mountain. Dealers have cleverly displayed their vintage prints, hardbacks and paperbacks, fiction and non-fiction, cookbooks and children's books amidst vintage linens and paintings. Be sure to check out the collection of vintage Nancy Drew, Hardy Boys and Bobbsey Twins books, and enjoy coffee, snacks and soft drinks while you browse this charming store. Main Street Emporium, 129 Main St., is open daily 10 am-6 pm. For more information, call 706-663-7721.

Artists & Art Galleries

FEATURING THINGS TO ENTERTAIN THE EYE!

This unique fine art and gift gallery in Pine Mountain features the combined collections of two very talented artists—Alexander Kalinin and Anne Tutt Kalinin. Anne Tutt Gallery has been dubbed by visitors as, "the spend the day place." Anne showcases her jewelry designs—including her amazing "Pocket Crosses" and Christian necklaces—fine pottery, etched and blown glass, sculpture, and Asian antiques. Alexander's art fills the walls, including original paintings, giclees, limited-edition prints, and much more. Located in Chipley Village fronting on Hwy.27 at intersection of Hwy. 354 and open Monday-Saturday 10 am-6 pm. Call 706-663-8032, 888-282-0021 for orders, or visit www.annetuttgallery.com or www.kalinin.fotopic.net.

Cason J. Callaway and his wife Virginia fashioned this stunning naturalized landscape. Their purpose was to create a wholesome family environment where all could find relaxation, inspiration, and a better understanding of the living world. The beauty of every season blooms throughout Callaway Gardens, from the breathtaking Azalea Bowl and incredible Overlook Garden to the Cecil B. Day Butterfly Center and Mountain View Golf Course. More than 1,000 tropical butterflies freely flutter among tropical plants and birds in the conservatory, and year round programs allow guests the chance to explore and discover nature's glorious array. The gardens' Gothic stone chapel has become a favorite place for weddings, and there are three different types of lodging accommodations on the property. Guests love Robin Lake Beach, the world's largest man-made white beach that stretches a mile around the beautiful 65-acre lake. Callaway Gardens is an enchanting place, with gorgeous vistas and peaceful places for retreat. It is nestled in the foothills of the Appalachian Mountains, just outside of Pine Mountain. For more information and directions, call 706-663-2281, 800-225-5292 or visit www.callawaygardens.com.

Chipley Murrah House Bed & Breakfast

Ask Donna and Paul Haynes how they do it all and Donna will answer, "after surviving breast cancer and raising triplets, this is easy!" This beautiful Victorian mansion at 207 W. Harris St., was built in 1895 by T.T. Murrah and is the only bed and breakfast in Pine Mountain. The property offers four large guest bedrooms featuring 12-foot ceilings, private baths and beautiful antiques, as well as three cozy cottages. Guests of the Chipley Murrah House will also enjoy an inviting swimming pool, a perfectly manicured putting green, a large wrap-around porch and a full breakfast served each morning. Call 888-782-0797, 706-663-9801 or visit www.chipleymurrah.com online.

PINE MOUNTAIN CLUB CHALETS RESORT

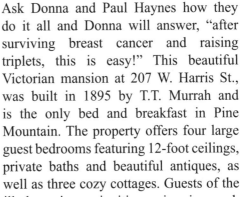

Nestled around a beautiful 12-acre lake, surrounded by magnificent dogwoods and azaleas, the Pine Mountain Club Chalets Resort, 14475 Ga. Hwy. 18, offers four seasons of enjoyment in a charming Swiss Alpine setting. This second generation, family-owned-and-operated resort originally opened in 1971 and continues to be a family favorite today. The three-bedroom Chalets include a living and dining room, a fully equipped kitchen and charcoal grill, and can accommodate up to six people. For more information or reservations, visit www.pinemountainclubchalets.com online or call 800-535-7622, 706-663-2211.

HOTEL WARM SPRINGS
BED & BREAKFAST INN
GIFT SHOP & ICE CREAM PARLOR

It has hosted such guests as the King and Queen of Spain, the Queen of Mexico, President Osmena of the Philippines, and movie star Bette Davis, as well as frequent daytime visitor President Franklin D. Roosevelt. Hotel Warm Springs Bed & Breakfast, 47 Broad St., is indeed steeped in history, and offers guests a memorable stay in one of the state's most gracious inns. Gerrie Thompson purchased the grand old hotel in 1988, and for five years, painstakingly scraped and painted, laid tile, refinished floors, hung light fixtures, gardened the grounds and decorated the hotel to its remarkable present-day

beauty and historical authenticity. The rooms are filled with beautiful antiques and furniture manufactured in Eleanor Roosevelt's Val-Kill shop in New York, and Roosevelt memorabilia is displayed throughout the 1907 building. Be sure to ask about the romantic Honeymoon Suite, which features a king-size bed with suspended canopy, Queen Anne furniture and a large red heart-shaped tub. A "Southern Breakfast Feast" is served each morning, including the award-winning cheese grits.

Hotel Warm Springs Bed & Breakfast is within walking distance of fine specialty shops and great restaurants, but if you are looking for a delicious ice cream cone, a cup of homemade Georgia peach ice cream or maybe a milkshake, stop by the Inn's ice cream parlor and gift shop. For more information or reservations, call 800-366-7616 or 706-655-2114 or visit www.hotelwarmspringsbb.org.

Books

THE CHRISTIAN CONNECTION CHRISTIAN BOOKSTORE

Chad and Rebecca Bishop say that their store is "Christ owned and Christian operated." With a mission to serve God and tell others about His love, they opened The Christian Connection Christian Bookstore, 88 Broad St. in Warm Springs. Their sons, Tye and Tanner "help" in the store, welcoming customers to browse and enjoy the variety of inspirational gifts and books. You will find Bibles, books, gifts, music, witness wear, church supplies and more. They will personalize and gift wrap your purchases for free, and they special order weekly. With a desire to give back to ministries who have their same mission at heart, Chad and Rebecca created "the Ministries Mall" within their store. They post names of nonprofit organizations dedicated to spreading God's word, and 2 percent of everything sold is divided between the organizations. In addition, the Bishops select a visitor who has signed their guest book each month, and that blessed individual receives a wonderful gift basket. The Christian Connection Christian Bookstore is open Monday-Friday 10 am-5 pm, Saturday until 6 pm and Sunday 1-5 pm. Visit www.thechristianconnection.ws or call 706-655-2166.

Cabins, Camping & RV Parks

PINE MOUNTAIN CAMPGROUND

Jim and Chris Jennings fell in love with the people and the town of Pine Mountain when they purchased the Pine Mountain Campground in 1999. The area is a vacationer's dream, and for tent campers and RV travelers, this is the best place to enjoy it all. The campground offers paved sites with patios, privacy fences and grills, as well as full and partial hookups and rental cabins. Campers will also enjoy an activity building and a pavilion, which is perfect for group events and celebrations. Guests can also enjoy the swimming pool, miniature golf and volleyball pit. Experience all of the comforts of home at Pine Mountain Campground, 8804 Hamilton Rd. Call 706-663-4329 or visit www.camppinemountain.com online.

Town and Country Fashions

Lois Boyd opened Town & Country Fashions in 1983, and the store has since become one of the most loved places to shop in Pine Mountain. Customers say that it has a "Home Away From Home" appeal, and that they are always treated like family. Lois and her mom worked in the shop side-by-side for more than 20 years, so it was almost like their home. You will be pleasantly surprised at what you will find in this small town shop, including designer handbags by Mary Frances, Jantzen Swimwear for ladies, Rafaella Sportswear for missy and large sizes, Izod for men and New Balance and Merrell for the entire family. You will also find everything from baby gifts and children's accessories to bath and body products and hand-made birdhouses. There truly is a little of everything and something for

everyone in this charming boutique. Town & Country Fashions is located in Chipley Village at the corner of US Hwy. 27 and GA Hwy. 354, just outside Callaway Gardens. Stop by and browse Monday-Saturday 10 am-6 pm. For more information, call 706-663-4449.

Furniture, Gifts & Home Décor

MOUNTAIN CRAFTS

Located at the foothills of beautiful Pine Mountain in the Historic Village of Warm Springs, Mountain Crafts lives up to its name and reputation. From the fine display of sterling silver jewelry to the Big Green Egg Smoker and Grill for the man in your life—you will love it here. "Red Hat Ladies" will find lovely accessories, as well as unique costume jewelry, hand-stitched quilts, and many great collectibles. Be sure to explore out-

side, behind the store in the garden area, where you'll discover garden accessories, swings and more. Mountain Crafts is located at 55 Broad St., and is open daily 10:30 am-5:30 pm. Call 706-655-3606.

Canterbury's

Ted and Valerie Merry visited Warm Springs after hearing about the area and the wonderful local attractions. They were so intrigued by the historic town that they felt it would be enjoyable to make it a more permanent vacation. In August 2002, Ted and Valerie purchased Canterbury's, located at 50 Broad St. The 100-year-old building offers the classic charm of wood floors and original rolling ladders. Ted, Valerie and their staff always extend a sincere welcome to customers visiting this delightful shop. Specialty collectors will find treasured items like Willow Tree and Prayers & Promises from Demdaco, exquisite doilies and scarves from Heritage Lace, fragrant Colonial Candles, as well as bath and body products from Camille Beckman, Caswell-Massey and Lady Primrose's. Canterbury's is open Monday-Saturday 10 am-6 pm and Sunday noon-5 pm. Call 706-655-2545 or visit www.canterburys.biz online.

The BOUTIQUE

Established in 1984 by three women as a side business to their stay-at-home Mom jobs, The Boutique began as a small craft shop in the back courtyard, before becoming so successful it had to move to its present location at 60 Broad St. Simone Bernard is now the sole proprietor of The Boutique, as well as the only original shop owner from the resurrection years, when Jeanne Kidd put Warm Springs back on the map. It

is a fabulously fun store with a selection of wonderful gifts. It is not only an upscale year round Christmas shop, but also a place to find fine china, silver and collectibles of all sorts. You will love all the Red Hat Society accessories, and delicious gourmet foods and preserves. Don't miss the opportunity to shop one of the most delightful and charming stores in Warm Springs. Stop by Monday-Saturday 10 am-6 pm and Sunday 1-6 pm. For more information, call 706-655-3894.

Country Classics

Warm, friendly people combined with exceptional old-fashioned service and classically designed furniture is the best way to describe this store. It may sound like something out of the past, but it is available right now at Country Classics. Housed in one of the first three buildings built in Warm Springs around 1880, Country Classics offers fine furniture lines such as Timberlake, Palmer, Tommy Bahama and Howard Miller grandfather clocks. Popular collectible lines like Department 56, Precious Moments, Jim Shore, Fenton and many more, add up to make this a shoppers dream come true. Stop in at 56 Broad St. and say hello to owners Phil and Linda Drummond or their friendly staff. Open Monday-Saturday 10 am-6 pm or Sundays 1-6 pm. For more information, visit www.countryclassicsonline.com or call 888-655-2609 or 706-655-2609.

Hotels & Inns

WHITE HOUSE INN

A beautiful, gracious inn atop glorious mountains had been a long time dream for Janet Lawand's husband. When she was widowed with four small children, Janet determined to make that dream come true. The Best Western White House Inn, 2526 White House Pkwy., is a realization of that dream. It is pure Southern comfort with incredible views, beautiful amenities and a friendly, hospitable staff. All of the 52 oversized, luxurious rooms have a microwave and a refrigerator, as well as a coffeemaker, a hairdryer, an iron and ironing board. Twelve of the rooms have a pullout sofa bed, and some even have a Jacuzzi. The continental breakfast includes make-your-own waffles, and you can enjoy a free daily newspaper with your coffee. Business travelers will appreciate access to the Internet and nice meeting rooms. Guests also enjoy an outdoor patio and pool that overlooks an amazing view of the valley below. Just minutes from the historic site of the Little White House, this Inn is one of the nicest, most comfortable properties in the Warm Springs area—perfect for family reunions, parties or a weekend get away. For more information, call 800-667-7506, 706-655-2750 or visit www.bestwestern.com online.

DAVIS INN

Southern hospitality, tastefully appointed rooms and personal friendly service will make your stay at Davis Inn delightful. Don't be surprised to wake to the sights and sounds of cardinals feeding outside your window, or see wild deer or turkey roaming the beautifully landscaped property. Davis Inn is located at 5585 State Park Rd. in Pine Mountain, just 15 minutes from Warm Springs, and is your host to Callaway Gardens, F.D. Roosevelt State Park and the Little White House. Owners Dan and Didi Taylor welcome you to a beautiful mountain "home away from home." Call 888-346-2668, 706-663-2522 or visit www.davisinn.com online.

FDR'S LITTLE WHITE HOUSE

People have been drawn to the healing, therapeutic "warm springs" of Georgia since the late 1800s. In the fall of 1924 Franklin Delano Roosevelt, then a private citizen, came to Warm Springs for therapy for his crippling condition. The visit set events in motion that gave the tiny village a bright future. Roosevelt was instrumental in forming the Georgia Warm Springs Foundation, and he established the first modern treatment center for infantile paralysis in the United States. His love for the area grew and he built his family home here. FDR's Little White House at 401 Little White House Rd. is now open to the public with exhibits that chronicle Roosevelt's life. You will learn about his role in the Great Depression, his leadership of the country during World War II, and his own struggles with polio. You will see the wheelchair he designed using a kitchen chair, his hand controlled Ford convertible, the stagecoach he used during parades, and a film about his life narrated by Walter Cronkite. The cottage has been kept as it was the day he suffered a fatal stroke while posing for a portrait. For more information on calendar events and tours, call 706-655-5870 or visit www.fdr-littlewhitehouse.org online.

Restaurants & Tearooms

Gourmet Magazine recently received a request from a loyal Rose Cottage customer, asking the magazine to feature chef/partner Shannon Klein's "Lemon Custard" recipe. The magazine liked it so much that they agreed. Rose Cottage, 111 E. Broad St. in Pine Mountain, has become a favorite destination for groups looking for a day of extraordinary shopping and upscale lunching. The shop replicates a true English Tearoom, and the decorative accents are all for sale. The creation of Phillip Rogers and Bruce Thompson, this lovely tearoom also teams with Food Blossoms Catering to provide special occasion menus for dinners, weddings and receptions. It's always teatime at Rose Cottage. You'll love the full traditional English Tea, including rosemary and apricot scones with crème fraiche, tartlettes with lemon curd, assorted tea sandwiches, and of course delicious teas. Rose Cottage is open daily 10 am-6 pm. Lunch is served from 11 am-3 pm and Saturday until 4 pm. For additional information or reservations, call 706-663-7877.

VICTORIAN TEA ROOM

The charming and elegant historic building at 70 Broad St. is the perfect setting for the wonderful Victorian Tea Room in Warm Springs. A columned balcony allows guests to enjoy a beautiful view, while dining on some of the most delicious fare imaginable. Owners Ted and Valerie Merry have renovated this 1906 building with a sense of respect to its original grandeur, creating a gracious essence of "days gone by." Come and enjoy Italian and Southern cuisine; steaks, seafood, pasta and fresh baked desserts—it is well worth the visit! The Victorian Tea Room makes every occasion unforgettable. Reservations are available for individual parties, banquets, receptions and weddings. For more information, call 706-655-3508 or visit www.victoriantearoom.biz online.

CARRIAGE & HORSES

The words unique, romantic, gorgeous, peaceful and delicious don't even begin to describe Carriage & Horses restaurant at 607 Butts Mill Rd. in Pine Mountain. Owner B. Dagher calls it "a piece of heaven on earth," and we

agree! You will enjoy romantic fine dining, a gorgeous scenic view, and live entertainment in a wonderful Victorian house. From unique appetizers like spanakopita and escargot to entrees like Seared North Alaskan Salmon and Lobster Tails to the "House Cake" and the wine cellar—everything is outstanding. Carriage & Horses is open for lunch 11:30 am-2 pm and dinner 6 pm until closing! Call 706-663-4777 or visit www.cometodagher.com.

This charming little Italian bistro is located at 408 N. Main St. in one of the original 1930s buildings in Pine Mountain. Owner Bessie McGee features authentic Italian dishes from recipes her family brought with them from Sicily during the early 1800s. Everything is delicious! From the generous appetizers, soups, salads and sandwiches to the unforgettable pizza pies and hearty entrees—you'll love it all. They use only the freshest ingredients in preparing their dishes from scratch. In fact, they have the Italian sausage over-nighted from a small town in northwestern Wisconsin. Mandella's Italian Restaurant is open for lunch Tuesday-Saturday 11 am-2 pm and for dinner 5-9 pm. Call 706-663-7736.

CRICKET'S RESTAURANT

This charming Pine Mountain restaurant has become known far and wide for its deliciously authentic New Orleans cuisine. Cricket's Restaurant is located at 14661 Hwy. 18—on the way to Callaway Gardens. Perfectly seasoned dishes include New Orleans Blackened Fish, Catfish Orleans, Jambalaya, Crawfish Etouffe, and grilled to perfection steaks and chicken. Save just a little room for the perfect ending to a perfect meal—Chocolate Praline Cake, Almond Cream Crepes or Bread Pudding. Cricket's Restaurant is open for dinner daily 5-9 pm. For more information, call 706-663-8136 or visit www.cricketsrestaurant.com online.

Established 1892

KIMBROUGH BROTHERS

GENERAL STORE

Originally known as the Murrah Bros. General Store in 1892, the pioneer citizens of Pine Mountain were provided with livery, seed, dry goods, groceries, boots, tobacco, coffins, buggies and wagons. In 1908, brothers Henry and Heywood Kimbrough purchased the Murrahs' business and building at 44 Main St., and it has remained in the family since. Kimbrough Brothers General Store has survived lean war times, the pestilence of influenza, and the Great Depression, remaining an extraordinary piece of Pine Mountain's history. The store has flourished through each generation of Kimbroughs, changing with the times to provide the latest fashions for men and women, toys for children of all ages, kitchen accessories, unique gifts and even fun Coca Cola and John Deere collectibles. Of course, you still can pick up a bag of feed or seed, get your fishing license, or buy a pair of overalls. And, you will still feel the warm welcome of the Kimbrough family that has endured. Stop by Monday-Saturday 8 am-6 pm. For more information, call 706-663-2528.

Value

Chipley Discount From caviar to pig's feet and everything in between, you just never know what you'll discover at Chipley Discount, 134 N. McDougald Ave. in Pine Mountain. This location was the original livery station, then in the 1960s opened as a grocery store. Now, at this discount and grocery store, you will find items like Avon products, greeting cards, gourmet coffee, school supplies and many other treasures. Locals know that in addition to finding what they need at great prices, they will always be treated like family. Ask about the daily specials! Chipley Discount is open Monday-Saturday 9 am-6 pm. For more information, call 706-663-9898.

Discover
Warner Robins

The vibrant, thriving community of Warner Robins has been called the "International City" because of its cultural diversity and many choices in cuisine, entertainment and shopping. Originally known as Wellston, Warner Robins was chartered in 1943. The United States Air Force established the Robins Air Force Base here in 1941, and the community sprang up around the military depot. The town's name was changed to honor Brigadier General Augustine Warner Robins, who is generally recognized as the father of modern air force logistics. Robins Air Force Base remains today as Georgia's largest single industry. The community is a friendly, diverse group of individuals whose military roots account for their openness, acceptance and tolerance. No one is a stranger in this progressive city. Locals welcome visitors with true hospitality and pride in all that their city has to offer.

Up, Up and Away

The city is just "Plane Fun!" The absolute must see in Warner Robins (for all ages) is the Museum of Aviation. The 43-acre aviation museum is the fourth largest in the United States, with more than 93 displays of aircraft and missiles. The three story main museum was built in the shape of the Air Force's Stars & Bars insignia. The Eagle Building houses exhibits, aircraft and archives, as well as the Victory Café and the Museum Gift Shop. Hangers hold restored Presidential and combat helicopters, Pre–WWII, Vietnam, Korean and Cold War aircraft, and America's Black Eagles: The Tuskegee Pioneers. The Heritage Building opens Windows to a Distant Past, with unique sight and sound exhibits that explore the culture of Georgia's first inhabitants. The Museum is also home to the Georgia Youth Science and Technology Center and the Georgia Aviation Hall of Fame.

Wings and Wheels Car Show

Every October a collection of more than 250 vehicles show up at the annual Wings and Wheels Car, Truck and Motorcycle Show at the Museum of Aviation. Custom, classic and modified vehicles from throughout the southeast are displayed alongside the Museum's collection of over 93 vintage aircraft and missiles. There's always an added bonus to the show such as NASCAR drivers, radio controlled and plastic model airplanes, performances by the Southern Flare Clogging Team, and runway races for the kids. Youngsters can bring their 6-volt and 12-volt battery operated vehicles to the Museum for races down a 200-foot simulated runway in the Museum's picnic area. And while there are nominal fees for participating in the vehicle display, admission to the Museum is free.

Military Tattoo Ceremony

If you've ever had the good fortune to observe the Tattoo Ceremony in Edinburgh, Scotland, you won't be disappointed at the marvelous production every year at Robins Air Force Base. The tattoo traditional ceremony traces its roots to the British Army of King William, III serving in the Netherlands. King William's troops were housed in the towns and villages around the battlefield and went to the local pubs to spend the evening. Drummers marching through the streets signaled when it was time for innkeepers to stop selling beer and the soldiers to leave the pubs. When the drummers completed their rounds, they would return to the fort where the sergeant major would command them to "sound tattoo." In the language of the time, "doe den tap toe" meant, "turn off the taps." However, the troops learned only the last words "tap toe" which over time became "tattoo." On that signal, the freshly assembled troops were marched back to the garrison. As the custom developed, flutes and other musical instruments accompanied the drums. Eventually, full bands played for the whole garrison, and the tradition of the military tattoo came into being. The tradition today is held worldwide, showcasing the excellence and readiness of service members. Events differ from one to the other, but typically a tattoo will tell a story of the past to the future and will highlight a flyover and precision teams.

Fore!

Two of Georgia's gorgeous pine tree-lined golf courses are located here in Warner Robins—the International City Golf Club and the Landings Golf Club. With the outstanding scenic beauty and the various levels of challenge, both the beginner and the professional golfer will equally find entertainment.

Beautiful Bouquets Abound

Who doesn't love flowers? The American Camellia Society National Headquarters is located at Massee Lane Gardens, just a stones throw away from Warner Robins (about 20 miles). Enjoy nine breathtaking acres of ever changing color from October to March as vibrant hues of azaleas, hydrangeas, roses and others burst into bloom. In the formal garden, bricks used as ballast on ships coming from England into the port of Charleston in the late 1700s, take on a new life in the pierced brick walls decorating the paths. And if your senses need just a little more, the world's largest public display of Edward Marshall Boehm porcelains can be found in two galleries as you stroll through the gardens.

For more information about Warner Robins, contact the Warner Robins Convention and Visitors Bureau at 888-288-WRGA(9742), 478-922-5100 or visit www.warner-robins.org/cvb.htm online.

Warner Robins
Fairs Festivals & Fun

January
Museum of Aviation
1/2 Marathon • 5K Run/Walk

February
Houston Arts Alliance Open House

March
Museum of Aviation Young
  Astronauts Day

April
Mossy Creek Barnyard Festival
Annual Golf Tournament
GIs on Wheels Show & Swap Meet
Southern Wings Art Show

May
Gospel Concert
Memorial Day Activities
Southern Wings Art Show

June
Hangar Talks

July
Independence Day Concert
Patriotic Film Festival

August
A Night of Swing

September
Gospel Sing
Georgia Golden Olympics
Georgia Invitational Golf
  Tournament

October
Mossy Creek Barnyard Festival
Wings and Wheels Car, Truck
  and Motorcycle Show

December
Christmas Parade

JEFFERSON DAVIS HERITAGE TRAIL

Warner Robins is located in the Historic Heartland, only 90 minutes south of Atlanta. Known as Georgia's "International City" because of its cultural diversity, great shopping and varied family entertainment from clogging to cricket. It is home to the Robins Air Force Base and the Museum of Aviation. Civil War buffs will love following the Civil War Trails of Georgia through the Jefferson Davis Heritage Trail, which follows the grueling march of Davis and his confederate soldiers through 15 counties until their final stop in Macon. Stop by the CVB located at 99 N. First St. in the charming E.L. Greenway Welcome Center at the Historic Train Depot site. For more information, visit online at www.warner-robins.org/cvb.htm or call 888-288-9742, 478-922-5100.

WARNER ROBINS
GEORGIA, USA
CONVENTION & VISITORS BUREAU

The Antique Mall

You will find incredible quality antiques, furniture, gifts and collectibles at very reasonable prices when you find your way to The Antique Mall, 1815 Watson Blvd. in Warner Robins. More than 20 professional dealers are located throughout this 12,000 square foot mall, where you'll also find primitives, beaded bags and estate jewelry—there is something for everyone in this wonderful antique mall. Open Tuesday-Saturday 10 am-6 pm and Sunday 1-5 pm. For information, call 478-929-3925.

Attractions, Entertainment & Museums

The Museum of Aviation in Warner Robins is called the "Crown Jewel" of Middle Georgia. It is the second largest museum in the United States Air Force, and draws more than 525,000 visitors each year. Located in four buildings across 51 acres at Russell Pkwy. and Hwy. 247, it includes an interactive theater, more than 100-restored aircraft, hundreds of exhibits—some even suspended in air! Open daily 9 am-5 pm. Visit www.museumofaviation.org or call 478-926-6870.

You will certainly feel as though you've stepped onto a tropical island here. Kokomo's Island Café, 4086 Watson Blvd. in Warner Robins, is decorated with bright, fun colors, real Koi ponds, and aquariums filled with fish in every hue imaginable. The menu is equally as tempting and exciting—one of the most unique in the state. Feast on ceviche made from the freshest of ingredients and fish tacos that are prepared just right. The menu includes a variety of delicious seafood, steak and chicken dishes that are all wonderful. The women behind the success of Kokomo's Island Café are mother and daughter team Belinda and Missy Evans (the prettier two of the Georgia Bob's and Danielle's Bistro family). Open daily 11 am-10 pm. For more information, call 478-971-4801.

What's for dinner? Let Kathryn Kile do the cooking! In fact, you can place your order for an entire week and pick-up a meal that is hot from the oven. Kathryn's Bakery-Café is an inviting bakery and eatery at 1801-E Watson Blvd. in Warner Robins that specializes in delicious cakes, desserts and pastries. You'll also enjoy incredible breakfasts and lunches. Call 478-922-4438 or visit www.kathrynsbakery.com. Hours are Monday-Friday 6 am-6 pm and Saturday 8 am-3 pm.

Chef Audrey's
Bistro & Bakery

Chef Audrey's Bistro & Bakery is a fun, friendly restaurant that will become one of your favorites in the time it takes for one meal. The star of her own cable television show "Now We're Cooking!," Chef Audrey George is a delight to meet in person. And, you will have that opportunity when dining at the Bistro located at 115-A Margie Dr. in Warner Robins. But as delightful as Chef Audrey is in person and in media and as warm and friendly the ambience at the Bistro, the meals are the main attraction.

Chef Audrey hails from Birmingham, Ala. where she trained as an apprentice with a German Master Chef and French Pastry Chef. She obviously studied earnestly, as evidenced by her mouth-watering creations and awards, named one of the "Chefs of the South" by the *Atlanta Journal-Constitution*.

Chef Audrey's masterful culinary skills are evidenced in every aspect of her menu at the Bistro & Bakery. From homemade mayonnaise and original recipe salad dressings to the refreshing peach tea served any hot summer to such offerings as Salmon Wellington, Herb & Pepper Crusted Pork Tenderloin, you will be delighted with every menu item. But, don't stop with the main course, for the pastry case is just as varied and delectable.

Chef Audrey's Bistro & Bakery serves lunch Monday-Friday 10:30 am-3 pm and Saturday 11:30 am-3 pm. Dinner is served Monday-Saturday 5:30-8 pm. For more information, call 478-953-7480 or visit www.chefaudrey.com online. And, while you're visiting, be sure to fill out a CABB Friends information slip so you can learn of all the upcoming events at Chef Audrey's Bistro &

Bakery. If you have a special occasion to plan, request a catering menu. Chef Audrey will be happy to make your occasion an extraordinary event— culinary speaking, that is! *(Color photo featured in front section of book.)*

DANIELLE'S
⚜ NEW ORLEANS BISTRO ⚜

Fresh seafood and steaks all cooked with a delicious "Cajun Flair." Danielle's New Orleans Bistro, 2922 Watson Blvd. in Centerville just minutes from Warner Robins, is a charming restaurant decorated with a definite "Big Easy" atmosphere. It features the finest and most sophisticated Cajun fare in the area. Feast on traditional Cajun dishes like Crawfish Etoufée, Shrimp Créole and Blackened Red Fish. Or, try one of the house specialties, like the Stuffed Shrimp or Filet Chadwick—a nine-ounce Black Angus steak, topped with fried oysters and béarnaise sauce. No matter what you choose, you won't be disappointed. This elegant, but relaxed, restaurant will satisfy your taste buds and your love for a bit of the unexpected. Open for dinner Tuesday-Saturday 5-10 pm. Call 478-971-4408.

A visit to this incredible Warner Robins restaurant is must! Georgia Bob's Barbecue Company, 1882 Russell Pkwy., is the result of father Bob Evans' barbecue experience and son Chad's romantic ideas. Everything is cooked over a real pit outside. And, when they aren't cooking up the best pulled pork and old-fashioned Brunswick Stew in the South—you'll find them singing somewhere. Chad fronts a band called Hank Vegas. Open Monday-Saturday 6 am-9 pm and Sunday 11 am-9 pm. For catering information, call 478-971-1341.

Hotels & Inns

Ideally located near the Museum of Aviation and the Georgia National Fairgrounds, Comfort Suites, 3101 Watson Blvd., is a top choice for visitors to Warner Robins. The 64 luxurious suites and Jacuzzi suites include two phone lines with data port, cable TV, micro-fridge, and in-room coffee service. Guests will enjoy a complimentary buffet breakfast bar, USA Today, as well as access to the heated pool, spa, and fitness center. For information or reservations, call 478-953-5240, 877-424-6423 or visit www.choicehotels.com.

Jewelry

 Yelverton Jewelers

Yelverton Jewelers is the premier jewelry and gift store in Warner Robins. Owner Darrell Yelverton has more than 20 years experience and is certified in GIA grading of diamonds. His creativity and knowledge makes a big difference in the service you will receive. You'll find one-of-a-kind and custom-designed pieces; ranging from traditional to contemporary. You'll also discover innovative gemstones and colors. Yelverton Jewelers is your one-stop bridal registry at 198 S. Houston Lake Rd. Open Monday-Friday 10 am-6 pm and Saturday until 4 pm. For more information, call 478-971-1600 or 800-354-3723.

KITCHEN GALLERY

For the finest in cookware and bakeware you must visit the Kitchen Gallery, 504 Russell Pkwy. in Warner Robins. You'll find gobs of gadgets and gifts galore, as well as a wide selection of gourmet coffees and teas. Ferrelle and John Bagley love entertaining and cooking, and they love being able to share their passion with others. The Kitchen Gallery is an authorized Lampe Berger dealer and carries a full-line of Scanpan and All-Clad cookware. You will find the latest in new products, such as bamboo cutting boards, French rolling pins, micro-plane graters, and silicon spatulas, whisks and oven mitts. Be sure to ask about the Kitchen Gallery's popular cooking classes offered throughout the year. Stop by Monday-Friday 10 am-6 pm and Saturday until 4 pm. Call 478-923-0090.

Index

119 Chops – 205
A Child's Garden – 125
A Touch of Country – 116
A Victorian Cowgirl – 156
A-1 Vacation Rentals – 160
Adrianna's Café Bistro – 71
Alexis Maternity Collections – 29
Amelia's & The Ruffled Rooster – 177
Amici Italian Café – 119, 176
Anasazi – 100
Andrea's China Cabinet, Inc. – 32
Anne Tutt Gallery – 287
Antebellum Inn Bed & Breakfast – 198
Antique Sweets – 178
Antiques & Crafts Unlimited Mall – 286
Antiques from The Shed – 218
Antiques of Vinings – 23
Antiques On Broad – 231
Appointments at Five – 79
Athens Antique Mall – 80
Athens Interiors Market – 78
Atkins Park Tavern – 261
Atlanta Antique Gallery – 22
Baldwin Antiques – 266
Belles Choses – 35
Bert's – 72
Best Western White House Inn – 295
Beth Ann – 28
Betty's Vintage Boutique – 99
Beverly Bremer Silver Shop – 9, 43, III
Biscuit Inn – 161
Black Sheep Antiques – 195
Blue Ridge Antiques & Mall – 94
Blue Ridge Inn Bed & Breakfast – 97
Blue Willow Inn Restaurant – 269
Boxwoods Gardens & Gifts, Inc. – 34
Brenda's House of Flowers – 186
British Bits and Bobs – 99
Buckhead Ornamentals – 36

Bulloch Hall & Archibald Smith Plantation Home – 247
C.R. Rader Jewelers – 66
Callaway Gardens – 288
Camellia Cottage Antiques – 195
Canterbury's – 293
Card Carousel – 225
Carlton Interiors – 221
Carriage & Horses – 298
Carrie Lynn's Antiques – 218
Caruso's – 129
Celebrity on Paces – 27, XIII
Chamblee's Antique Row District – 22
Chanticleer – 285
Chappelle Gallery – 81
Chef Audrey's Bistro & Bakery – 8, 307, XI
Chipley Discount – 300
Chipley Murrah House Bed & Breakfast – 289
Choby's at Little River – 6, 204
Chocolate Moose – 139
Christa's etc. – 232
Circa Antiques & Gardens – 80
City of Smyrna – 253, XI
Classics – 164
Claws & Paws – 161
Coldwell Banker High Country Realty – 102
Collectors' Corner – 212, VI
Comfort Inn – Newnan – 213
Comfort Suites – 309
Cottage Hill Antiques – 53
Country Classics – 294
Country Cousins – 235
Country Roads Antique Mall – 232
Cranberry Corners – 126
Cream of the Crop – 57
Creter's – 61
Cricket's Restaurant – 299
Crowne Plaza Macon – 64, X
Dahlonega Tasting Room – 132
Danielle's New Orleans Bistro – 308
Dante's on the Square – 129

Dasha Style & Color – 237
Davis Inn – 295
Dawson County Chamber of Commerce – 133, 135
Dawsonville Pool Room – 138
Decatur Downtown Development Authority – 142, 145
DeKalb History Center – 150
Design Finds – 140
Dish – 40
Dog Ear Books – 174
Dolls & Stuff – 270
Dory's – 90
Douglas Inn & Suites – 101
Douglass Theatre – 56
Dragonfly Dreams – 234
Dreams – 59
Dreamscape – 54
DuPre's Antiques & Interiors – 185
Easy Living Garden Center – 218
Edelweiss German Inn & Restaurant – 159, 162
Eden'z Vegetarian Restaurant – 71
Enchanted Pieces – 63
Endless Treasures – 136
Fairfield Inn & Suites – 38
FDR Warm Springs Welcome Center – 278, 284
FDR's Little White House – 296
Felicity Gifts and Home Décor – 36
Fine Gifts by Glass, Etc. – 33
First Class Cabin Rentals – 96
Forrest Hills Mountain Resort & Conference Center – 128
Frogtown Cellars – 132
Frontier – 87
Full Cup Bread, Books, Gifts – 34
Gabriel's – 266
Garden House Bed & Breakfast – 148
Gathering Place Café & Events – 138
Gautreau's Cajun Café – 89

Georgia Bob's Barbecue Company – 308
Georgia Gameday Center – 83
Georgia Market House – 62
Georgia Music Hall of Fame and Museum – 67
Georgia National Fairgrounds and Agricenter – 219
Georgia Originals – 81
Georgia Prime Real Estate, LLC – 102
Georgia Sports Hall of Fame – 68
Georgia's Old Capital Museum – 203
Gigi's Salon and Day Spa – 179
Ginger Howard Selections – 28
Ginger's Dollings & Cattywags – 233
Golden Classics – 126
Grapevine Antiques & More – 196
Greater Rome CVB – 226, 230
Greenstone Soap Company – 164
Habersham Vineyards & Winery – 165
Hallie Jane's Market Catering – 176
Hampton Inn – Madison – 179
Hampton Inn – Perry – 222
Happy Valley Pottery – 81
Harvest Moon Café – 241
Hawthorn Suites – 239
Hay House – 69
Heart to Heart for Kids, Inc. – 29
Helen Black Bear Resort – 160
Henry's of Bolingbroke – 106
Heritage Hall – 173
High Country Art & Antique – 95
Highridge Gallery – 98
Historic Roswell CVB – 243, 250
Homeplace Gifts & Toys – 82
Hoopla – 149
Hotel Warm Springs Bed & Breakfast Inn – 290

House to House Furnishings Consignment – 88
Impressions – 25, VIII
Ingleside Village Antique Centre – 52
Ingleside Village Pizza – 72
J.C. Grant Company Jewelers – 201
Jameson Inn – 238
Jane Marsden Antiques & Interiors – 20, VIII
Jingles – 87
Jolie Home – 146, XIII
Jones Jewelers, Inc. – 223
Joycine's – 59
Kaleidoscope – 150
Karen's Gifts – 259
Karla's Shoe Boutique – 60
Kathryn's Bakery-Café – 306
Kimbrough Brothers – 300
Kitchen Gallery – 310
Kokomo's Island Café – 306
Kreature Komforts of Marietta, Inc. – 188
L & L Beanery – 97
La Quinta Inn & Suites – 65
Ladyslipper Rare Plant Nursery, Inc. – 187
Lavender Loft – 139
Lily Creek Lodge – 137
Little European Bakery – 24
Little River Park Campground & Marina – 6, 199
Love Street Gifts & Gardens – 258
Love Street Home – 260
Macon Arts – 55
Macon-Bibb CVB – 44, 51
Madison Interiors Market – 170
Madison Museum of Fine Art – 174
Madison-Morgan Cultural Center – 172
Magretta Hall – 242
Main Street Covington – 109, 112
Main Street Emporium – 286
Main Street Yarns and Fibers – 89
Mandala Wellness Retreat & Day Spa – 163
Mandella's Italian Restaurant, LLC – 299

Martha Jane's Homestyle Fudge – 238
Me & Thee – 70
Mel & Mimi – 234
MeMe's on Carroll – 220
Merci Woman – 30
Merle Norman Cosmetics Studio – 114
Michael Gibson Antiques & Design, Inc. – 19, IV, V
Milledgeville-Baldwin County CVB – 190, 194
Mitchell's Last Chance Gift Shop – 214
Mittie's Tea Room Café – 248
Morgan County African-American Museum – 172
Mountain Crafts – 293
Museum of Arts and Sciences – 70
Museum of Aviation – 305
My Mountain Cabin Rentals LLC – 96
N & N Florist – 98
Nacoochee Grill – 163
Nature's Health & Christian Bookstore – 137
New Perry Hotel – 222
Nicklaus Golf Club Birch River – 127
Oak Hill & The Martha Berry Museum – 240
Ocmulgee Arts, Inc. – 55
Oh! Fine Lingerie – 30
Old Town Antiques & Gifts – 211, X
Opulence – 86
Paula's Silver and Gold – 235
Payne Mill Village Antique Mall – 53
Perry Area CVB – 215, 217
Petit Sweets Confectionery – 56
Piazza Italian Restaurant – 130
Pine Mountain Campground – 291
Pine Mountain Club Chalets Resort – 289
Pine Mountain Tourism Association – 278, 284
Planet Me – 255
Pura Vida USA – 128, XI

Ramada Limited – Blue Ridge – 101

Ramsey's Furniture – 116

Razzle Dazzle – 28

RE/MAX Properties Plus – 106

Red Door Interiors – 259

Richards Studio of Photography – 214

RL's Off The Square – 119

Rome Area Council for the Arts – 232

Rose Cottage – Madison – 173

Rose Cottage – Pine Mountain – 297

Ruby Jean's – 256

Rue de Leon – 147

Sally's – 169

Salon Red & Salon Red Kids – 151

Savvy Snoot – 31

Scentimentals – 251

Scrappin' Sisters – 120

Serenity Garden Café – 94

Serenity Medical Health and Beauty Spa – 141

Serenity Wellness Spa & Salon – 6, 206

Sew Memorable – 141

Shapiro's – 157

Simpler Times Realty – 268

Simply Sophie – 140

Simply Southern – 170

Slippers – 85

Smartypants – 233

Social Circle Better Hometown – 263

Southern Artistry – 274

Southern Belles and Beaus – 82

Southern Comforts – 88

Southern Cross Guest Ranch – 175

Southern Heartland Art Gallery – 112

Spires Interiors & Gifts – 117

Stan Milton Salon – 42

Staybridge Suites – 38

Steffen Thomas Museum and Archives – 173

Stiles Properties – 84

Stone Mountain General Store – 276

Stonebridge Western Treasures and Fine Art – 171

Stones – 277

Sugarplum Tree – 220

Sunshine Village, Ltd. – 80

Susan Lee – 26, IX

Swan Coach House – 41

Swan Galleries – 276

Swan House – 39, FC

Sweet Home Antiques – 285

Sweet Repeats – 26

T. Martooni's – 242

The Antique Mall – 305

The Avenue – 189, VII

The Back Burner Restaurant – 72

The Barnes House – 58

The Boutique – 294

The Cannonball House – 70

The Cat's Pajamas – 86

The Christian Connection Christian Bookstore – 291

The Columns – 53

The Country Craftsman – 237

The Fickle Pickle – 248

The Forrest Interior Design & Gifts – 236

The Front Porch Tearoom – 224

The Gardens at Great Oaks – 249, XIII

The Guest House – 198

The Holly House – 268

The Ivy Garden – 184

The McGuire House – 130

The Oar House – 130

The Old Governor's Mansion – 202, XII

The Plantation Shop – 21, IX

The Posh Pup – 151

The Red Tomato – 107

The Restaurant at the New Perry Hotel – 224

The Rogers House – 172

The Roman Antique Mall & Expo – 231

The Scarlet Tassel – 35

The Seen Gallery – 147

The Shoppe in the Back – 256

The Shoppes of Plum Tree Village – 252, XIII

The Society Gardener – 63

The Squished Grape – 178

The University of Georgia – 90

The Village Corner – 277

The Village Inn Bed & Breakfast – 275

The Whistle Stop Café – 108

The Wild Honeysuckle – 185

The Willows Pottery – 158

Three Sisters Fudge – 94

Timeless Reflections – 94

Tina's Shoes – 57

Town & Country Fashions – 292

Town Center Breads – 113

Tré Bella – 200

Trinkets – 118

Tubman African American Museum – 69

Two Friends – 221

Utopia Day Spa – 115

Victorian House Restaurant – 103

Victorian Rose Tearoom and Café – 241

Victorian Tea Room – 298

Village Green Flowers & Gifts – 257

Villane's Art Glass Studio – 197

Visual Praise Fine Art Studio & Gallery – 267

Warner Robins CVB – 301, 304

White County Chamber of Commerce – 152, 155

Willow on Fifth – 73

Wingate Inn Macon – 65

Wolf Mountain Vineyards – 131

Wyndham Hotels & Resort – 37

Yelverton Jewelers – 309

Yonah Treasures – 158

Zucca Bar and Pizzeria – 262

Cross Reference

Antiques

A Victorian Cowgirl – 156
Antiques & Crafts Unlimited Mall –286
Antiques from The Shed – 218
Antiques of Vinings – 23
Antiques On Broad – 231
Appointments at Five – 79
Athens Antique Mall – 80
Athens Interiors Market – 78
Atlanta Antique Gallery – 22
Baldwin Antiques – 266
Belles Choses – 35
Beverly Bremer Silver Shop – 9, 43, III
Black Sheep Antiques – 195
Blue Ridge Antiques & Mall – 94
Boxwoods Gardens & Gifts, Inc. – 34
Buckhead Ornamentals – 36
C.R. Rader Jewelers – 66
Camellia Cottage Antiques – 195
Carrie Lynn's Antiques – 218
Chamblee's Antique Row District – 22
Chanticleer – 285
Chipley Murrah House Bed & Breakfast – 289
Christa's etc. – 232
Circa Antiques & Gardens – 80
Collectors' Corner – 212, VI
Cottage Hill Antiques – 53
Country Roads Antique Mall – 232
Cranberry Corners – 126
DuPre's Antiques & Interiors – 185
Easy Living Garden Center – 218
Endless Treasures – 136
Frontier – 87
Gabriel's – 266
Grapevine Antiques & More – 196
Henry's of Bolingbroke – 106

High Country Art & Antique – 95
House to House Furnishings Consignment – 88
Ingleside Village Antique Centre – 52
Jane Marsden Antiques & Interiors – 20, VIII
Jingles – 87
Love Street Home – 260
Madison Interiors Market – 170
Madison-Morgan Cultural Center – 172
Main Street Emporium – 286
Michael Gibson Antiques & Design, Inc. – 19, IV, V
Old Town Antiques & Gifts – 211, X
Payne Mill Village Antique Mall – 53
Perry Area CVB – 215, 217
Rose Cottage - Pine Mountain – 297
Rue de Leon – 147
Simply Sophie – 140
Southern Comforts – 88
Sunshine Village, Ltd. – 80
Sweet Home Antiques – 285
The Antique Mall – 305
The Columns – 53
The Ivy Garden – 184
The Plantation Shop – 21, IX
The Roman Antique Mall & Expo – 231
The Shoppes of Plum Tree Village – 252, XIII
The Society Gardener – 63
Timeless Reflections – 94
Trinkets – 118

Artist/Art Galleries/ Framing/Photography

Andrea's China Cabinet, Inc. – 32
Anne Tutt Gallery – 287
Antiques & Crafts Unlimited Mall – 286
Antiques of Vinings – 23
Appointments at Five – 79
Athens Interiors Market – 78

Buckhead Ornamentals – 36
Chanticleer – 285
Chappelle Gallery – 81
Chipley Murrah House Bed & Breakfast – 289
Chocolate Moose – 139
Collectors' Corner – 212, VI
Dreamscape – 54
Georgia Originals – 81
Greater Rome CVB – 226, 230
Happy Valley Pottery – 81
Heart to Heart for Kids, Inc. – 29
High Country Art & Antique – 95
Joycine's – 59
Karen's Gifts – 259
Macon Arts – 55
Madison Museum of Fine Art – 174
Main Street Covington – 109, 112
Michael Gibson Antiques & Design, Inc. – 19, IV, V
Mitchell's Last Chance Gift Shop – 214
Museum of Arts and Sciences – 70
Ocmulgee Arts, Inc. – 55
Richards Studio of Photography – 214
Rome Area Council for the Arts – 232
Rue de Leon – 147
Shapiro's – 157
Southern Artistry – 274
Southern Comforts – 88
Southern Heartland Art Gallery – 112
Steffen Thomas Museum and Archives – 173
Stonebridge Western Treasures and Fine Art – 171
Stones – 277
Sunshine Village, Ltd. – 80
Swan Coach House – 41
The Avenue – 189, VII
The Country Craftsman – 237
The Seen Gallery – 147

The Shoppes of Plum Tree Village – 252, XIII
The Willows Pottery – 158
Tubman African American Museum – 69
Villane's Art Glass Studio – 197
Visual Praise Fine Art Studio & Gallery – 267
Yonah Treasures – 158

Attractions/Entertainment
Blue Willow Inn Restaurant – 269
Bulloch Hall & Archibald Smith Plantation Home – 247
Callaway Gardens – 288
Choby's at Little River – 6, 204
Dawon County Chamber of Commerce – 133, 135
Dawsonville Pool Room – 138
Decatur Downtown Development Authority – 142, 145
DeKalb History Center – 150
Dish – 40
Douglass Theatre – 56
FDR Warm Springs Welcome Center – 278, 284
FDR's Little White House – 296
Georgia Music Hall of Fame and Museum – 67
Georgia National Fairgrounds and Agricenter – 219
Georgia Sports Hall of Fame – 68
Georgia's Old Capital Museum – 203
Greater Rome CVB – 226, 230
Hay House – 69
Heritage Hall – 173
Historic Roswell CVB – 243, 250
L & L Beanery – 97
Little River Park Campground & Marina – 6, 199
Macon-Bibb CVB – 44, 51
Madison Museum of Fine Art – 174

Madison-Morgan Cultural Center – 172
Main Street Covington – 109, 112
Milledgeville-Baldwin County CVB – 190, 194
Morgan County African-American Museum – 172
Museum of Arts and Sciences – 70
Museum of Aviation – 305
Oak Hill & The Martha Berry Museum – 240
Perry Area CVB – 215, 217
Pine Mountain Tourism Association – 278, 284
Rose Cottage – Madison – 173
Steffen Thomas Museum and Archives – 173
Swan House – 39, FC
The Cannonball House – 70
The Guest House – 198
The Old Governor's Mansion – 202, XII
The Restaurant at the New Perry Hotel – 224
The Rogers House – 172
The Willows Pottery – 158
Tubman African American Museum – 69
Warner Robins CVB – 301, 304
White County Chamber of Commerce – 152, 155
Zucca Bar and Pizzeria – 262

Bakeries
Chef Audrey's Bistro & Bakery – 8, 307, XI
Full Cup Bread, Books, Gifts – 34
Harvest Moon Café – 241
Kathryn's Bakery-Café – 306
L & L Beanery – 97
Len Berg's – 71
Little European Bakery – 24
Petit Sweets Confectionery – 56
The Avenue – 189, VII
The Village Corner – 277
Town Center Breads – 113
Victorian Tea Room – 298

Bed & Breakfasts/Cabins/Cottages
A-1 Vacation Rentals – 160
Antebellum Inn Bed & Breakfast – 198
Blue Ridge Inn Bed & Breakfast – 97
Chipley Murrah House Bed & Breakfast – 289
Edelweiss German Inn & Restaurant – 159, 162
First Class Cabin Rentals – 96
Forrest Hills Mountain Resort & Conference Center – 128
Garden House Bed & Breakfast – 148
Helen Black Bear Resort – 160
Hotel Warm Springs Bed & Breakfast Inn – 290
Lily Creek Lodge – 137
My Mountain Cabin Rentals LLC – 96
Pine Mountain Campground – 291
Pura Vida USA – 128, XI
Southern Cross Guest Ranch – 175
The Guest House – 198
The Holly House – 268
The Village Inn Bed & Breakfast – 275

Books
A Child's Garden – 125
Baldwin Antiques – 266
Dog Ear Books – 174
Full Cup Bread, Books, Gifts – 34
Henry's of Bolingbroke – 106
Homeplace Gifts & Toys – 82
Ingleside Village Antique Centre – 52
Main Street Emporium – 286
Nature's Health & Christian Bookstore – 137
The Avenue – 189, VII
The Christian Connection Christian Bookstore – 291

Bridal/Weddings
Antebellum Inn Bed & Breakfast – 198
Appointments at Five – 79

Beth Ann – 28
Beverly Bremer Silver Shop
  – 9, 43, III
Brenda's House of Flowers
  – 186
C.R. Rader Jewelers – 66
Callaway Gardens – 288
Celebrity on Paces – 27, XIII
Comfort Suites – 309
Cottage Hill Antiques – 53
Creter's – 61
Edelweiss German Inn &
  Restaurant – 159, 162
First Class Cabin Rentals – 96
Forrest Hills Mountain Resort
  & Conference Center – 128
Frogtown Cellars – 132
Gathering Place Café &
  Events – 138
Hallie Jane's Market Catering
  – 176
Helen Black Bear Resort
  – 160
Henry's of Bolingbroke – 106
Impressions – 25, VIII
J.C. Grant Company Jewelers
  – 201
Jones Jewelers, Inc. – 223
Kaleidoscope – 150
Kathryn's Bakery-Café – 306
Kitchen Gallery – 310
Lily Creek Lodge – 137
Little European Bakery – 24
Mandala Wellness Retreat &
  Day Spa – 163
Merci Woman – 30
Nicklaus Golf Club Birch
  River – 127
Oh! Fine Lingerie – 30
Opulence – 86
Petit Sweets Confectionery
  – 56
Rose Cottage - Pine Mountain
  – 297
Scrappin' Sisters – 120
Simply Southern – 170
Spires Interiors & Gifts – 117
Susan Lee – 26, IX
The Cat's Pajamas – 86
The Gardens at Great Oaks
  – 249, XIII
The Oar House – 130
The Restaurant at the New
  Perry Hotel – 224

The Village Inn Bed &
  Breakfast – 275
The Wild Honeysuckle – 185
Victorian House Restaurant
  – 103
Victorian Rose Tearoom and
  Café – 241
Victorian Tea Room – 298
Village Green Flowers &
  Gifts – 257
Wolf Mountain Vineyards
  – 131
Wyndham Hotels & Resorts
  – 37
Yelverton Jewelers – 309

Camping/RV
Little River Park Campground
  & Marina – 6, 199
Pine Mountain Campground
  – 291

Catering
119 Chops – 205
Adrianna's Café Bistro – 71
Amici Italian Café – 119, 176
Atkins Park Tavern - 261
Bert's – 72
Blue Willow Inn Restaurant
  – 269
Chef Audrey's Bistro &
  Bakery – 8, 307, XI
Dawsonville Pool Room
  – 138
Eden'z Vegetarian Restaurant
  – 71
Gathering Place Café &
  Events – 138
Gautreau's Cajun Café – 89
Georgia Bob's Barbeque
  Company – 308
Hallie Jane's Market Catering
  – 176
Harvest Moon Café – 241
Kathryn's Bakery-Café – 306
Magretta Hall – 242
Mandella's Italian Restaurant,
  LLC – 299
Mittie's Tea Room Café – 248
Nacoochee Grill – 163
Rose Cottage - Pine Mountain
  – 297
Serenity Garden Café – 94

The Back Burner Restaurant
  – 72
The Fickle Pickle – 248
The Red Tomato – 107
The Restaurant at the New
  Perry Hotel – 224
The Shoppes of Plum Tree
  Village – 252, XIII
The Whistle Stop Café – 108
Victorian Rose Tearoom and
  Café – 241
Willow on Fifth – 73
Zucca Bar and Pizzeria – 262

Children's
A Child's Garden – 125
Alexis Maternity Collections
  – 29
Antique Sweets – 178
Belles Choses – 35
Buckhead Ornamentals – 36
Callaway Gardens – 288
Card Carousel – 225
Cream of the Crop – 57
Creter's – 61
Dasha Style & Color – 237
Dog Ear Books – 174
Dolls & Stuff – 270
Douglass Theatre – 56
Felicity Gifts and Home
  Décor – 36
Frontier – 87
Ginger's Dollings &
  Cattywags – 233
Heart to Heart for Kids, Inc.
  – 29
Henry's of Bolingbroke – 106
Homeplace Gifts & Toys – 82
Hoopla – 149
Jingles – 87
Jolie Home – 146, XIII
Karen's Gifts – 259
Kimbrough Brothers – 300
Lavender Loft – 139
Little European Bakery – 24
Museum of Arts and Sciences
  – 70
Planet Me – 255
Salon Red & Salon Red Kids
  – 151
Scentimentals – 251
Simply Southern – 170
Smartypants – 233

Southern Belles and Beaus – 82
Sugarplum Tree – 220
Swan Coach House – 41
Swan House – 39, FC
Sweet Repeats – 26
The Avenue – 189, VII
The Cat's Pajamas – 86
The Front Porch Tearoom – 224
The Ivy Garden – 184
The Plantation Shop – 21, IX
Tina's Shoes – 57
Utopia Day Spa – 115
White County Chamber of Commerce – 152, 155

Coffee
Adrianna's Café – 71
Blue Ridge Antiques & Mall – 94
Card Carousel – 225
Chipley Discount – 300
Dasha Style & Color – 237
Kathryn's Bakery-Café – 306
Kitchen Gallery – 310
L & L Beanery – 97
Main Street Emporium – 286
Martha Jane's Homestyle Fudge – 238
The Avenue – 189, VII
The Barnes House – 58
The Ivy Garden – 184
The Shoppes of Plum Tree Village – 252, XIII
The Village Corner – 277

Condominiums/Resorts/ Rentals
A-1 Vacation Rentals – 160
Callaway Gardens – 288
First Class Cabin Rentals – 96
Forrest Hills Mountain Resort & Conference Center – 128
Georgia Gameday Center – 83
Georgia Prime Real Estate, LLC – 102
My Mountain Cabin Rentals LLC – 96
Pine Mountain Club Chalets Resort – 289

Pura Vida USA – 128, XI
Southern Cross Guest Ranch – 175
Staybridge Suites – 38
Stiles Properties – 84

Cosmetics/Health & Beauty Products
Beth Ann – 28
Canterbury's – 293
Chipley Discount – 300
Dragonfly Dreams – 234
Gigi's Salon and Day Spa – 179
Greenstone Soap Company – 164
Joycine's – 59
Lavender Loft – 139
Mandala Wellness Retreat & Day Spa – 163
Merle Norman Cosmetics Studio – 114
Nature's Health & Christian Bookstore – 137
Opulence – 86
Pura Vida USA – 128, XI
Salon Red & Salon Red Kids – 151
Scentimentals – 251
Serenity Medical Health and Beauty Spa – 141
Serenity Wellness Spa & Salon – 6, 206
Simply Southern – 170
Stan Milton Salon – 42
Sugarplum Tree – 220
The Barnes House – 58
The Shoppe in the Back – 256
Utopia Day Spa – 115

Fashion/Accessories
A Child's Garden – 125
A Victorian Cowgirl – 156
Alexis Maternity Collections – 29
Amelia's & The Ruffled Rooster – 177
Atlanta Antique Gallery – 22
Beth Ann – 28
Carlton Interiors – 221
Celebrity on Paces – 27, XIII
Chamblee's Antique Row District – 22

Country Cousins – 235
Cream of the Crop – 57
Dragonfly Dreams – 234
Dreams – 59
Felicity Gifts and Home Décor – 36
Ginger Howard Selections – 28
Heart to Heart for Kids, Inc. – 29
Homeplace Gifts & Toys – 82
Hoopla – 149
Joycine's – 59
Kaleidoscope – 150
Karla's Shoe Boutique – 60
Kimbrough Brothers – 300
Love Street Gifts & Gardens – 258
Main Street Emporium – 286
Mel & Mimi – 234
MeMe's on Carroll – 220
Merci Woman – 30
Oh! Fine Lingerie – 30
Opulence – 86
Paula's Silver and Gold – 235
Planet Me – 255
Razzle Dazzle – 28
Ruby Jean's – 256
Scentimentals – 251
Simply Southern – 170
Slippers – 85
Southern Belles and Beaus – 82
Sugarplum Tree – 220
Susan Lee – 26, IX
Sweet Repeats – 26
The Avenue – 189, VII
The Barnes House – 58
The Boutique – 294
The Cat's Pajamas – 86
The Shoppe in the Back – 256
The Shoppes of Plum Tree Village – 252, XIII
Timeless Reflections – 94
Tina's Shoes – 57
Town & Country Fashions – 292
Tré Bella – 200
Two Friends – 221
Victorian Rose Tearoom and Café – 241
Yonah Treasures – 158

Fishing
Callaway Gardens – 288
Little River Park Campground & Marina – 6, 199

Florists
Brenda's House of Flowers – 186
Georgia Market House – 62
Jingles – 87
N & N Florist – 98
Village Green Flowers & Gifts – 257

Furniture
A Touch of Country – 116
Anasazi – 100
Andrea's China Cabinet, Inc. – 32
Antiques & Crafts Unlimited Mall – 286
Antiques from The Shed – 218
Antiques On Broad – 231
Appointments at Five – 79
Athens Antique Mall – 80
Athens Interiors Market – 78
Baldwin Antiques – 266
Black Sheep Antiques – 195
Camellia Cottage Antiques – 195
Carlton Interiors – 221
Carrie Lynn's Antiques – 218
Chamblee's Antique Row District – 22
Chanticleer – 285
Chocolate Moose – 139
Christa's etc. – 232
Collectors' Corner – 212, VI
Country Classics – 294
Country Roads Antique Mall – 232
Design Finds – 140
Dory's – 90
Dreamscape – 54
Easy Living Garden Center – 218
Enchanted Pieces – 63
Endless Treasures – 136
Grapevine Antiques & More – 196
Henry's of Bolingbroke – 106
Highridge Gallery – 98

House to House Furnishings Consignment – 88
Ingleside Village Antique Centre – 25, VIII
Jingles – 87
Jolie Home – 146, XIII
Karen's Gifts – 259
Ladyslipper Rare Plant Nursery, Inc. – 187
Love Street Home – 260
Madison Interiors Market – 170
Main Street Emporium – 286
Michael Gibson Antiques & Design, Inc. – 19, IV, V
Mountain Crafts – 293
Old Town Antiques & Gifts – 211, X
Payne Mill Village Antique Mall – 53
Ramsey's Furniture – 116
Savvy Snoot – 31
Simply Sophie – 140
Simply Southern – 170
Southern Comforts – 88
Spires Interiors & Gifts – 117
Sunshine Village, Ltd. – 80
Sweet Home Antiques – 285
The Antique Mall – 305
The Columns – 53
The Country Craftsman – 237
The Forrest Interior Design & Gifts – 236
The Scarlet Tassel – 35
The Shoppes of Plum Tree Village – 252, XIII
Timeless Reflections – 94

Gardens/Nurseries
A Victorian Cowgirl – 156
Boxwoods Gardens & Gifts, Inc. – 34
Buckhead Ornamentals – 36
Callaway Gardens – 288
Circa Antiques & Gardens – 80
Dory's – 90
Easy Living Garden Center – 218
Endless Treasures – 136
Ladyslipper Rare Plant Nursery, Inc. – 187
Love Street Gifts & Gardens – 258

Opulence – 86
Payne Mill Village Antique Mall – 53
Ruby Jean's – 256
Stone Mountain General Store – 276
The Scarlet Tassel – 35
The Society Gardener – 63

Gifts/Home Décor
A Child's Garden – 125
A Touch of Country – 116
A Victorian Cowgirl – 156
Amelia's & The Ruffled Rooster – 177
Anasazi – 100
Andrea's China Cabinet, Inc. – 32
Anne Tutt Gallery – 287
Antique Sweets – 178
Antiques from The Shed – 218
Antiques of Vinings – 23
Antiques On Broad – 231
Appointments at Five – 79
Athens Antique Mall – 80
Athens Interiors Market – 78
Atlanta Antique Gallery – 22
Belles Choses – 35
Beth Ann – 28
Betty's Vintage Boutique – 99
Black Sheep Antiques – 195
Blue Ridge Antiques & Mall – 94
Blue Willow Inn Restaurant – 269
Boxwoods Gardens & Gifts, Inc. – 34
Brenda's House of Flowers – 186
British Bits and Bobs – 99
Buckhead Ornamentals – 36
Bulloch Hall & Archbald Smith Plantation Home – 247
C.R. Rader Jewelers – 66
Callaway Gardens – 288
Camellia Cottage Antiques – 195
Canterbury's – 293
Card Carousel – 225
Carlton Interiors – 221
Carrie Lynn's Antiques – 218
Celebrity on Paces – 27, XIII

Chamblee's Antique Row District – 22
Chanticleer – 285
Chappelle Gallery – 81
Chipley Discount – 300
Chocolate Moose – 139
Christa's etc. – 232
Circa Antiques & Gardens – 80
Classics – 164
Claws & Paws – 161
Collectors' Corner – 212, VI
Cottage Hill Antiques – 53
Country Classics – 294
Country Cousins – 235
Country Roads Antique Mall – 232
Cranberry Corners – 126
Cream of the Crop – 57
Creter's – 61
Dahlonega Tasting Room – 132
Dasha Style & Color – 237
Design Finds – 140
Dolls & Stuff – 270
Dory's – 90
Dreamscape – 54
DuPre's Antiques & Interiors – 185
Easy Living Garden Center – 218
Enchanted Pieces – 63
Endless Treasures – 136
Felicity Gifts and Home Décor – 36
Fine Gifts by Glass, Etc. – 33
Frontier – 87
Full Cup Bread, Books, Gifts – 34
Gabriel's – 266
Georgia Market House – 62
Georgia Music Hall of Fame and Museum – 67
Georgia Originals – 81
Ginger's Dollings & Cattywags – 233
Golden Classics – 126
Grapevine Antiques & More – 196
Habersham Vineyards & Winery – 165
Happy Valley Pottery – 81
Henry's of Bolingbroke – 106
Highridge Gallery – 98

Homeplace Gifts & Toys – 82
Hoopla – 149
Hotel Warm Springs Bed & Breakfast Inn – 290
House to House Furnishings Consignment – 88
Ingleside Village Antique Centre – 52
J.C. Grant Company Jewelers – 201
Jane Marsden Antiques & Interiors – 20, VIII
Jingles – 87
Jolie Home – 146, XIII
Jones Jewelers, Inc. – 223
Karen's Gifts – 259
Kimbrough Brothers – 300
L & L Beanery – 97
Ladyslipper Rare Plant Nursery, Inc. – 187
Lavender Loft – 139
Little European Bakery – 24
Love Street Gifts & Gardens – 258
Love Street Home – 260
Macon Arts – 55
Madison Interiors Market – 170
Madison Museum of Fine Art – 174
Main Street Emporium – 286
Main Street Yarns and Fibers – 89
Martha Jane's Homestyle Fudge – 238
Me & Thee – 70
Mel & Mimi – 234
Merle Norman Cosmetics Studio – 220
Michael Gibson Antiques & Design, Inc. – 19, IV, V
Mitchell's Last Chance Gift Shop – 214
Mountain Crafts – 293
Museum of Arts and Sciences – 70
Ocmulgee Arts, Inc. – 55
Old Town Antiques & Gifts – 211, X
Opulence – 86
Paula's Silver and Gold – 235
Payne Mill Village Antique Mall – 53
Planet Me – 255

Ramsey's Furniture – 116
Red Door Interiors – 259
Rome Area Council for the Arts – 232
Ruby Jean's – 256
Rue de Leon – 147
Sally's – 169
Savvy Snoot – 31
Scentimentals – 251
Serenity Wellness Spa & Salon – 6, 206
Sew Memorable – 141
Shapiro's – 157
Simply Sophie – 140
Simply Southern – 170
Southern Artistry – 274
Southern Comforts – 88
Southern Heartland Art Gallery – 112
Spires Interiors & Gifts – 117
Stone Mountain General Store – 276
Stonebridge Western Treasures and Fine Art – 171
Stones – 277
Sunshine Village, Ltd. – 220
Swan Coach House – 41
Swan Galleries – 276
Sweet Home Antiques – 39, FC
The Antique Mall – 305
The Avenue – 189, VII
The Barnes House – 58
The Boutique – 294
The Cannonball House – 70
The Cat's Pajamas – 86
The Christian Connection Christian Bookstore – 291
The Columns – 53
The Forrest Interior Design & Gifts – 236
The Front Porch Tearoom – 224
The Ivy Garden – 184
The Old Governor's Mansion – 202, XII
The Plantation Shop – 21, IX
The Posh Pup – 151
The Scarlet Tassel – 35
The Seen Gallery – 147
The Shoppe in the Back – 256
The Shoppes of Plum Tree Village – 252, XIII

The Society Gardener – 63
The Squished Grape – 178
The University of Georgia – 90
The Wild Honeysuckle – 185
The Willows Pottery – 158
Timeless Reflections – 94
Town & Country Fashions – 292
Trinkets – 118
Tubman African American Museum – 69
Two Friends – 221
Utopia Day Spa – 115
Victorian House Restaurant – 103
Village Green Flowers & Gifts – 257
Villane's Art Glass Studio – 197
Visual Praise Fine Art Studio & Gallery – 267
Yelverton Jewelers – 309
Yonah Treasures – 158

Golf
Callaway Gardens – 288
Chipley Murrah House Bed & Breakfast – 289
Nicklaus Golf Club Birch River – 127

Gourmet & Specialty Foods
Antique Sweets – 178
Brenda's House of Flowers – 186
British Bits and Bobs – 99
Buckhead Ornamentals – 36
Chanticleer – 285
Chef Audrey's Bistro & Bakery – 8, 307, XI
Chipley Discount – 300
Cranberry Corners – 126
Creter's – 61
Eden'z Vegetarian Restaurant – 71
Endless Treasures – 136
Gautreau's Cajun Café – 89
Georgia Market House – 62
Georgia Originals – 81
Ingleside Village Pizza – 72
Jingles – 87
Kathryn's Bakery-Café – 306
Kitchen Gallery – 310

L & L Beanery – 97
Little European Bakery – 24
Martha Jane's Homestyle Fudge – 238
Merle Norman Cosmetics Studio – 114
Petit Sweets Confectionery – 56
RL's Off The Square – 119
Rose Cottage – Pine Mountain – 297
Sally's – 169
Simply Southern – 170
Stone Mountain General Store – 276
Stonebridge Western Treasures and Fine Art – 171
The Avenue – 189, VII
The Back Burner Restaurant – 72
The Barnes House – 58
The Boutique – 294
The Cannonball House – 70
The Ivy Garden – 184
The Shoppes of Plum Tree Village – 252, XIII
The Village Corner – 277
Three Sisters Fudge – 94
Town Center Breads – 113

Hotels/Inns
A-1 Vacation Rentals – 160
Best Western White House Inn – 295
Biscuit Inn – 161
Comfort Inn – Newnan – 213
Comfort Suites – 309
Crowne Plaza Macon – 64, X
Davis Inn – 295
Douglas Inn & Suites – 101
Fairfield Inn & Suites – 38
Forrest Hills Mountain Resort & Conference Center – 128
Georgia Gameday Center – 83
Hampton Inn – Perry – 222
Hampton Inn – Madison – 179
Hawthorn Suites, Ltd. – 239
Hotel Warm Springs Bed & Breakfasts Inn – 290
Jameson Inn – 238

La Quinta Inn & Suites – 65
Lily Creek Lodge – 137
New Perry Hotel – 222
Perry Area CVB – 215, 217
Pine Mountain Campground – 291
Pine Mountain Club Chalets Resort – 289
Ramada Limited – Blue Ridge – 101
Staybridge Suites – 38
The University of Georgia – 90
The Village Inn Bed & Breakfast – 275
Wingate Inn Macon – 65
Wyndham Hotels & Resorts – 37

Ice Cream Parlors
Card Carousel – 225
Hotel Warm Springs Bed & Breakfast Inn – 290

Interior Design
Anasazi – 100
Antiques of Vinings – 23
Athens Antique Mall – 80
Athens Interiors Market – 78
Carlton Interiors – 221
Chanticleer – 285
Chocolate Moose – 139
Country Classics – 294
Design Finds – 140
Enchanted Pieces – 63
Gabriel's – 266
Highridge Gallery – 98
Ingleside Village Antique Centre – 52
Jane Marsden Antiques & Interiors – 20, VIII
Love Street Home – 260
Madison Interiors Market – 170
Michael Gibson Antiques & Design, Inc. – 19, IV, V
Ramsey's Furniture – 116
Red Door Interiors – 259
Simply Sophie – 140
Spires Interiors & Gifts – 117
The Forrest Interior Design & Gifts – 236
The Roman Antique Mall & Expo – 231

The Shoppes of Plum Tree Village – 252, XIII
The Wild Honeysuckle – 185
Timeless Reflections – 94

Jewelry
A Child's Garden – 125
Andrea's China Cabinet, Inc. – 32
Anne Tutt Gallery – 287
Antiques from The Shed – 218
Antiques On Broad – 231
Athens Antique Mall – 80
Athens Interiors Market – 78
Atlanta Antique Gallery – 22
Beth Ann – 28
Betty's Vintage Boutique – 99
C.R. Rader Jewelers – 66
Canterbury's – 293
Carlton Interiors – 221
Celebrity on Paces – 27, XIII
Chamblee's Antique District Row – 22
Christa's etc. – 232
Circa Antiques & Gardens – 80
Country Cousins – 235
Creter's – 61
Dasha Style & Color – 237
Dragonfly Dreams – 234
Felicity Gifts and Home Décor – 36
Fine Gifts by Glass, Etc. – 33
Frontier – 87
Gigi's Salon and Day Spa – 179
Ginger Howard Selections – 28
Grapevine Antiques & More – 196
High Country Art & Antique – 95
Homeplace Gifts & Toys – 82
J.C. Grant Company Jewelers – 201
Jones Jewelers, Inc. – 223
Joycine's – 59
Kaleidoscope – 150
Karen's Gifts – 259
L & L Beanery – 97
Lavender Loft – 139
Macon Arts – 55
Main Street Emporium – 286

Mel & Mimi – 234
MeMe's on Carroll – 220
Merci Woman – 30
Merle Norman Cosmetics Studio – 114
Michael Gibson Antiques & Design, Inc. – 19, IV, V
Mountain Crafts – 293
Oh! Fine Lingerie – 30
Opulence – 86
Paula's Silver and Gold – 235
Payne Village Antique Mall – 53
Planet Me – 255
Razzle Dazzle – 28
Ruby Jean's – 256
Scentimentals – 251
Serenity Medical Health and Beauty Spa – 141
Simply Southern – 170
Slippers – 85
Southern Comforts – 88
Stonebridge Western Treasures and Fine Art – 171
Stones – 277
Susan Lee – 26, IX
The Avenue – 189, VII
The Barnes House – 58
The Boutique – 294
The Cat's Pajamas – 86
The Columns – 53
The Ivy Garden – 184
The Roman Antique Mall & Expo – 231
The Shoppe in the Back – 256
The Shoppes of Plum Tree Village – 252, XIII
Timeless Reflections – 94
Town & Country Fashions – 292
Tré Bella – 200
Victorian House Restaurant – 103
Villane's Art Glass Studio – 197
Yelverton Jewelers – 309
Yonah Treasures – 158

Museums
Bulloch Hall & Archibald Smith Plantation Home – 247
DeKalb History Center – 150

FDR Warm Springs Welcome Center – 278, 284
FDR's Little White House – 296
Georgia Music Hall of Fame and Museum – 67
Georgia Sports Hall of Fame – 68
Georgia's Old Capital Museum – 203
Hay House – 69
Heritage Hall – 173
Historic Roswell CVB – 243, 250
Macon-Bibb CVB – 44, 51
Madison Museum of Fine Art – 174
Madison-Morgan Cultural Center – 172
Milledgeville-Baldwin County CVB – 190, 194
Morgan County African-American Museum – 172
Museum of Arts and Sciences – 70
Museum of Aviation – 305
Oak Hill & The Martha Berry Museum – 240
Rome Area Council for the Arts – 232
Rose Cottage – Madison – 173
Steffen Thomas Museum and Archives – 173
Swan House – 39, FC
The Cannonball House – 70
The Old Governor's Mansion – 202, XIII
The Rogers House – 172
Tubman African American Museum – 69
Warner Robins CVB – 301, 304

Orchard/Produce
Georgia Market House – 62

Pampered Pets
Biscuit Inn – 161
Claws & Paws – 161
Kreature Komforts of Marietta, Inc. – 188
The Posh Pup – 151

Quilts/Needlework/Stitchery

Antiques & Crafts Unlimited Mall – 286
L & L Beanery – 97
Main Street Emporium – 286
Main Street Yarns and Fibers – 89
Me & Thee – 70
Mitchell's Last Chance Gift Shop – 214
Sew Memorable – 141
Simply Southern – 170
Southern Comforts – 88

Realtors

Coldwell Banker High Country Realty – 102
Georgia Prime Real Estate, LLC – 102
RE/MAX Properties Plus – 106
Simpler Times Realty – 268

Restaurants

119 Chops – 205
A Touch of Country – 116
Adrianna's Café – 71
Amici Italian Café – 119, 176
Atkins Park Tavern – 261
Bert's – 72
Blue Willow Inn Restaurant – 269
Callaway Gardens – 288
Carriage & Horses – 298
Caruso's – 129
Chamblee's Antique Row District – 22
Chef Audrey's Bistro & Bakery – 8, 307, XI
Choby's at Little River – 6, 204
Cricket's Restaurant – 299
Crowne Plaza Macon – 64, X
Danielle's New Orleans Bistro – 308
Dante's on the Square – 129
Dawsonville Pool Room – 138
Dish – 40
Edelweiss German Inn & Restaurant – 159, 162
Eden'z Vegetarian Restaurant – 71
Forrest Hills Mountain Resort & Conference Center – 128
Frogtown Cellars – 132
Gathering Place Café & Events – 138
Gautreau's Cajun Café – 89
Georgia Bob's Barbecue Company – 308
Hallie Jane's Market Catering – 176
Harvest Moon Café – 241
Hawthorn Suites – 239
Ingleside Village Pizza – 72
Kathryn's Bakery-Café – 306
Kokomo's Island Café – 306
Little European Bakery – 24
Magretta Hall – 242
Mandella's Italian Restaurant, LLC – 299
Mittie's Tea Room Café – 248
Nacoochee Grill – 163
Nicklaus Golf Club Birch River – 127
Piazza Italian Restaurant – 130
RL's Off The Square – 119
Rose Cottage - Pine Mountain – 297
Serenity Garden Café – 94
Southern Cross Guest Ranch – 175
Swan Coach House – 41
T. Martooni's – 242
The Avenue – 189, VII
The Back Burner Restaurant – 72
The Fickle Pickle – 248
The Front Porch Tearoom – 224
The McGuire House – 130
The Oar House – 130
The Red Tomato – 107
The Restaurant at the New Perry Hotel – 224
The Shoppes of Plum Tree Village – 252, XIII
The University of Georgia – 90
The Village Corner – 277
The Whistle Stop Café – 108
Victorian House Restaurant – 103
Victorian Rose Tearoom and Café – 241
Victorian Tea Room – 298
Willow on Fifth – 73
Wolf Mountain Vineyards – 131
Zucca Bar and Pizzeria – 262

Salons/Spas/Indulgence

Forrest Hills Mountain Resort & Conference Center – 128
Gigi's Salon and Day Spa – 179
Greenstone Soap Company – 164
Hawthorn Suites – 239
Mandala Wellness Retreat & Day Spa – 163
Pura Vida USA – 128, XI
Salon Red & Salon Red Kids – 151
Serenity Medical Health and Beauty Spa – 141
Serenity Wellness Spa & Salon – 6, 206
Stan Milton Salon – 42
The Avenue – 189, VII
Utopia Day Spa – 115

Soda Fountains

A Touch of Country – 116

Special Events/Groups/Corporate

119 Chops – 205
A Child's Garden – 125
A Victorian Cowgirl – 156
A-1 Vacation Rentals – 160
Adrianna's Café – 71
Amici Italian Café – 119, 176
Antebellum Inn Bed & Breakfast – 198
Atkins Park Tavern – 261
Bert's – 72
Best Western White House Inn – 295
Blue Ridge Inn Bed & Breakfast – 97
Blue Willow Inn Restaurant – 269
Brenda's House of Flowers – 186
Bulloch Hall & Archibald Smith Plantation Home – 247
Callaway Gardens – 288
Carriage & Horses – 298

Caruso's – 129

Chef Audrey's Bistro & Bakery – 8, 307, XI

Choby's at Little River – 6, 204

Comfort Inn – Newnan – 213

Comfort Suites – 309

Cricket's Restaurant – 299

Crowne Plaza Macon – 64, X

Danielle's New Orleans Bistro – 308

Dante's on the Square – 129

Davis Inn – 295

Dawsonville Pool Room – 138

Decatur Downtown Development Authority – 142, 145

DeKalb History Center – 150

Dish – 40

Douglas Inn & Suites – 101

Douglass Theatre – 56

Edelweiss German Inn & Restaurant – 159, 162

Fairfield Inn & Suites – 38

FDR Warm Spings Welcome Center – 278, 284

FDR's Little White House – 296

Forrest Hills Mountain Resort & Conference Center – 128

Frogtown Cellars – 132

Gathering Place Café & Events – 138

Gautreau's Cajun Café – 89

Georgia Bob's Barbecue Company – 308

Georgia Music Hall of Fame and Museum – 67

Georgia National Fairgrounds and Agricenter – 219

Georgia Sports Hall of Fame – 68

Georgia's Old Capital Museum – 203

Ginger's Dollings & Cattywags – 233

Greater Rome CVB – 226, 230

Hallie Jane's Market Catering – 176

Hampton Inn – Perry – 222

Hampton Inn – Madison – 179

Harvest Moon Café – 241

Hawthorn Suites – 239

Hay House – 69

Helen Black Bear Resort – 160

Heritage Hall – 173

Historic Roswell CVB – 243, 250

Ingleside Village Antique Centre – 52

Jameson Inn – 238

Kokomo's Island Café – 306

La Quinta Inn & Suites – 65

Lily Creek Lodge – 137

Little European Bakery – 24

Macon-Bibb CVB – 44, 51

Madison Museum of Fine Art – 174

Madison-Morgan Cultural Center – 172

Magretta Hall – 242

Main Street Covington – 109, 112

Mandella's Italian Restaurant, LLC – 299

Milledgeville-Baldwin County CVB – 190, 194

Morgan County African-American Museum – 172

Museum of Arts and Sciences – 70

Museum of Aviation – 305

My Mountain Cabin Rentals LLC – 96

Nacoochee Grill – 163

New Perry Hotel – 222

Nicklaus Golf Club Birch River – 127

Oak Hill & The Martha Berry Museum – 240

Perry Area CVB – 215, 217

Pine Mountain Campground – 291

Pine Mountain Club Chalets Resort – 289

Pine Mountain Tourism Association – 278, 284

Pura Vida USA – 128, XI

Ramada Limited – Blue Ridge – 101

RL's Off The Square – 119

Rome Area Council for the Arts – 232

Rose Cottage – Madison – 173

Rose Cottage – Pine Mountain – 297

Serenity Garden Café – 94

Serenity Medical Health and Beauty Spa – 141

Southern Cross Guest Ranch – 175

Steffen Thomas Museum and Archives – 173

T. Martooni's – 242

The Back Burner Restaurant – 72

The Cannonball House – 70

The Fickle Pickle – 248

The Front Porch Tearoom – 224

The Gardens at Great Oaks – 249, XIII

The Holly House – 268

The McGuire House – 130

The Oar House – 130

The Old Governor's Mansion – 202, XII

The Red Tomato – 107

The Rogers House – 172

The Squished Grape – 178

The University of Georgia – 90

The Village Corner – 277

The Village Inn Bed & Breakfast – 275

The Whistle Stop Café – 108

Tubman African American Museum – 69

Victorian House Restaurant – 103

Victorian Tea Room – 298

Village Green Flowers & Gifts – 257

Visual Praise Fine Art Studio & Gallery – 267

Warner Robins CVB – 301, 304

White County Chamber of Commerce – 152, 155

Willow on Fifth – 73

Wingate Inn Macon – 65

Wolf Mountain Vineyards – 131

Wyndham Hotels & Resorts – 37

Zucca Bar and Pizzeria – 262

Specialty Shop
A Victorian Cowgirl – 156
Alexis Maternity Collections
– 29
Amelia's & The Ruffled
Rooster – 177
Andrea's China Cabinet, Inc.
– 32
Antique Sweets – 178
Appointments at Five – 79
Athens Antique Mall – 80
Beth Ann – 28
Betty's Vintage Boutique – 99
Beverly Bremer Silver Shop
– 9, 43, III
British Bits and Bobs – 99
Canterbury's – 293
Card Carousel – 225
Chappelle Gallery – 81
Chipley Discount – 300
Classics – 164
Claws & Paws – 161
Country Cousins – 235
Cream of the Crop – 57
Creter's – 61
Dahlonega Tasting Room
– 132
Design Finds – 140
Dolls & Stuff – 270
Dory's – 90
Dreams – 59
Eden'z Vegetarian Restaurant
– 71
Fine Gifts by Glass, Etc. – 33
Georgia Market House – 62
Georgia Originals – 81
Ginger Howard Selections
– 28
Ginger's Dollings &
Cattywags – 233
Golden Classics – 126
Greenstone Soap Company
– 164
Habersham Vineyards &
Winery – 165
Happy Valley Pottery – 81
Homeplace Gifts & Toys – 82
Hoopla – 149
Hotel Warm Springs Bed &
Breakfast Inn – 290
Impressions – 25, VIII
Jingles – 87

Jones Jewelers, Inc. – 223
Karla's Shoe Boutique – 60
Kimbrough Brothers – 300
Kitchen Gallery – 310
Kreature Komforts of
Marietta, Inc. – 188
Lavender Loft – 139
Main Street Yarns and Fibers
– 89
Me & Thee – 70
MeMe's on Carroll – 220
Merci Woman – 30
Mitchell's Last Chance Gift
Shop – 214
Nature's Health & Christian
Bookstore – 137
Oak Hill & The Martha Berry
Museum – 240
Oh! Fine Lingerie – 30
Planet Me – 255
Red Door Interiors – 259
Sally's – 169
Savvy Snoot – 31
Scentimentals – 251
Scrappin' Sisters – 120
Sew Memorable – 141
Shapiro's – 157
Simply Southern – 170
Slippers – 85
Smartypants – 233
Southern Artistry – 274
Southern Belles and Beaus
– 82
Southern Comforts – 88
Southern Heartland Art
Gallery – 112
Stone Mountain General Store
– 276
Stones – 277
Sugarplum Tree – 220
Swan Coach House – 41
Swan Galleries – 276
The Avenue – 189, VII
The Barnes House – 58
The Boutique – 294
The Forrest Interior Design &
Gifts – 236
The Posh Pup – 151
The Seen Gallery – 147
The Shoppe in the Back – 256
The Shoppes of Plum Tree
Village – 252, XIII
The Squished Grape – 178
The Wild Honeysuckle – 185

Tina's Shoes – 57
Tré Bella – 200
Two Friends – 221
Village Green Flowers &
Gifts – 257
Villane's Art Glass Studio
– 197
Yonah Treasures – 158

Sports & Fitness
Callaway Gardens – 288
Little River Park Campgroud
& Marina – 6, 199
Nicklaus Golf Club Birch
River – 127
Southern Cross Guest Ranch
– 175

Tea Rooms
Chamblee's Antique Row
District – 22
Collectors' Corner – 212, VI
Kathryn's Bakery-Café – 306
Mittie's Tea Room Café – 248
Rose Cottage – Pine
Mountain – 297
Southern Belles and Beaus
– 82
The Front Porch Tearoom
– 224
Victorian Rose Tearoom and
Café – 241
Victorian Tea Room – 298

Value
Chipley Discount – 300
Heart to Heart for Kids, Inc.
– 29
House to House Furnishings
Consignment – 88
Savvy Snoot – 31
Smartypants – 233
Southern Comforts – 88

Wines/Winery
Bert's – 72
Carriage & Horses – 298
Caruso's – 129
Dahlonega Tasting Room
– 132
Dante's on the Square – 129
Frogtown Cellars – 132
Habersham Vineyards &
Winery – 165

Nacoochee Grill – 163
RL's Off The Square – 119
The Back Burner Restaurant
   – 72
The McGuire House – 130
The Squished Grape – 178
Wolf Mountain Vineyards
   – 131
Zucca Bar and Pizzeria – 262

Dear Adventurer,

If you are reading this book chances are you are an 'Adventurer.' An 'Adventurer' is a person with a sense of adventure and a curiosity for new and exciting places, people and experiences—both long and short distances. All of the Lady's Day Out books appeal to that sense of adventure and cater to the natural curiosity in all of us.

A Lady's Day Out, Inc., would like to share this gift of the perfect combination between work and travel with our loyal following of readers.

In an effort to expand our coverage area we are looking for adventurous travelers who would like to help us find the greatest places to include in our upcoming editions of A Lady's Day Out. This is a wonderful opportunity to travel and explore some of the best destination cities in the United States.

If you would like more information, we would love to hear from you. You may call A Lady's Day Out, Inc. at 1-888-860-ALDO (2536) or e-mail us through www.aladysdayout.com online.

Best wishes and keep on exploring, from all of us at A Lady's Day Out, Inc.

"A Lady's Day Out Giveaway" Entry Form

Have five of the businesses featured in this book sign your entry form and you are eligible to win one of the following: weekend get away at a bed and breakfast, dinner gift certificates, shopping spree gift certificates or $250 cash.

1. _____
   (NAME OF BUSINESS)   (SIGNATURE)

2. _____
   (NAME OF BUSINESS)   (SIGNATURE)

3. _____
   (NAME OF BUSINESS)   (SIGNATURE)

4. _____
   (NAME OF BUSINESS)   (SIGNATURE)

5. _____
   (NAME OF BUSINESS)   (SIGNATURE)

NAME: _____

ADDRESS: _____

CITY: _____ STATE: _____ ZIP: _____

PHONE#: _____ E-MAIL: _____

Where did you purchase book? _____

Other towns or businesses you feel should be incorporated in our next book.

_____

_____

No purchase necessary. Winners will be determined by random drawing from all complete entries received. Winners will be notified by phone and/or mail.

Mail To:
A Lady's Day Out, Inc.
8563 Boat Club Road
Fort Worth, Tx 76179

Fax To: 817-236-0033
Phone: 817-236-5250
Web-Site: www.aladysdayout.com